INTERPRETING
CULTURAL DIFFERENCES
the challenge of intercultural
communication

INTERPRETING CULTURAL DIFFERENCES

the challenge of intercultural communication

Margaret C. McLaren

Peter Francis Publishers

Peter Francis Publishers
The Old School House
Little Fransham
Dereham
Norfolk NR19 2JP
UK

A CIP catalogue record for this book
is available from the British Library

ISBN 1-870167-29-5

Printed and bound in Great Britain by Biddles Ltd,
Guildford and King's Lynn.

CONTENTS

PREFACE

'A journey of a thousand miles
Begins with a single step'

Tsu-ssu

On the first page of *Beyond the Chinese Face*, Michael Bond says: 'This book's distinctiveness must lie in its claim to scientific status.' For *Interpreting Cultural Differences: the challenge of intercultural communication* I can make no such claim. The method is distinctly interpretive, drawing substantially on the quantitative research of others and on the rich personal insights my intercultural students have shared with me over the years. The aim is to provide some help for teachers and administrators whose work involves international staff and students, and for teachers and students who are, or may be, working outside the culture they were raised in.

If a positive climate exists, international staff and students and host staff and students can feel comfortable about asking questions when they are unsure of what to do, free to take risks and inclined to share their different cultures with one another. Relationships prosper and tasks are completed.

Educators want to produce a climate in which everyone will flourish. In this we have the support of scholars like Young Yun Kim (1992: 346) who both sees the importance of providing a conducive climate for interaction with international students and realises that hosts themselves grow in understanding as they communicate:

> One of the most critical factors that promote or deter the immigrants' development of interpersonal relationships with the natives is host communication competence ... This theoretical relationship also operates in the reverse direction, that is, the process of developing host communication competence is enhanced by participating in interpersonal relationships with the natives. One learns to communicate by communicating, so to speak, as one learns to swim by swimming.

How well we communicate depends on what we know, what we feel and how we behave – not necessarily in that order. These correlate closely with the three aspects of communication competence isolated by Brian Spitzberg and William Cupach (1984): knowledge, motivation and skills. Gudykunst and Kim (1995) stress the same three, though in a different order and with slightly different wording – awareness, knowledge and skills. Whatever the wording, this text will be concerned with all three, interrelated as they are.

We can work at improving intercultural communication in two ways: as a difficult challenge or as a learning experience. The first, concentrating on outcome, has been called the intercultural communication-as-problem approach (in, for instance, Kim and Rubin, 1988). The second, emphasising process, has been called the intercultural communication-as-learning-growth approach (Adler, 1975). This book will work with both approaches, but the emphasis will be on the second. In the words of Langer (1992: 53), 'A pre-occupation with outcome can make us mindless.'

In recent decades scholars have worked steadily to develop a theoretical base for communication in general and intercultural communication in particular. In Kurt Lewin's (1951) frequently quoted words, 'There is nothing so practical as a good theory.'

Practice without theory can be a recital of what to do and not do, which could encourage stereotyping and hurt rather than help intercultural under-standing. But reading provides only a beginning. Mingling, living, working with others is necessary also. Articles, books and training courses can be useful shortcuts but on their own they are not enough. What they can do, though, is provide vicarious experience, through stories of other people, other times and other cultures.

With some reluctance I have used the terms 'eastern' and 'western' throughout the book. For one thing they are inaccurate. Inuit, Mãori, Australian aborigine, various African cultures are far from being 'western' in the usual meaning of the word, and yet the term 'eastern' does not apply geographically to them whatever location a writer takes as base. For another, as a New Zealander for whom India and China, for example, are the Near North and certainly not the Far East, I find the terms even geographically disconcerting. Yet almost all the literature uses the terms. The alternatives for 'eastern' are 'Oriental' a term which Edward Said (1979) has shown is even more objectionable, and 'Asian', preferred by scholars like Samovar and Porter (1991; 1995) but not used in this text because it excludes South America and the Middle East. The other popular alternative, 'stranger', used originally by Georg Simmel (1906) in *Der Fremde*, seems to me to suggest a distance I am not prepared to accept.

Even if a suitable term could be found, using it would raise the danger of generalising rashly. For example, as Jules Wohl and Amnuay Tapingkae (1972) pointed out, there are striking differences between the 'relatively practical, realistic approach' to essay writing of Thai students and the aesthetic, mystical approach of Burmese students (Smith and Luce, 1979). Yet the terms 'eastern', 'Asian' and even 'Oriental' would have grouped Thai and Burmese students together.

There are two reasons for using 'eastern' and 'western'. The main reason is that so much of the literature uses either or both of these terms. The second reason is that Peter Francis are British publishers and many of those who will use the book are British, and for them the term is at least geographically appropriate. I ask that the terms be taken as reference points only, never implying the ethnocentric view that 'western' is the norm and 'eastern' the other, but rather the competent communication view that cultures are different, and all must be recognised and valued for themselves. In the words of Abdu'l Baba, 'The east and the west must unite to provide one another with what is lacking' (Bond, 1991: vii).

Three people contributed sections of the text. The whole of Chapter 5 was written by Douglas Pratt who leads the Religious Studies programme at the University of Waikato. Understanding the various religions is indispensable to the study of intercultural communication so the expert explanation he provides is of great value. Yasuhiro Yoshioka, a friend and fellow teacher from Japan, and Samuel Coad Dyer, a colleague in the Department of Management Communication at the University of Waikato, contributed personal statements which raise several interesting intercultural issues. I am grateful to all three.

My thanks must also go to those who helped during and after the writing of this book. Philip Hills, who this time as on all previous occasions, has been supportive and patient at every stage. Jean Beaton has put many hours into improving my clumsy word-processing. My students, both local and international, from several years of masters classes and theses in intercultural communication, have given me much information and many anecdotes which have been used (and, of course, acknowledged) in this book. My colleagues, especially Rosemary de Luca, Ted Zorn, Ken Morse, Frances Nelson and Sandra Goodwin, all of whom read the text in draft, have checked some of my excesses and provided countless useful insights. Most of all I thank my husband, Ian McLaren, my harshest and best critic, for his always discerning, constructive and willing help at every stage of the writing.

Samuel Taylor Coleridge suggested that the true artist is one who can create a willing suspension of disbelief. Perhaps the true educator is similarly one who can accept others as they are, whatever his or her own culture. Whether or not Rumpelstiltskin really stamped through three storeys when he lost his temper, or the princess really felt the pea through twenty mattresses, simply does not matter as long as we are prepared to let go our own inbred sense of the reality of the world around us and accept another reality without judging it as better or worse than our own – only different, an exciting new world to explore.

1 A CELEBRATION OF DIFFERENCE

'An encounter with other cultures can lead to openness only if you can suspend the assumption of superiority, not seeing new worlds to conquer, but new worlds to respect.'

Mary Catherine Bateson

In January 1996 four graduate students from the University of Staffordshire went to Foshan University in Guangdong province in southern China. Their first lecture was given by a Chinese staff member who had completed his own graduate work – in intercultural communication – at the University of Waikato, New Zealand. Foshan University had taken enormous trouble to ensure that the technological facilities of the university, like computers and fax machines, were of the standard the students were used to.

At the same time, or a few months before, all over the United Kingdom and in other western countries, foreign staff and students were settling to study, sometimes in an atmosphere extremely unfamiliar to them. In different ways, the host institutions had made careful preparations for them. Yet the discontent sometimes aired by the expatriate students, their classmates and their teachers, suggests that the preparations are seldom enough, that some who come to study or teach abroad, despite their induction, still feel lonely, confused, alienated, and unable to make full use of the opportunities they have looked forward to for so long and now have. This kind of discontent showed itself, for instance, in the complaint made by members of the National Liaison Committee for International Students in Australia (1996) that only a small number of Australian universities had credible 'cross-cultural training' programmes for staff or for students.

In spite of the uneasiness and criticisms sometimes expressed by expatriate students, the wish to study abroad seems to increase all the time. Although rising fees, forced on most educational institutions by reduced government funding, create difficulties for some, the trend continues, bringing mutual benefits to both hosts and newcomers.

Within the educational institutions concerned, the flow of staff and students from other cultures brings richness in many forms. Consider benefits like these:

- The greater understanding of others that can develop in the student body.
- The subsequent benefit of having ambassadors all over the world after the students have graduated.
- The benefits of scale as a result of increased enrolments. (The institutions where the newcomers study may be able to afford resources they would otherwise have to do without.)
- Increased knowledge and new insights through the introduction of specialised skills like the idiomatic use of foreign languages, or of products like herbal medicines.
- Awareness by everyone involved of their own limitations through getting to know unfamiliar people and customs.
- The greater cognitive flexibility of both staff and students that may result from intercultural interaction.

Everyone in the institutions hosting significant numbers of international staff and students needs to be aware of the difficulties the newcomers face. For example, their notion of the role and status of a teacher may be very different from that of the locals, which could be disconcerting for international students, devastating for international teachers. When they come from a different cultural background with different values and often with a different mother tongue, they may find it difficult, even impossible, to conform to local conventions and practices. If the newcomers can know that their diverse cultures are understood and valued, the difficulties become a challenge they can more willingly accept.

If they feel outsiders, the 'culture shock', to use a term which will be explained more fully later in this chapter, can lead to missing classes and a reluctance to submit assigned work. Other students, and staff too, may find it hard relating to them, because of their different backgrounds and, very often, their problems with the local language. The newcomers, instead of communicating their difficulties and their confusion, tend to retreat into themselves, limiting their social dealings to people they find similar to themselves, usually fellow nationals. If the difficulties, real or imagined, are too daunting students may not persist with their studies, and in extreme cases may even consider suicide.

However, if understood in time, the problems can be avoided, or at least minimised, as long as both hosts and newcomers realise that goodwill and tolerance alone are not enough. To achieve the immense benefits of having a body of staff and students who move between academic institutions, goodwill and tolerance must be supplemented with knowledge, sensitivity and skills.

The aim of this book is to increase intercultural understanding, especially in an educational environment. For some, the concepts it presents will be a start, and for others one step more on a journey. By recognising our own culture and respecting the culture of others, we can work towards understanding cultural differences better than we otherwise would. We can develop the knowledge to understand how others think, the empathy to sense how others feel and the necessary skills to cope flexibly with differences. In more technical terms, we can develop cognitive, affective and behavioural skills. This book will suggest ways to enhance these skills.

People involved in education are unlikely ever to discriminate deliberately against those from other cultures, but that is not a reason for complacency. Paul Pedersen (1990: 2), in his work on counselling, reminds us that 'well-meaning, right-thinking, good-hearted, caring professionals . . . are probably no more or less free from cultural bias than other members of the general public.'

As long ago as 1983 James Lynch, examining the primary school curriculum in the United Kingdom, argued that, because British society is increasingly multicultural, only by taking a multicultural approach can 'person-respecting' decisions be made about what to include in a curriculum. In his words, 'Respect for others implies respect for their opinions and beliefs and willingness to engage in dialogue about them.'

Constructive dialogue between people of different cultures is possible only when speakers and listeners understand that the meaning of any communication resides not just in the message but in the minds of the sender and receiver as well. Even when speaker and listener come from the same background, they may interpret a message differently according to their personality, their accumulated experience or even their mood at the moment. When speaker and listener come from different cultural backgrounds, the potential for the message to mean different things is increased greatly.

The contention in this book is that knowledge, sensitivity and appreciation of cultural difference are prerequisites for effective intercultural communication for educators – especially those who are interacting with international students. Research by Gudykunst, Chua and Gray (1987) bears this out. They show that cultural dissimilarities appear to have a major influence on our communication in the early stages of a relationship. If culture is learned,[1] it is

---

[1]   See Chapter 2 for an explanation of this concept.

also learnable, both by newcomers and hosts.

As newcomers become less new, they absorb aspects of the host culture. Hosts, too, who ideally will themselves come from a range of different cultures, can take on some of the cultural perspective of newcomers they meet and mix with. As Stuart Hall (1992: 274) points out, cultural identity is not fixed but 'movable', something that changes continually as people interact with others. For those at home this is a process of growth but for those from elsewhere it may be extremely unsettling, even when circumstances are such that they decide to stay permanently in the host country.

Paul and Anne Pedersen's work (1989) on the cultural grid teases out the individual's personal cultural orientation from the variables within a particular social system. In the grid, the variables can be demographic, ethnographic, linked to status or linked to affiliation. A single variable, like age, might not matter; a cluster, such as age, nationality and military rank, might. Culture is more than learned behaviour. It is the result of ongoing, dynamic events and relationships affected by the environment and by individuals in countless ways. Those who have lived for many years away from the place in which they were raised have a complex cultural identity, sometimes to such an extent that they feel they belong nowhere. Both the host and the international student can work to ensure this feeling of being lost does not last.

The process of adaptation begins soon after the newcomer arrives. How can those responsible make it more comfortable?

Uncertainty Reduction

If a student comes to a staff member with an academic or personal worry, the person whose help is sought can:

(1)   ignore the problem or refuse to listen;
(2)   listen and give the best advice possible, being specific and explaining the rationale constructively;
(3)   be sympathetic and listen but change the subject as soon as possible, helping the student to become involved in doing something enjoyable; or
(4)   listen in a way that shows he or she can really understand but refrain from giving advice, simply helping the student talk the situation out enough to be able to sort it out him or herself.

The simple solution is to use the method approved and taught in one's own culture, adjusted for the personal preference of the speaker. For the westerner, especially if he or she has had counselling training, that is likely to be the fourth of the four methods, shifting when a solution seems in sight to the third method. A more useful solution would take into account the culture of *both* speaker and listener, the personal preference of *both* speaker and listener and the particular situation.

Western teachers, trained to separate the deed from the doer, may be reluctant to bolster the student who desperately wants approval or to accept the perceived deference to the teacher which many international students show. In any case, overt requests for help may be rare, since in some cultures to ask for help would be to admit failure. Isolating problems is natural to those who see life as a series of discrete events, but strange to those who see life as a unified whole. Yet giving specific advice may be the very way to reduce anxiety in difficult situations. Gudykunst and Hammer (1988) consider that intercultural adaptation is the process of reducing anxiety and uncertainty. If newcomers are to settle well into a culture they must be able to feel at ease with others.

Many of us, especially those outside our own culture, want to reduce the uncertainty which is part of every new meeting. This means that as both hosts and newcomers we need conscious control over our verbal and our nonverbal language so that the statements we make and the questions we ask help rather than hinder communication.

To have the ability to reduce uncertainty we need both to understand others, however different their cultural background may be from our own, and to be able to communicate with them sensitively. Charles E. Berger (1992: 6) spells out the need:

> To interact in a relatively smooth, co-ordinated, and understandable manner, one must both be able to predict how one's interaction partner is likely to behave, and, based on those predictions, to select from one's own repertoire those responses that will optimize outcomes in the encounter.

If any relationship is to be more than superficial, those involved will need to have some sense of the whole, complex, cultural background each brings into the situation. For instance, Gudykunst (1992) has shown that different strategies are used to reduce uncertainty by people from high context cultures like India from those used by people from low context cultures like Great Britain.[2] The challenge to understand the differences is considerable. The

---

[2]   High and low contexts are discussed in Chapter 2.

problem with understanding *strangers* is, he suggested (1983), that 'we are likely to attribute their behaviour to one particular characteristic – namely their cultural background' whereas with people from the same background we may look for other reasons.

Gudykunst and Kim and other intercultural theorists such as Kerry O'Sullivan favour the term 'stranger' from Georg Simmel's work, *Der Fremde* to describe people whose culture is different from our own. 'Stranger' does carry something of the worry and the discomfort of communicating with those outside our own culture. Dodd (1991: 3) calls the term a 'captivating metaphor' because of the sense of distance it can convey. In the same ways the Latin term, *barbarus*, the Japanese term, *gaijin*, and even the English term 'foreigner', seem to be excluding rather than including those who need acceptance. But surely we should accept an international student or staff member not as an outsider but as part of the culture of academia with something extra to contribute. If he or she must be a stranger at all, let it at least be as a 'privileged stranger'.[3]

The term, 'sojourner' is rather more welcoming but seems to emphasise the temporary nature of the stay. Furnham (1988) defines a sojourner as a person who spends a medium length of time, six months to five years, in a place, usually intending to return 'home'. The motives for spending time abroad are specific and goal-oriented. In that sense, students are often 'sojourners'. But whereas most sojourners may return to their homes or move on elsewhere if their culture shock is too severe, students may feel bound to endure hardship and personal unhappiness in order to achieve the qualifications they are working for and their families want them to have.

International Students

Though all students are likely to suffer some of the kinds of stress described below because of the high expectations placed on them, studies show that international students suffer significantly more stress than local students (Furnham, 1988). The major problems are these:

- Those demoralising stresses that many foreigners face – racial discrimination, language difficulties, accommodation trouble, unfamiliar diet, financial stress, misunderstandings and loneliness. (For students these may not be as severe as the problems con-

---

[3]   The term was first used in this way to describe not foreign students but anthropologists by Morris Freilich, throughout *Marginal Natives: Anthropologists at Work* (1970).

fronting refugees and immigrants but they are compounded by other factors.)

- Those that face any adolescents and young adults as they try to become emotionally and financially self-supporting.
- Academic stress, a common feature of university life involving very hard work, with complex material.
- The stress of being constantly forced into the role of being ambassadors or representatives of their countries.

Assem al-Hajj (1994) adds others, such as occur when a grant is frozen during a political crisis at home or when a huge and unanticipated bill comes in for something not used or needed at home, such as heating.

Ward (1967: 430-40), describing what he called 'foreign student syndrome', argued that depressed international students, to save face, tended to somatise their problems, using them as a reason to attend medical clinics. This in turn gave them a ready excuse for substandard, late or unfinished work.

Another strategy international students often adopt and are criticised for, is to form their own groups, rarely mixing with others. To do so is, of course, natural. We all like people similar to ourselves. Students in the first western universities, Paris, Bologna and Oxford, formed 'nations' for many of the same reasons as today's international students form their own groups.

Communication

To consider how to improve the communication climate for international staff and students, we need to consider communication itself. Communication is sending and receiving messages. Since understanding of meaning resides in people and not in the verbal or nonverbal language, messages will rarely if ever be identical for sender and receiver. However, to communicate effectively the sender and receiver must understand similar meaning in the message.

Imagine a person wanting a pen to write with, saying: 'Could you get me a pen, please?' If a pen usually means a ballpoint to one person and a fountain pen to another, the variation would probably not be serious. However, if the listener looked for a wooden pen for a baby to play in, or an outdoor pen for a sheep or pig to be put into, real miscommunication would have occurred. Linguistic sources of miscommunication, such as the vocabulary confusion in this example, will be discussed in the language chapters. They form one part of the complex of cultural issues involved in the communication process.

Nonverbal cues can be even more troublesome than verbal language if they mean different things to sender and receiver. Since they are more likely to be unconscious, the misunderstanding may never be recognised. A Māori child who shrugs her shoulders in answer to a question will mean: 'I'm truly sorry, I realise I ought to know but I don't.' To a person unfamiliar with the Māori culture it might be assumed to mean: 'Don't know, don't care, so there!'

A major problem exists when misunderstandings occur: often people – teachers included – are completely unaware of them. The New Zealand anthropologist, Joan Metge (1978), calls this phenomenon 'talking past each other'. Statements of fact may be seen as statements of conceit. Behaviour may be interpreted in a way that was never intended. Arriving late for a function is seen as rudeness. Winnie Mandela's being refused admission to the opening of the International Women's Conference in Beijing in September 1995 because she was late was reported on television throughout the world. Was transport the problem, did exact time not matter in her culture, or was she making a theatrical gesture? Who is to say?

Such problems exist with any communication, but may be especially serious with international students. The miscommunication may be exacerbated by what has been called the 'fundamental attribution error' (Ross, 1977), that is, a tendency – which may itself be a western phenomenon – to over-estimate the influence of personality traits and underestimate the influence of the situation when making decisions about people's behaviour.

Yet situations alone do not control communication. Communication is a dynamic process, always changing, each participant affecting and being affected by others. Like any other learned process it can be improved by learning from others through the literature, through formal courses of instruction and through practice. We all learn to communicate from others and by communicating ourselves.

As the chapter on ethnocentrism will show, it is important to accept differences and ambiguity. Stereotypes can get in the way of communication. We are better than we were. We have come a long way since any senior diplomat would dare write:

> The European is a close reasoner; his statements of fact are devoid of any ambiguity; he is a natural logician, albeit he may not have studied logic; he is by nature sceptical and requires proof before he can accept the truth of any proposition; his trained intelligence works like a piece of mechanism. The mind of the oriental, on the other hand, like his picturesque streets, is eminently wanting in symmetry. His reasoning is of the most slipshod nature. (Baring, 1908: II, 16)

We understand our world by putting its nations into categories like 'developed' and 'developing'. Such a division can have extraordinary results. For instance, since *per capita* income is the criterion, New Zealand, with its recent history, is 'developed' and China for all its long and dignified history, 'undeveloped'.

Advances in transport and communication technology have shrunk the world into the 'global village' as McLuhan (1989) predicted. Time and space no longer block communication but cultural barriers still can, often unintentionally.

Communication may be deliberate, as when a teacher gives a class an assignment. It may also be unconscious, as when people stare at someone who is very different in any way, tap their fingers on the table indicating impatience or wring their hands in front of an audience from anxiety. If those watching respond to these actions, communication is occurring.

Responses differ towards, say, deep sniffing or spitting in the west, or to nose blowing or handing something to someone with the left hand in the east. Dodd (1991: 202) explains that spitting, treated as disgusting in most western cultures, can 'represent an act of kindness among American Indians, for example the medicine man spitting on a sick person to cure him'. And in Islamic cultures in which Muslims must fast from dawn to dusk during Ramadan, and may not even imbibe their own saliva, they may constantly spit, to the shock and horror of those from other cultures (Dodd, 1991: 58). In a student setting such behaviour may have disproportionate effects. And the student may never notice. He or she may be exhausted by fasting many more hours than at home, because in countries far from the equator, daybreak in summer comes earlier and dark later than in any Islamic countries.

Culture Shock

Culture shock is the disorientation that comes from being plunged into an unfamiliar setting. Everything people do is different: travelling, ordering meals, telephoning – all can be exhausting in an unfamiliar culture. Add to this the loneliness, unfamiliar attitudes towards time, towards women and family, dress, customs, finance, food, accommodation, and different ideas about cleanliness, medicine, transport, privacy, tips, and levels of formality. No wonder sojourners feel tired, incompetent, confused and worried about seeming stupid to the hosts.

At least students travelling today are not under the stresses of Hans

Staden, the young German who, in the sixteenth century, wanting to see more of the world than his homeland, travelled to Brazil where he was captured and made to say, 'I your food have come' to the villagers. The natives did not eat him because he was able to convince them he had supernatural powers, but he certainly feared they would (Letts, 1957).

The study of culture shock began with Kalvero Oberg who called it an occupational hazard of those suddenly transplanted abroad, with, like most ailments, its own symptoms and cure. He identified six aspects of culture shock: strain, a sense of loss, rejection, confusion, anxiety and feelings of impotence. These make the newcomer want to reject the new environment. In Oberg's (1960) words, the newcomer feels, 'The ways of the host country are bad because they make us feel bad.'

Depending on the degree of differences between the home and host cultures, the pain may include the fatigue of constant adaptation, irritable behaviour to the point of constant anger, insomnia, the sense of loss of friends, home comforts and familiar food, rejection of the host population or rejection by it, confusion of values or identity, discomfort at violation of values, and a feeling of incompetence at dealing with the environment (Taft, 1977; Gudykunst and Kim, 1992).

Sufferers may be worn out by the effort taken by things that would have been easy at home, like deciding what is clean enough to eat or drink, working out transport and even crossing the road, and using or not being able to use the telephone. Making decisions on insufficient information and having to adjust to different attitudes to gender can make the strain worse.

Symptoms include preoccupation with cleanliness, a feeling of being cheated, touchiness about any adverse criticism which becomes particularly hurtful when combined with a cultural sense of face, constant tiredness and severe depression. These emotional reactions caused by differences beyond the individual's control result in a feeling of helplessness, sometimes called anomie.

For students the different attitudes to education, discussed later in Chapter 7, are a major concern. And, when the language of instruction is not the language students are most used to, language itself – which people rely on to *help* them communicate – can become a constant barrier. But that is only the beginning. Other factors, like climate, can cause great distress. Foshan students going to Staffordshire, like Samoan students going to New Zealand, can be miserable with cold.

The housing available may be very different from that international staff and students are used to. Is the place a person lives in somewhere to study or just somewhere to sleep and eat? Is it acceptable to entertain in the bedroom in some countries and not in others? Is it clean for the toilet and shower to be in the same room? What privacy is wanted or can be expected? A student who has shared a bedroom-cum-study with seven others may feel desperately cut off living in a separate room whereas one who has always had a single room may resent sharing. Altman and Chemers argue that when crowding is perceived, psychological stress is generated (Gudykunst and Kim, 1992a).

Though culture shock is itself an unpleasant and negative experience, writers like Adler (1987) have shown that it may lead to self-development and personal growth: 'The transition the person goes through is one of personal growth ... a movement from a state of low self- and cultural awareness to a state of high self- and cultural awareness.' And later he added: 'Rather than being only a disease for which adaptation is the cure, culture shock is likewise at the very heart of the cross-cultural learning experience. It is an experience in self-understanding and change.' Bock (1970: xi), who treats culture shock very much as an unpleasant emotional stage, similarly sees it has a positive side to it:

> Its value lies in the liberation and understanding that can come from such an experience: the full realization that strange customs are not quaint or meaningless to those who practise them; that other languages are not gibberish or merely awkward substitutes for English; and that other perceptions of reality are just as valid to those who live according to them as our own belief and value systems are to us.

Dodd (1991) describes four possible ways of coping with culture shock: fight, flight, filter and flex. 'Filtering' means accepting the things you want to accept, so denying some aspects of reality. Flexing, or trying everything in a positive frame of mind, is the only way that leads to final balanced acceptance of the new culture. The culture shock can then be followed by the next stages, adaptation and acculturation.

The Process of Adaptation

It is this positive view of culture shock that educators can use to help themselves and international staff and students enjoy differences. Several scholars have described the process of adapting to culture shock, usually dividing it into four stages.

Most of the time, but not always, the stages come in this order. First comes what Oberg (1960) called the honeymoon, a time of excitement, when everything is new and fascinating. The second is a time of distress, when everything seems unduly hard and individuals from the same culture try to group together to share their sense of frustration with the difficult common host. Holmes and Rahe (1967) have suggested that this may continue for the whole of the first year, a long time for students with examinations to face well before the first year ends. The third reflects adaptation, and is usually marked by improved use and understanding of the host language and culture. Finally, the fourth is worry-free and shows full acceptance and enjoyment of the host culture. At this final stage, the individual has passed through culture shock, to become truly intercultural.

Although Oberg (1960) calls culture shock 'an occupational disease of people who have been suddenly transplanted overseas' the process of adaptation to such shock is not a sudden one, nor is it to be viewed as a disease. It may last six months or two or three years, and may repeat itself again and again. Argyle (1982) analyses the process:

> Those going abroad for a limited period, like a year, show a U-shaped pattern of discomfort; in the first stage they are elated, enjoy the sights, and are well looked after. In the second stage they have to cope with domestic life, and things get more difficult; they keep to the company of expatriates and are in some degree of culture shock. In the third phase they have learned to cope better and are looking forward to returning home. There may be problems when they do return home, and many people experience problems on re-entry, due for example to a loss of status, or a less exciting life.

At the adaptation stage a firm base with others of the same culture is a great help. Very often international students have friends both from their home country and the host country. Although it is natural and comfortable to have friends from home, Jin Kim (1980) found that too strong a network of ethnic friendships can slow down adaptation.

Even Adler (1987), who sees the process as one of personal growth, puts the responsibility for overcoming culture shock squarely on the newcomer's head. But if, as Oberg (1960) taught so long ago, adjustment can be complete only when all the cues of social intercourse are completely grasped, surely the responsibility must be shared with hosts? Even if, in Oberg's words, the visitor takes the attitude: 'This is my problem and I have to bear it,' the hosts are not absolved from a share in responsibility. All the research on communication of the past forty years sees the overcoming of culture shock as a two way process. When the communication is with a group like international students whose stay is specifically arranged by an organisation which will itself benefit from their presence, responsibility is more than ever shared.

The aim of this chapter has been to create an awareness of difference, of the responsibility for alleviating any problems this difference may cause, and of the excitement of appreciating the new insights this difference may bring. The focus is on interacting with international students but international staff are mentioned also, especially teaching staff, since they may well be involved yet overlooked. Both bring such value to any academic community that their differences need to be explained and celebrated, to the advantage of host and visitor alike.

Issues to Consider

With relation to the last international student or staff member you talked to:

(1)   In what ways did your own culture affect what you said and did?

(2)   Consider an international staff member you think of as an asset to your institution. To what extent may your own preconceptions have accounted for your assessment?

(3)   Consider an international student you think troublesome. To what extent do your own preconceptions account for your assessment?

(4)   Do you think it worthwhile to learn to distance yourself from your own assumptions, actions and judgments? Why or why not?

(5)   How easy is it to distance yourself from your own subjective biases?

(6)   Were you aware of any misunderstandings? Was there any 'talking past each other'?

(7)   Ask an international staff member or student you know what particular problems caused worry in the early days of work in your institution. Are they still causing problems? Ask yourself if you have ever done, or could now do, anything to alleviate the problems.

2 CULTURE

'I do not want my house to be walled in on all sides and my windows to be stuffed. I want the cultures of all lands to be blown about my house as freely as possible. But I refuse to be blown off my feet by any.'

Mahatma Gandhi

The Enigma, Culture

To understand the culture shock international staff and students may suffer, we need to understand culture itself. Culture is a human phenomenon; it is the way we are, both physically and mentally. It is both a state in which each of us exists and a process which changes constantly according to the individual, the time and the place. This combined state and process called culture affects us all as we respond to others, to events and to the environment. Although Mahatma Gandhi refused to be 'blown about' by culture, his very use of the phrase 'my house' suggests a personal place for him, a place where he belongs, a 'security blanket', to use Korzenny's phrase (1991: 56-61).

The subsidiary meanings of culture, refinement and the arts, are part of culture in the sense it is used in this book, but only a small part. Refinement is the kind of superficial polish referred to in a sentence like, 'She is a cultured person' – or, less kindly, 'She is an uncultured person'. The arts are referred to when, for example, a country has a ministry of culture to foster poetry, music, drama, the fine arts, mime, ballet and other forms of dance.

Culture changes within a community all the time, sometimes momentously but more often imperceptibly. Discoveries such as electricity, the telephone, television, computer technology, and laser beams all conspicuously changed the cultures where they were developed and those in which they are now used. Attitudes towards marriage, education, health and sport change radically also, though not suddenly.

Culture, pervasive as it is, has been explained many more ways than can be seen in the 300 definitions Kroeber and Kluckhohn collected in 1954. The definitions can be grouped into four categories: learned behaviour, sharing of values, a dialectic process and an interactive process. Each of these requires explanation.

(1) **Learned Behaviour** Explaining culture as learned behaviour is no more than a start for useful work with international students. However it can be extended to cover perception, which according to Hall (1972: 46-55) includes what we are going to do about something, what we see and what we are blind to: 'In its simplest sense, perception is the internal process by which we select, evaluate, and organize stimuli from the external environment.'

(2) **Sharing of Values** This, based on definitions like Hofstede's 'the collective programming of the mind' (1984: 21), and 'the software of the mind'(1991: 237), blurs the distinction between culture and values discussed in Chapter 4 and may also encourage stereotyping. However it does indicate the depth and importance of culture.

(3) **A Dialectic Process** This is similar except that it recognises differences among members of a group and throughout a single cultural system; in this view culture is limited to a process *within* people in one society.

(4) **An Interactive Process** This is the result of a combination of the person's personality, values and the context. This approach is implied in definitions like 'the sum total of ways of living' (Sikkema, 1987), 'the total accumulation of an identifiable group's beliefs, norms, activities, institutions and communication patterns (Dodd, 1991), or 'the totality of beliefs and practices of a society' (Nida, 1991). It tells an English person that he or she must eat with the mouth closed, quietly, while an Indian knows that the mouth should be open while a person is chewing and an African knows that to show appreciation it is important to make noises with gusto. This approach is the most useful for understanding the culture of those international staff and students out of their home environment and working to establish roots in another context.

These categories, especially the fourth one, imply that culture is learned, transmitted by each generation to the next, capable of constant change, transmissible, encompassing the physical and the mental, and shared by a group. Culture includes, among other things, appearance, clothes, food, shelter, attitudes towards family, work, leisure, time, dress, what is beautiful and what is ugly. Its coverage is vast and its consequences major. In a familiar environment it helps people behave appropriately and understand the behaviour of others. But unless those of us involved in education are conscious of the ways it tints our own behaviour and understanding, our culture may blur our vision so that we behave in a way damaging to our relationships with those whose culture differs from our own.

This blurring was seen by Edward T. Hall (1972) as a highly selective screen between people and their outside worlds, a filter which effectively designates what people attend to as well as what they choose to ignore. Culture helps mould the individual but does not prevent individuals varying from one another within it.

Although our own culture can affect our vision in this way, it is not something to reject in order to be clear sighted. The aim is rather is to be aware of and respect both our own and others' values. The term 'cultural relativism' (Gudykunst and Kim, 1992) has been used to label the view that all cultures are of equal value, and the values and behaviour of a culture can only be judged using that culture as a frame of reference. Jewish laws about eating pork, Islamic laws about eating beef, and Hindu laws about eating flesh of any kind have a long-established rationale behind them. Michael Bond (1991: v), an American psychologist who has spent many years teaching in a university in Hong Kong, tells readers he always tried to ask, 'Under what cultural rule can that puzzling behaviour possibly make sense?'

Culture, Ethnicity and Nationality

Culture is sometimes, but certainly not always, the same as ethnicity and nationality. A Japanese person, brought up in Japan in a Japanese household would be Japanese by culture, by ethnicity (that is, physically he or she would be recognisably Japanese to another Japanese) and by nationality. A Japanese born in Australia, adopted and brought up by English-speaking Australians would be Japanese by ethnicity but Australian by culture and nationality. In some cultures ethnicity is easy to recognise. For example, Gotanda, a Japanese-American living in Japan suddenly recognising his ethnicity, expressed his feelings:

> I looked ahead and saw a sea of people coming towards me, all about my same height, with black hair, with skin that looked exactly like mine ...

What I experienced for the first time was this extraordinary thing called anonymity – the sense of being able to be part of a group. (Gudykunst and Kim, 1992b: 71)

Distinctions are not always so easy to make. Ethnicity can be readily established and sometimes easily recognised, but culture and nationality can depend on the choice of the individual and on political decisions. For instance, what is now the Czech Republic was formerly part of Czechoslovakia so people who consider themselves Czech would previously have called themselves Czechoslovakian by nationality. Yet nationality itself is a complex, difficult concept. The word 'nationality', which derives from the Latin *nasci* (to be born) and originally had no political connotations, does now. When Mazzini united Italy and Bismarck, Germany, they were creating nations in the sense we think of them today. And when the Union of Soviet Socialist Republics (the USSR) disintegrated, old nations were recreated.

Certainly a person brought up in one nation as a young child may be placed or may place him or herself in another. At the time this book is written, a child brought up in New Zealand with one parent born in Britain may claim to have British nationality. Even when place is the deciding criterion, that place may be much narrower than national borders. A Roman, a Sydneyite, a Mäori or a (Scottish) Lowlander may claim a culture different in marked ways from that of compatriots. Only the choice of the individual can finally decide the culture; the choice of individual and a particular government together can finally decide nationality.

Others may not recognise ethnic, national or cultural differences. Many westerners cannot tell whether a person is Thai, Chinese or Japanese. Nationality is even more difficult to tell. Malay, Chinese, Indians, people of other ethnic backgrounds and people of mixed ethnicity can be equally Malaysian.

Culture is not fixed. Dress, food, housing, attitudes to inheritance, sex, marriage, health, education and many other matters change. In a western community it now seems extraordinary that two centuries ago possessions passed normally only to male members of a family, and a married woman had no income of her own. Even fifty years ago, it was exceptional for a man and woman to live together outside marriage in a western community. Twenty years ago in New Zealand the hosts' first job after a party was to open all windows to get rid of the cigarette smoke. Now it is rare for anyone to smoke inside someone else's house, at least without specially asking for, and being given, permission.

Within a culture, variation occurs. Subcultures, or groups similar in age, education, wealth, interests, sports and many other factors, may exist within a larger culture. Most people belong to more than one subculture, even when in a foreign country.

High and Low Context

A major cultural difference is that between high and low contexts, a distinction first analysed by Edward T. Hall. Both high and low contexts exist in all communities, but one or other predominates. Hall defines context as whatever surrounds an event and is bound up in it. He shows that the elements that combine to produce any given meaning are in different proportions according to the culture and so it is possible to order the cultures of the world on a scale from high to low context:

> High context messages are placed at one end and low context messages at the other end of a continuum. A high-context (HC) communication or message is one in which most of the information is either in the physical context or internalized in the person, while very little is in the coded, explicit, transmitted part of the message. A low-context (LC) communication is just the opposite; i.e. the mass of the information is vested in the explicit code. Twins who have grown up together can and do communicate more economically (HC) than two lawyers in a courtroom during a trial, a mathematician programming a computer, two politicians drafting legislation, two administrators writing a regulation, or a child trying to explain to his mother why he got into a fight. (1987: 79)

People from high context cultures can become impatient with people from low-context cultures when they are required to give information which they think should be known and understood. Conversely, people from low-context cultures are uncomfortable when not given the details they expect. To quote Hall again:

> Too much information frequently leads people to feel they are being talked down to; too little information can mystify them or make them feel left out. Ordinarily, people make these adjustments automatically in their own country, but in other countries their messages frequently miss the target. (1987: 11)

In a high-context culture, there are distinctions between ingroups and outgroups. People expect more of others. High-context people, because of their intense involvement with each other and their extensive cohesive networks are more elastic; there is more 'give' in their system. (1987: 31)

Asian and indigenous cultures tend to be high context cultures. In them most of the information is either in the setting or the person, with very little in the message as it is explicitly transmitted to others. Children are trained not to show emotions publicly. People expect others to understand the unspoken, interpreting messages as part of the whole context, not as discrete contributions by the individual.

High context actions tend to be made by the group, to be rooted in the past, to be slow to change and highly stable. In them emphasis is on personal relationships with a high degree of obligation on both sides, on oral communication and on preserving personal dignity. Both occupations and business relationships last for a long time and are based on the well being of the group.

Low context cultures tend to be western cultures, like those of the United Kingdom, the United States and Europe, often those which colonised less advanced countries in order to draw on their natural wealth. In them, most of the information is recorded in writing and ruled on by the laws of the land. Facts lie outside those communicating and those communicated with. Individuals make decisions both about business and about career paths. Even in a western community, spelling out every detail as though the listener is a child, or knows nothing, can irritate others. What is happening is that the speaker is assuming that more context needs to be supplied than the listener considers necessary.

Victor (1990: 144) gives five main differences between high and low culture:

(1)   Different emphasis on personal relationships
(2)   Different attitude to explicit communication, the law, contracts
(3)   Different reliance on verbal communications
(4)   Uncertainty avoidance variations
(5)   Different versions of face-saving

Conscious recognition of these differences can help a person from one cultural context understand those from another. They will be discussed in more detail in Chapter 4 and Chapter 6.

Individualism and Collectivism

Many theorists have seen cultures as predominantly individualist or collectivist. Just as no culture is completely high or low context, so no culture is completely individualist or collective. Most, however, have a tendency one way or the other, and usually that tendency is strongly marked. For instance, Israel is shown in Hofstede's research to have relatively strong individualism, yet Victor (1992: 105) points out that its *kibbutz* system for farming and some industries, including high tech industries, is 'the most purely collectivist managerial system of any culture'. Significant research on the individualist and collectivist tendencies has been carried out by several intercultural specialists, in particular, Hofstede (1980; 1984; 1986; 1991) and Triandis (1987; 1991).

More recently, theorists have put forward the idea that individualism and collectivism co-exist and interact and should not be seen as opposites. Yoke Leng Thomas (1996: 10), for example, writes:

> It is entirely conceivable for a culture to display highly individualistic as well as collectivist attributes. The Malaysian Chinese executive demonstrates this when on the one hand he is self-reliant, seeking to start his own business. On the other hand he is interdependent, fulfilling his family obligations to provide employment for his sister and help for his aging father. His actions are guided by his consideration for himself and for his family interests.

A similar dichotomy can exist with Koreans who are collectivist in their relationships yet can be fiercely determined to achieve personal success and intensely competitive in business, perhaps because of their country's harsh historical experiences. The country suffered prolonged occupation by the Japanese who the Koreans accuse of attempted cultural genocide; the political division of the Korean peninsula at the 38th parallel into the communist north and the capitalist south after the defeat of the Japanese in 1945; and the destruction wrought by the contending armies during the Korean war of the early 1950s. The aggressive attitude which resulted, though, is not used to win benefits for the individuals themselves but for the group, whether the group is the extended family, the company or the country.

Usually individualists tend to be competitive; collectivists, co-operative. Nepotism, frowned on in individualist cultures, is assumed and taken as right in collectivist cultures. Achievement can be important in either individualist or collectivist societies but in a different way. In an individualist culture achievement is fulfilment of the individual; in a collectivist culture achievement is for the benefit of the group.

Attitudes to ownership and sharing of possessions differ according to the culture. If family money is a shared possession in a collectivist culture, so is responsibility to pay for education or large scale hospitality like weddings or funerals.

From there it is a natural step to see intellectual property as a shared benefit, public, not private. In the west people see that individual time and so money has gone into producing something, and therefore treat it as privately owned. In Asia, time and costs are shared, so the group benefits. Dissension over journals, videotapes, films and computer programmes produced in the west and copied in Asia is considerable. While individualists tend to work from the equity principle, what an individual deserves according to his or her effort, the collectivists work on the equality principle, what a person should have in relation to what others have and he or she needs.

Even concepts of 'face' are different. In collectivist cultures, people are concerned that others will be embarrassed. In individualist cultures, the concern is that the self, the individual, will be embarrassed.

Stella Ting-Toomey (1988: 129) points out the contrast, defining 'face' as the claimed public self-image of a person in a particular situation:

> In the individualistic cultures the 'I' identity is most vulnerable to attack and to relational hurt. In the collectivistic cultures the 'face' identity is most sensitive to hurts and violations. To hurt someone's 'I' identity in individualistic cultures means direct violation of the other person's sense of personal privacy, the betrayal of private information to a third person, or the bringing up of deeply personal taboo topics that hurt the other person's ego. To hurt someone's face identity in the collectivistic cultures means verbally assaulting the other person's face in front of a third party, separating the other person's connection with family and kinship network ties, or bringing up taboo topics that deal with in groups' ineffectiveness or inadequacy.

Since, as has been mentioned above, no culture is completely individualist or collective, both kinds of hurt are possible. The difference may be in degree.

In a predominantly individualist society people are used to work and leisure being kept separate. In the east, work and leisure are blended. An employer could be expected to be responsible for the total life of employees, including health, family, personal problems and children's welfare.

There are, of course, individual differences between people within both collectivist and individualist cultures. As Triandis *et al.* (1991) wrote:

> It is not enough to know the culture of the other person. It is also necessary to know something about demographic and biographic information, because individuals from urban, industrialized, mobile, migrating, affluent environments with much exposure to the media are likely to be idiocentric, even if they come from collectivist cultures.

Individualism: 'I' before 'We'

Individualism as a term was first used by the French social philosopher, Alexis de Tocqueville in the 1830s. Soon after, John Stuart Mill writing in 1859 'of individuality as one of the elements of wellbeing' cited Wilhelm von Humboldt as giving a person's ultimate human goal as 'the highest and most harmonious development of his powers'. Mill goes as far as saying that what he calls 'individuality' is the same thing as development. He sees it as the belief that each person is more important than the group in which he or she belongs and should have the right to full development according to personal choice. Maslow's (1954: 12) hierarchy of needs, with self-actualisation at the summit, is based on this belief.

Both Judaism and Christianity emphasise the worth of each separate being: 'Inasmuch as you do it unto the least of these my brethren, you do it unto me,' said Christ. The same theme was repeated by Blake in the *Songs of Innocence and Experience,* by the United States in the *American Declaration of Independence,* by the French in the *Complément à Déclaration des Droits de l'homme* of 1936, by the General Assembly of the United Nations *Declaration of Human Rights* and in many other political and religious documents.

Individualism includes the belief that each person should have the right to develop him or herself according to personal choice, whether or not that suits the society. H.G. Wells (1940: 14) wrote:

> Every man ... is entitled ... to realise his full possibilities of physical and mental health ... to enjoy the utmost freedom of discussion and to suggest employment for himself and have his claim publicly considered.

Sayings like 'Every man for himself and the devil take the hindmost' encapsulate this attitude.

Further, each person is entitled to privacy. This right was recognised in statements like this from Jules Renard, a nineteenth century French author, 'I prefer to look after myself rather than others in case they say: "Why is he interfering?"' Virginia Woolf's autobiographical essay, "A Room of My Own", was an early twentieth century cry for the right of a woman author for space to work to her full potential.

In an individualist culture, confrontation is part of law, and is generally seen as a way of sorting things out. Work is done through contracts, usually written, more than through relationships. Employment and contracts can be changed or broken by either party. Networking exists and is powerful but usually depends on deliberate choice. When the 'old boy network' operates, it is, perhaps, a glimpse of collectivism in a western society. However, it still involves using others for personal gain, not for the good of the group.

Initiative and assertiveness are encouraged. People belong to groups but by choice. They create their own groups, they try out groups others have created and they move in and out of groups at will.

Collectivism: 'We' before 'I'

In a collectivist society, relationships are permanent and all important. A child is taught from infancy to place the group above the individual in family matters, in education, in politics and in business. Proverbs like 'Loud thunder brings little rain', 'A single arrow is easily broken but not a whole bunch' and 'The nail that sticks up will be hammered down' reinforce this teaching. The Japanese word *amae,* meaning a feeling of closeness and dependency, encapsulates the concept of collectivism.

As travel becomes easier, some collectivist cultures are changing, but not with full approval. The words of Anwar Ibrahim (1996), Malaysian Deputy Prime Minister, could have been spoken by many Asians: 'There is an excessive and unbridled individualism today in our country. This has caused the downfall of many civilisations in the past. If the motivation is materialistic and individualistic, we will be in trouble.'

A person will belong to several groups, one of which will be more important than the others. In Japan the main group tends to be the company; in India, the family; in China, the state. Since in many collectivist cultures housing is provided with work, colleagues are likely to be neighbours and highly trusted. Public and private life are inseparable and an employer is responsible for the wellbeing of his – for the employer is seldom a woman – workforce. And whereas in individualistic cultures the group may be temporary, in Asia it is usually permanent and settled by tradition.

The sense of loyalty to the group is built up by intensive education and training. The same kind of induction into togetherness was and still is deliberately fostered in the United States by the procedure of swearing the oath of allegiance in front of the American flag in schools at the beginning of each day.

Since the group goes on forever, harmony within it is important and confrontation avoided at all costs. If a group go out to dinner the person who suggested the outing pays and the others remember and return the kindness later, in the same or a different way. 'Going Dutch', or each paying his or her share, would be unthinkable.

Membership of a group confers privileges and incurs obligations. The Chinese word, *guanxi* (literally 'connected'), the Filipino phrase, *utang na loob* (gratitude), the Japanese *nemawashi* (literally 'root-binding'), all convey the same sense of the binding and reciprocal nature of relationships. Gift-giving, arranging jobs for members of the family, accepting responsibility for paying for education of family including siblings, caring for parents in old age, are all aspects of commitment to the group. The three Confucian principles of *jen* (warm human feelings), *i* (loyalty) and *li* (respect for social order) underlie this sense of membership of a group. The bonding is so strong that young people train for work they would not choose to do, young parents leave their babies with their families while they go abroad for further education and nations can implement policies totally against their tradition, like the one-child policy in China.

In an educational situation, the implications are legion. A young man from a collectivist culture on a scholarship in an individualist culture will send home to elderly parents, money intended to enable him to live and buy the materials he needs. A young woman in a western country, from say, Mexico or the Middle East will not go to see a doctor because for that she should be accompanied by the eldest member of the family. When possible, as in the latter example, structures need to be set up to enable requirements of the home culture to be satisfied.

Business Strategies

In individualist cultures, business is separate from home, and is supposed to be open and honest. Accountants preparing audit reports are required to say that the books give a 'true and fair' account of records kept. Terms like 'under the counter deals', 'through the back door' and 'nepotism' are derogatory. A senior executive who has an 'open door policy' is admired. An employee who does outstanding work is publicly commended and rewarded.

In the west, hospitality is often enough a part of business but does not necessarily mean much. In contrast in the east, hospitality is an essential part of the relationship. Business and private life overlap. Strangers are suspect so business people use go-betweens to introduce them. Establishing rapport and trust through gifts and through dining together and building a warm personal relationship is a necessary early step in business.

Everyone depends on everyone else, but individuals do not expect recognition. Singling out individuals in the classroom or workforce for praise would embarrass them. Motivation must always be intrinsic; the good of the organisation, not the promotion of the individual, is what matters.

The business person must always be sensitive to saving face. In an individualist society this is achieved by working to avoid misunderstanding by a clear and direct statement of purpose and by written records of meetings and agreements. In a collectivist society it is achieved by establishing trust before negotiations begin, maintaining harmony and avoiding confrontation.

In the west anyone, young or old, new or of long standing in the relationship, can be the negotiator, with full authority to clinch agreements. In the east only the senior person has authority, even if the organisation has experts far more knowledgeable about a particular matter. Not that the authority is always visible. The Japanese, for example, consider it offensive for an individual to make or to claim to make decisions about any issue. Even at a business meeting the person with most weight in the decision-making process is usually not obvious to the outside party. The decision must be seen to come from the group. Obligation, which is a burden in some cultures where people say 'I owe you one' and want to repay indebtedness openly, is seen as a benefit in others, to be savoured long-term and never forgotten.

Business and study may both be affected by cultural habits such as the widespread practice of taking a break for sleeping around midday in countries with hot and humid weather. The Mediterranean and South American custom of taking a noon siesta is well known but the Chinese habit of *xiu-xi* has become just as much a ritual since 1949 when it was written into the Chinese Constitution as Article 49. Butterfield (1982: 272) tells of an incident in the South China Sea in which an oil rig was running delicate tests with an air-pressure gun to find out whether there was oil in the area. The equipment cost $50,000 a day to operate and, besides, it was technically dangerous to halt the testing. However the American engineer sent to inspect was astonished to find drilling had completely stopped during *xiu-xi* and the rig crew had disappeared for their sleep. It is no wonder then, that students who have for the first two decades of their lives had 'nap time' straight after lunch sometimes find tests and scheduled study in the early afternoon a great strain.

Family

The family is important in all cultures but more in some than in others. In western cultures it tends to be small, including those in the household, and possibly also parents or children living elsewhere. The western family used to be often called the nuclear family – father, mother and children – but divorce and re-marriage have so changed the pattern that 'nuclear' is rarely used now. In eastern cultures it can be a great web, the size depending on the particular society. Polynesian cultures, for example, are based on extended families. The *matai*, or chief of a Samoan extended family, has formal, established power and responsibility. New Zealand Mäori, whatever their work or educational commitments, are expected to attend the *tangi* (funeral) of anyone in the tribe, which could comprise four or five thousand people so that there may be a number of to attend in a year. Since a *tangi* takes several days, major disruptions to study or work can occur.

According to Mbiti (1970), in the traditional African family, the individual owed existence itself to all the members, living, dead and yet-to-be-born, of the family, tribe or clan. Each person is an integral part of a close-knit collective unity that is the family.

The role of the family differs very much according to the culture. In the Middle East, arrangements, including responsibility for education, tend to be based on the family who are bound by the *Qur'an* to take care of their members. The senior male member has the authority openly, unlike in Japan where consensus of the group at least appears to rule.

Marriages are still arranged by the family in many eastern societies and those who support arranged marriages claim a high rate of success. Divorce is comparatively rare and only allowed for some measurable reason, such as failure of the woman to conceive. In western cultures divorce has become common and is usually seen as a sort of safety valve though in some societies it does still have some stigma. Ireland, for example, only legalised divorce on 25 November 1995.

Gender

Attitudes of men and women to each other differ significantly across cultures, just as they have differed significantly with the passing of time. Similarly, attitudes to what Hofstede (1980) called masculinity and femininity differ across cultures.

Hofstede's research on this matter, which will be cited and referred to in depth and detail in Chapter 4, has been criticised for three reasons. First, it was based on a quantitative study, originally carried out in 1980. Although it has been updated and extended several times since, the situation in some countries has changed so radically that the very questions asked on the gender issue seem inappropriate now. Second, he and his team surveyed IBM employees in only fifty countries and three regions. These countries excluded China, not open to the western world when the research was originally done but too significant to omit now in a comprehensive survey, containing as it does almost a quarter of the world's population. Third, certainly in 1980 and to some degree even now, a computer industry might be expected to employ a disproportionate number of white collar males and so might not be truly representative of views on masculinity and femininity in the culture. All the same, though Hofstede's findings may not be entirely reliable, the thinking behind them provides a useful starting point for discussion of this issue.

Hofstede's understanding of masculinity and femininity was in itself idiosyncratic. He associated masculinity with a society where strength, performance, achievement, competition and ambition were admired. He associated femininity with a caring society where the young, the old and people with disabilities were cherished and nurtured. A society with a welfare system giving all those people over sixty 80 per cent of the average wage and supplying free education and medicine to all who wanted it, as New Zealand did at the time of the survey but does not now do, could be expected to rank high on the femininity scale, yet it came close to mid way, fifteenth of the thirty-nine countries, making it relatively masculine.

In individualist cultures, where each individual matters, it might be expected that men and women would have equal status. Yet still men 'hold better jobs, gain higher wages and have more opportunities for success than their female counterparts' (Verburg, 1988: 246). However in most western societies a serious attempt is being made to give women equal opportunities with men. Often overt discrimination on grounds of sex is illegal.

In some cultures discrimination is still open and legal. The Algerian saying 'Women have but two residences – the house and the tomb' shows the extreme position. In predominantly Islamic cultures like Saudi Arabia, Libya and Qatar, women do not work outside the home. They can be stoned to death for adultery, though the law requires four witnesses to the sexual act to establish guilt. And according to Cherry and Charles Lindholm (1988), strict Muslims such as the Yusufzai Pakhtum in Pakistan allow men to beat their wives and boast about the beatings they have administered. It may be difficult for students from such places to accept women, especially women of perceived lower academic status like secretaries, as worthy of deference. Yet it must be remembered that the *Qur'an* says 'Men and women are of the same family, and as such have similar rights and duties.'[1] The differences of status in the Muslim perception are not intended to downgrade women. Rather, they are a reflection of the different status of, and attitude towards home – where women preside – and the outside world, where men have the major responsibility.

Attitudes to sport illustrate the point. In Iran, for example, women's sports are continually being condemned. In 1996 four separate ayatollahs issued religious edicts saying women should not practise such sports as cycling, riding and canoeing in public, and one said they should not practise them at all. On the same day, France decided women could become fighter pilots, allowing them to enter the airforce academy's next training programme.[2]

In education girls do not always have even approximately the same rights as their brothers. The United Nations Children's Fund reported in early 1997 that schools had re-opened in Afghanistan after the winter recess 'but there were no girls in sight'. According to *The Waikato Times* on 3 April 1997 the Afghan Government in Kabul, headed by the extremist Islamic Taliban movement, had barred girls from schools as well as women from the workplace.

When women are a recognisable part of the work force, as in Indonesia where nearly 50 per cent of the women of working age are gainfully employed, they have been publicly reminded that they should 'strike a balance between the two facets of their lives' and not neglect household chores. Western influence has led women's groups to reject such advice which came from Vice-President Try Sutrisno. Women are beginning to claim such comments are a way to justify the wage disparity between men and women, and are not basic to their religion.[3] Muslim women, according to the *Qur'an*, do have their economic rights protected and some of their personal rights. For instance, they have to be paid 'maintenance on a reasonable scale' (Naila Minae, 1988) though they cannot keep their children after divorce. They cannot be made to marry against their will. 'None, not even the father or the sovereign, can lawfully contract in marriage an adult woman without her permission, whether she be a virgin or not' (Minae, 1988). In making these rulings Mohammad had been enormously influenced by his own wife, Khadija.

Arranged marriages, still preferred by many in cultures such as the

---

[1]   The *Qur'an* 3: 195.

[2]   Reuter, published in the *Waikato Times* (Friday 3 May 1996: 5).

[3]   "Women irate at comments on work role", AAP Jacarta, quoted in *The New Zealand Herald* (16 November 1996: 3).

Punjabi, do not indicate that women are chattels to be disposed of at will by the family. Rather they are a serious attempt on both sides of a family to match two people in a way that will ensure that their marriage will last, be happy, and will contribute to the well-being of the whole group.

Certainly the Confucian saying about the three pathways for a woman still affects the status of Asian women: 'In her youth, she must follow her father. In her adulthood, she must follow her husband. In her later years, she must follow her oldest son' (Montiero, Kenneth P., 1995). In Japan many women work in business organisations though in low level jobs and with no guarantee of the lifelong employment men often have. They do control the purse strings in the home, perhaps because the men work long hours away from the home.

Women usually work outside the home in China and do sometimes rise to high positions in some places. Bond (1991: 45), whose experience has mostly been in Hong Kong, writes 'Despite the egalitarian cant, women are conspicuously absent from positions of political authority and are still lumbered with the primary responsibility for child care.' However, at Foshan University in Guangdong Province, I saw very different customs. Even the male guards in full uniform at the university gates were looking after small children at the same time as they were on duty, as were many of the male builders on site. Zhi Lin, an academic at the same university, said that one third of university presidents in China are women, a situation very different from that in the west.[4] This kind of information, as explained in Chapter 8, is almost impossible to check. And because China is such a vast country, any generalisation has limited validity.

Certainly it is easy to assume that the culture we know privileges women more than those we do not know, until facts prove us wrong. The International Labour Organisation, discussing employment in Asia in 1994, collected data which show that 'women in employment in Asia in all the main minority groups were a little *more*[5] likely than their white counterparts to be professional' (Amit-Talai & Knowles, 1996: 291).

Many cultures insist that the different attitudes to men and women do not imply that one is lesser; simply that they are different. In the Māori culture, for instance, women do not go on to building sites. A young Māori woman, asked how she felt about this, acknowledged strong conflict in herself. On the one hand, her education made her feel that if a woman wants to become, say, an electrician, then she should be able to. On the other hand, she could feel what

---

[4] Personal communication 20 December, 1995.

[5] Emphasis added.

she called the *tapu* in her bones and the respect for the *kaumatua* (older person in authority) is very strong. 'I would have to give up being a Mäori just to make a point. It's too big to think about' (Nelson, Frances, 1995). Such pressure, for students outside their own culture, must add to the other stresses of being an international student.

Age

Attitudes to age differ greatly according to the culture. In some cultures, age is scorned, resented or discounted with terms like 'Old fuddy-duddy'. In western cultures because there is a tendency to see anyone over 65 as non-productive, they may become so. As Dodd (1991: 47) writes, 'In a type of self-fulfilling prophecy, some elderly people actually perform less efficiently, develop more health problems, and feel alienated because of societal expectations.' In other cultures age is seen as experience and valued. The Ashanti in Ghana greet elderly people with words which, roughly translated, mean 'my grandfather' or 'my grandmother' (Dodd, 1991: 47). The New Zealand Mäori address their elders with similar respect and affection, using terms of relationship to signify respect for age. Frances Nelson put it this way:

> Today I walked past Pehiaweri, our local *marae,* and saw elderly Mäori people working with younger people on various projects. Whenever the older people were speaking, the young were listening; and whenever the younger people were working, the older people were supervising. … I mentioned my observations to Henie, one of my students and she told me that for Mäori, maturity means exchanging manual work for the work of keeping tradition alive and guiding the people. At this time of their lives, Mäori work harder than before they gained their mana. (1995: 2)

This respect can have a downside. On farms young Mäori trained at horticultural colleges sometimes cannot use their knowledge while the old people are in charge, so that farms continue to lose money when they might be turned into thriving businesses.

As in Mäori communities, in Asian cultures the elderly are looked up to. If a western company or university sends a young person to represent it, its Asian counterpart will be insulted or at least unimpressed. The most impressive job titles and often the most responsibility tend to be held by the elderly though that does not mean they are expected to do the most work (Varner and Beamer, 1995: 96). In China after retirement, they continue to draw the same wage and live in the same supplied accommodation so that a factory or a university will have many people living in its grounds but no longer formally working for it. They still give guidance and private tutoring as required. Again this may have a downside. Young people, with up-to-date knowledge from leading MBA schools may have to wait for years before introducing their ideas into family companies. By the time they are the revered seniors their knowledge might be of little use.

In some Asian cultures, it is customary for the oldest son to have responsibility for looking after parents and grandparents, and this responsibility is treated as a norm by young and old alike. The responsibility can mean that students send part of their scholarship money home to cover living costs for their elderly. But in places this assumption that the young care for the old is changing. A 102-year-old woman in Hong Kong was reported to have tried to commit suicide because she did not want to be a burden to her family (*Sunday-Star Times*, 1997).

Death

Death is seen very differently according to the culture. In western countries the colour for mourning is black but in the east it is more often white, symbolised by white roses which brides wear in the west.

How long do people grieve? Mäori people hold a special service to honour and remember a year after a person has died and only then is the funeral over.

How public is death? In the west some nuclear families want to hold a small private service to keep their grief to themselves and the wish is then respected by giving them time and space to recover. It would be unthinkable in other cultures where a funeral is very public. In the Fijian-Indian culture all members of the family including distant aunts, uncles and cousins are expected to visit the bereaved every night for ten days. In China members of the extended family are expected to crawl on their knees from the gate of the house to the room where the body lies, to show respect. In Malaysia a small funeral will take place in a public street, a large one will take over part of a city. It is not uncommon for a company or a professional organisation such as a law partnership to put a half-page advertisement in the newspaper to extend sympathy to the family of someone with whom its staff have had much to do on his or her 'demise', the usual term when English is used. When the familiar customs cannot be observed, as when a student is far from home and cannot afford to travel, the grieving process must be even harder than it would otherwise have been.

A folk belief in Thailand is that parents of Buddhist monks can hang on to the saffron robe of their monk son and be carried up to heaven when they die. This may be one of the reasons why sons are so valued in Thailand, for every Buddhist male there is expected to spend some time as a Buddhist monk. Such folk beliefs, definitely not part of the religion itself, attach themselves to many religions.

Is death the end or not? The Hindus believe in reincarnation, in the circular nature of life. Yet in Asian cultures death is dreaded. The worst gift of all is a clock which symbolises the ticking away of life. In Mandarin the very word for death is avoided and in south China since it sounds like the word for four, four is an unlucky number and used as little as possible. On the day of the dead, a nationally observed day throughout China, candles are lit, words chanted and food prepared and laid out for ancestors. In Japan similar rites are performed but the food is eaten by the celebrants. In Mexico, equally a predominantly collective society though for different reasons, solemn services are held on *El Dia de Los Muertos.*

In western cultures, ancestor commemorations are rare but attitudes can be very different. In Russia death is welcomed. In Alaska among the Inuit it is ignored. Is death a private or a public concern, a time for unobtrusive grieving or public appreciation? Are funerals limited to close family or does everyone become involved? Evelyn Waugh's novel *The Loved One,* about American commercialisation of death, though written half a century ago, still shows how different American and British attitudes towards death are.

Environment

The physical environment affects people, especially when they are not used to it. Consider the natural environment which includes latitude, weather and topography; the man-made environment which includes housing, classrooms, transport and, unfortunately, pollution; and also the social environment which involves family groupings, crowding, lack of privacy and so on. A person used to open country may feel oppressed in a city. A person who has shared a room with several others may feel utterly cut off when living alone.

In collectivist cultures the environment is seen as something precious lent for proper care, something to be guarded for future generations, while in individualist societies the environment is seen as something to be harnessed to improve the quality of life of people. This attitude is changing. Books like Rachel Carson's *Silent Spring* have alerted many western people to the danger and the ugliness of using the environment without due respect for it. Political parties have been founded with care of the environment as their main platform. One of these parties, The Green Independents, with five seats out of thirty five, held the balance of power in 1989 in Tasmania, Australia, neither of the two major parties being able to govern in its own right. In the rest of Australia, in Canada, in the United States, in Germany and in New Zealand environmental groups have been politically active. However, the idea behind them is relatively new. The words of Tuwhareoa ki Kawera (1996) cited in the *Regional Plan for the Tarawera River Catchment* reflect a view that could have been expressed by members of collectivist cultures all around the world: 'Sustainability is a modern catch phrase for something that has been fundamental to Mäori for generations – *tikanga.*' *Tikanga* is Mäori protocol, the way things are done, including love of and respect for land and sea and air.

In some parts of the world it is almost impossible to obtain personal privacy. Films like *City of Joy* [Calcutta] show whole families not only living in one room but pleased to have a room to live in. In Guangdong province in south China it is quite usual for eight students to share a bedroom, with eight double-decker bunks, boxes under the bottom bunks for personal possessions, and four chairs, on the assumption that if more than four students need to sit at once the bottom bunks will be used. The students seem not to regard this room sharing as a hardship. As William B Gudykunst and Stella Ting-Toomey (1992: 276) say, 'Personal privacy might not be as major a concern for people in collectivistic cultures as it is in individualistic cultures.'

Three environmental matters may cause special difficulty for international staff and students: climate, physical setting, both built and natural, and population density. These will be discussed in Chapter 8.

Time

Time-related behaviour involves both the attitude to pre-arranged time and the pace of carrying out any tasks.

Is time cyclical or linear? How are the hours of the day to be arranged? Airlines operate by a twenty-four hour clock; most western countries use two blocks of twelve hours, which are referred to as am (Latin *ante meridian*) and pm (Latin *post meridian*); the Thai people use four blocks of six hours; ships use six blocks of four hours. Do the seasons of the year and the seasons of life dictate how a society should work? Or should tasks to be completed be planned and then dictate the arrangement of time? Such questions are answered in different ways in different cultures.

In invitations in the west, time can be exact. 'Cocktails: 5-7' or 'At home: 2-6' may appear on a written card. Such information is intended to be considerate, allowing people to adjust other arrangements. In Asia it would be unthinkable, as though telling guests they can come at certain times but not others. Asians know when to go. It can be disconcerting to westerners used to loitering farewells to hear, 'Let's go' after dinner and find a whole group get up and leave, pleasantly but without any hesitation.

We all share the same time, admittedly, but not the same calendar. New Year's day in China comes on a different day each year, and is never the same as in the western calendar. This is the twenty-sixth century in Thailand and the fifteenth in Saudi Arabia. People in every culture have their own special days and can reasonably assume other cultures will respect them.

The importance of time is reflected in language. Western languages have time, in the form of tense, as part of every sentence. Asian and Polynesian languages, however, have no tenses. Time can be shown, of course, with adverbs, but does not have to be.

In his more recent research Hofstede (1991) has introduced a preference for short or long term planning as a major cultural dimension. This fifth dimension will be discussed in Chapter 4. It is, however, worth noticing here that short term planning tends to occur with monochronic attitudes to time and long term planning with polychronic attitudes to time.

Monochronic and Polychronic Time

In some societies people and relationships come before externally imposed schedules. Present-oriented societies tend to treat time casually, enjoying the moment while future-oriented societies are much more exact, segmenting time deliberately. In the first major study of the link between time and culture, Edward Hall (1959; 1976; 1983) used the terms 'monochronic' (one di-mensional) and polychronic' (many dimensional and open-ended) to label this distinction.

Speaking of the two systems, Hall (1983: 188) said firmly, 'Like oil and water, they don't mix'. Yet cultures are not necessarily – perhaps not ever – entirely one or the other. The Japanese are polychronic with each other, monochronic with others. The French are monochronic intellectually but polychronic in behaviour (1976).

Time can be seen as related to tasks or to people. People sometimes call the former attitude to time *hora inglesa* or *hora americana*. The Thai expression for the western notion of time is *nat ferang,* literally 'foreigner time'. The latter view, putting people before time commitments, is variously referred to as *jam karet* (Indonesian, literally meaning 'rubber time'), Polynesian time, or *hora mexicana.* The terms are friendly or pejorative, depending on the user. Problems come when the people from the two systems have to work together. Being late for an interview, for example, may be acceptable in one system but far from acceptable in the other.

In results-oriented cultures, time is divided into chunks which are allocated to separate events. In relationship-oriented cultures, time is a rich whole in which several things may go on simultaneously. In the words of Samovar and Porter (1995: 72):

> Most western cultures think of time in lineal-spatial terms. We are time-bound. Our schedules and our lists dominate our lives. The Germans and the Swiss are even more time-bound than we are. For them, trains, planes, and meals must always be on time. In many parts of the world, however, the activity, not the clock, determines action.

In monochronic societies there is a clear distinction between work and private time but not in polychronic societies. Colleagues and friends are the same people. Suppliers and customers are friends. This can go so far as to mean that in a polychronic culture, only those in the inner circle or with 'friends' can get promotion or the work they want.

Hall and Reed (1990: 15) describe monochronic people as likely to be low context, to do one thing at a time, to emphasise promptness, to adhere to plans and to be accustomed to short-term relationships, whereas polychronic people tend to be high context, to do many things at once, to base promptness on the relationship, to change plans often and easily and to have a strong tendency to build lifetime relationships.

The different approach to meetings can be interesting. In western cultures the sentence 'I have a meeting from four to five' implies that any arrangement will have to avoid that time. In China people say, 'Come down between four and five. I have a meeting then so I know I'll be there.' The Chinese see time as spiral. If something is not done according to the schedule, they believe it will be done in its own time. This is similar to the Māori view that there is a 'right time' for everything.

Monochronic Time In Christian monasteries days were divided up for prayer sessions, so developing the western idea of time. Now, for the glory of profit rather than God, timetabling orders life. In Victor's (1992) words, 'Time is viewed as a commodity; it is scheduled, managed and arranged with every event being viewed as separate from all others.' Time is money, to be used wisely, even exploited. Every act is compartmentalised. We talk of 'spending time', 'wasting time', 'making time up and 'saving time'. When a football or hockey player is injured the referee takes note of the 'time out'.

North America and northern Europe emphasise scheduled time in a way that can amuse or irritate others. In many western organisations employees 'clock in' or sign a book to show just when they arrive and leave work. Some professional people, for instance, many accountants, charge for time, dividing a day into 6 minute stretches and charging clients exactly for the time their work takes. In contrast Edward Hall (1959: 25) cites a Sioux Indian school superintendent who told him, 'My people have no word for 'late' or for 'waiting' for that matter.'

Polychronic (open-ended) Time 'Polychronic', as the word implies, means that many things can happen at the same time, rather than one after the other. In a polychronic culture, such as those of Mediterranean, South American, African, Pacific Island and some Asian nations, people and relationships matter more than appointments. A Pakistani teacher told his students, 'Westerners are totally concerned about time and live a mechanical life that controls their freedom'[6] (Cameron, William, 1993: 18). Scheduling is an estimate, not a commitment. The Mexican *mañana* is accepted. Hall (1976: 47) puts it this way: 'Matters in a polychronic culture seem in a constant state of flux. Nothing is solid or firm, particularly plans for the future.' In Indonesia there is a subtle shifting of responsibility if plans change.

> One woman remarked that even if she invited her best friend to come to her house this Friday at 7:00 for dinner, she knows her friend would reply and mean *Insya Allah'* (If God wills it). There is no blame laid except at the foot of fate. (Draine and Hall, 1986: 115)

This flexible attitude carries through to other visits. In Indonesia a person usually goes to see a doctor or dentist without making an appointment. If she has made an appointment but does not want to go, she simply does not turn up. There is no need to inform the doctor. Both lecturers and students can come to class ten to fifteen minutes late without anyone minding.[7] It may be impossible to arrive on time because of traffic delays that not only slow private transport but also disrupt bus schedules. In China it is nothing to have an appointment and be kept waiting an hour. In the Philippines, being late is a way of life and 'Just a minute' means a quarter of an hour. In Thailand, a similar flexibility is reported:

> If one party is more than forty-five minutes late for a meeting, the other party may either leave or proceed, with no ill feelings. Such a rule is a tacit

---

[6]   Citing an interviewee.

[7]   Cited from an interview with Indonesian students.

understanding by many people in the Thai capital, as the traffic there necessitates a rather flexible attitude towards fixed appointment times. (Marcus and Slansky, 1994: 310)

The Japanese are known to be time-conscious. March (1996: 80) describes how Tara Neilson, a bilingual American, working as a marketing specialist for a Japanese cosmetics company, negotiated with the president an arrangement to take her lunch whenever it was convenient. 'I never liked to have my lunch exactly at noon. I didn't like the way the buzzer goes off and everyone runs out and then comes back exactly at one.' But, in spite of the pre-arrangement Neilson still ran into trouble with other senior members of staff. Throughout the company, time management was seen as an aspect of power, or control. Every day even senior staff had to record who they had talked to, for how long and with what results. And Japanese management has almost unlimited power to impose economic penalties for lateness, up to a day's pay for being a few minutes late (1996: 143).

In New Zealand at a university graduation ceremony a student speaker is given five to six minutes to thank the university on behalf of fellow students. One year a Mäori student speaker was chosen. She spoke in Mäori for forty minutes and then took another ten minutes to translate. The organisers and most of the audience who had not walked out were seething with annoyance. But that was unimportant to the young speaker who had followed a ritual of acknowledging contributions of ancestors and, welcoming, one by one, the attendance at the ceremony of members of many other tribes – all before beginning her allotted task. The decision was not a selfish one. She simply followed a ritual needing a certain time and suitable for a formal ceremony.

In Nigeria it may take several days to wait your turn in a government office, so professional 'waiters' do it for you (Argyle, 1982).

In his description of Chinese culture Arne J. de Keijzer tells a story of a farmer who lost his valuable horse. The neighbours commiserate. The farmer shrugs his shoulders and says, 'You never know what will happen.'

Two days later the horse returns with a pack of wild horses. The farmer says, 'You never know what will happen.'

A few days later, the farmer's son breaks both legs in a fall off one of the wild horses. The farmer says, 'You never know what will happen.'

Finally, a group of the Emperor's soldiers rides through the town taking every fit young man. The farmer says, 'You never know what will happen' (de Keizjer, 1992).

Such stories, showing a view of time as something culturally determined, are, of course, in danger of oversimplifying any situation. Generalisations invite disagreement. Hall (1983: 191) describes Jews as polychronic yet they are surely an achievement-oriented race. Victor (1992) repeatedly calls British people monochronic whereas Hofstede (1984: 104) says that in Great Britain 'time is a framework for orientation rather than something to be mastered'. My own experience has led me to consider that, although the clock was invented in China, the Chinese concept of time is elastic, yet De Mente (1994: 183-4) advises his readers, 'The Chinese rationale is that if people are not punctual for meetings ... they cannot be trusted.'

Some of the research done may not really measure attitudes to time at all. Bond (1991) cites Robert Levine as examining the pace of life in six societies, using measures such as walking speed, the accuracy of bank clocks, and the promptness of financial transactions. Taiwan was one of the slowest. Later Levine decided Hong Kong was faster paced than Japan, the most time conscious of his original six (Bond, 1991: 49).

Those brought up in one system may find adapting to the other extremely difficult. Most of us in our daily lives shift at least occasionally from one system to the other. The statements below, adapted from Seelye and Seelye (1995: 25-6), may help you discover your own predominant attitude to time.

A Checklist for You

Which of these monochronic statements below describe your attitude to time:

- I like to do one thing at a time.
- I concentrate on the job at hand.
- ✓ I treat deadlines and appointments seriously.
- I am committed to the job and give it priority.
- I keep closely to plans.
- I respect others' time and do not like to disturb them.
- ✓ I am comfortable with short-term relationships.

Which of these polychronic statements seem to apply to you:

- ✓ I like to do several things at once.
- I am easily distracted, and frequently interrupt what I'm doing.
- I see appointments and deadlines as objectives rather than commitment.
- I am committed to personal relationships.
- I change plans often and easily.

- I put obligations to family and friends before work commitments.
- I consider intimacy with family and friends matters more than their privacy.
- I base promptness on the particular relationship.
- I like relationships to be lifelong.

3 ETHNOCENTRISM

'The people of the world are bigoted and unenlightened: invariably they regard what is like them as right and what is different from them as wrong. ... They do not realize that the types of humanity are not uniform and that their customs are also not one, that it is not only impossible to force people to become different but also impossible to force them to become alike.'

Yung-Cheng, Emperor of China, 1727

The aim of this chapter is to try to encourage readers to recognise our own, unavoidable ethnocentrism and to strive to ensure it does not interfere with our understanding of others as individuals though from cultures different from our own.

The concept of ethnocentrism goes back to the sociologist, William Graham Sumner (1906: 13), who defined ethnocentrism as 'the technical name for the view of things in which one's own group is the center of everything, and all others are scaled and rated with reference to it'.

Such a view is inevitable and not, in itself, objectionable. We all see things from our own viewpoint. Like culture, ethnocentrism is learned and often subconscious.

Sumner's definition, however, bypasses the side of ethnocentrism that is objectionable, the tendency to rate all other cultures as inferior to our own. The feeling of superiority can be accompanied by a feeling of hostility towards other cultures and by deep ignorance. It is illustrated by the story Hofstede (1991: 214) cites of the farmer from Kansas who was supposed to have said, 'If English was good enough for Jesus Christ, it is good enough for me.'

Research has supported the predictable concept that similarity of culture will be a determining factor in our attitude to others. 'We tend to like people who are similar to us and dislike those who are dissimilar' (Wanguri, 1996: 456). The trouble with ethnocentrism is not just that we like those like ourselves and tend to see our own 'culture' as the best, but that we do not recognise the fact that we do, and that we allow it to cloud our understanding of other cultures. In the words of Hellweg, Samovar and Skow (1991):

> What makes ethnocentrism such a powerful and insidious force in communication is that it often exists invisibly (for example, we only study western philosophers) and is usually invisible in its manifestations (for example, we approach problems with a western orientation) ... Other cultures may also demonstrate these feelings of conscious or unconscious superiority...

The danger has been pointed out by Korzenny (1991: 57):

> We are most likely to attribute positive traits to those similar to us, but because to do so is, paradoxically, a societal taboo, we deny it. The denial of ethnocentrism is one of the most crucial barriers to intercultural communication because such denial prevents confrontation, clarification and acceptance.

Even apart from the question of denial, many scholars believe that because we learn ethnocentrism so early in life, and primarily on the subconscious level, it might well be the single major barrier to intercultural communication.

We may think we are being culturally sensitive without being so. Edward Said, whose books, *Orientalism* and *Culture and Imperialism,* showed radically – and disturbingly – how the concept of orientalism has been forged not in the east but in the west, put it this way:

> For if it is true that no production of knowledge in the human sciences can ever ignore or disclaim its author's involvement as a human subject in his own circumstances, then it must also be true that for a European or American studying the Orient there can be no disclaiming the main circumstances of *his* actuality: that he comes up against the Orient as a European or American first, as an individual second.[1]

Said insisted that all scholars feel the pressure of their nationality and of the scholarly tradition in which they work. He referred constantly to the history of dominance which has now changed. Chinese criticism of the way contracts for the Hong Kong airport were assigned shortly before the return of Hong Kong

---

[1]   Since Said wrote *Orientalism* in 1979, the word 'his' here and elsewhere in work written before scholars like Casey and Swift had pointed out the importance of inclusive language, was not intentionally sexist.

to China in 1997 shows the welling resentment against Britain. Similarly, the public recitation of alleged British nineteenth century iniquities at certain government *Son et Lumière* presentations in Malaysia shows that even when using a European cultural format, Malaysia openly condemns earlier British treatment of the country.

The Link with Nationhood

The term 'ethnocentrism' comes from the Greek words *ethnos,* meaning 'nation' and *kentron,* meaning 'centre'. This suggests a different emphasis from that implied by Sumner and most other scholars who link ethnocentrism with culture rather than with nationality. We think of ethnicity as race which is broader than nationhood; a nation may comprise several races, as in Malaysia, and a race several nationalities, as in China. People who are of Chinese ethnicity will have certain common characteristics but these will vary depending on whether they are from China, pre-1997 Hong Kong, Singapore, Malaysia, Australia, Canada, the United States, Britain or anywhere else.

Yet however important race may be, nationality is important also, since being international in outlook implies recognising nationalism. Yet being nationalistic can diminish appreciation of others, especially in wartime when propaganda can blind people by distorting information and fanning national fervour.

What is important is not that bias exists but that people recognise the bias within themselves and within their nations. Bias has always existed. Britannia 'ruled the waves'. Aryan Germans were the 'master race'. China is called by the Chinese *Zhongguo* or Middle Kingdom or the centre of the earth. The people of Ruanda in Africa see God or *Imana* as ruling over the whole world but considering Ruanda as home (Maquet, 1970). Lederer and Burdeck's novel, *The Ugly American,* (1958) drew readers' attention to the kind of result ethnocentrism can have, however good the intentions. In that novel an American arrives in an imaginary county ravaged by war and receiving help from the United States to find that generous aid given by the United States is thought to come from Russia. The Americans lived in comfort in their own compound because they felt superior, while the Russians lived among the people in far less pleasant accommodation. The Russians did nothing to alleviate the famine, but they had taken the trouble to learn the language and familiarise themselves with the culture. They had then stamped, in the language of the place, 'This is a gift from Soviet Russia' on all the sacks of rice and other food distributed.

Stereotyping

Ethnocentrism results from stereotyping, which in turn is based on generalising about people and events, something we all do and must do to make sense of the world around us. The psychologist, Heider (1958), suggested we have to simplify our perceptions in order to make sense of them. In so doing we are influenced by our own cultural assumptions. In Barnlund's (1975) words: 'To survive, each person masters the perceptual orientations, cognitive biases and communicative habits of his own culture.' When we generalise we observe differences which certainly do exist among cultures. We differ in appearance, customs, living standards, beliefs, values and in economic and technological development. We differ also in thought patterns, being to a certain degree racist, sexist, ageist and unaccepting of people with disabilities, depending both on our culture and ourselves.

Stereotyping is the process of making judgments about groups of people and applying those judgments to others. Each time we make judgments about people we use both the stereotypes we have already and the particular information and feelings we have about the people we are currently judging. The danger in this process is two-fold. The original stereotype may not be reliable and the particular information may be incomplete. Krueger and Rothbart (1988) showed that both group stereotypes and individual behaviour information influenced judgments, and found that processes which make it possible to sort people into groups could eliminate social category effects only when the processes depended on clearly conveyed stable, trait-like behavioural information (Hamilton *et al.*, 1992). In other words, we rely on stereotypes unless we have strong evidence to the contrary.

We tend to see our own behaviour as normal, and different behaviour as odd. We believe the group we are part of is superior to that to which we do not belong. A structured situation in which we know the unspoken rules is so much more comfortable than one in which we feel the anxiety of being outsiders that we are inclined to assume we are right and others wrong. In the words of Stephan and Stephan (1992) 'because structure lowers ambiguity, it decreases anxiety'.

Consider students of two cultures, one of which considers independence important while the other considers group solidarity important, including the solidarity of the class and the teacher as a unit. To those valuing independence, a student who feels bound to follow instructions without ever questioning them may seem to be refusing to act intelligently. To those valuing solidarity, the questioning may seem an affront to social cohesion. Adverse judgments can increase the anxiety of the person judged, a result particularly unfortunate when that person is an outsider and so has other reasons for being anxious.

Stereotyping and making judgments based on those stereotypes from an ethnocentric viewpoint are not new. In 1860 the Japanese Foreign Minister, Muragaki Awajimori, visited the United States and was shocked at the White House by the overt evidence of low power distance:

> In spite of the fact that he is the President, he received us dressed in the same stovepipe trousers that are worn by merchants, devoid of any decoration, and without a sword. These barbarians make no distinction between upper and lower, and have no idea about proper ceremony. (March, 1996: 28)

At the same time, March tells his readers, foreign travellers in Japan were shocked at such things as the nude bathing of both sexes together and the habit of bathing almost on the footpath (1996: 31).

Whatever the time and place, tension always exists between the general and the specific, which extends the general. Each new person we meet, each new situation we face, has to be considered sensitively against the background of our previous general knowledge. Often specific information will contradict the general stereotype. The stereotype itself may be useful when it identifies tendencies, risky when it is used to justify judgments.

Attribution theory, originally developed by social psychologists like H.H. Kelley (1972), sheds light on the process. It posits that people use observed behaviour of some to predict and explain the behaviour of others. This can lead to negative interpretations of behaviour, including, among other kinds of stereotyping, ethnic stereotyping. What is called the 'fundamental attribution error' is the pervasive tendency to attribute behaviour to *internal* factors (for example, stable traits, personality) rather than to situational factors. This is particularly likely to occur when people are observing others and especially when the others' behaviour is perceived unfavourably.

Research supports commonsense in showing that attribution can lead to wrong judgments. Williams, Whitehead and Miller (1971) used videotapes of black, white and Mexican children assembling toy cars and describing what they were doing. Unknown to the observers the voices were dubbed, *all* children being heard to use standard English. The observers still judged the Mexican and black children as non-standard, ethnic and not confident in comparison with the white children. Since then many similar experiments have shown that teacher expectations influence their judgment.

Many scientists in the past decade have argued that the concept of race, as distinct from ethnicity, has no basis in human biology. Race is a social and political rather than a biological concept. Somatic differences like skin and eye colour, and face and skull size and shape have been shown to be unreliable indicators of racial difference. In spite of this, stereotyping on the grounds of skin colour and other physical characteristics is not uncommon and can carry prejudice with it. William Blake's "Little Black Boy" cried out against it two hundred years ago:

My mother bore me in the southern wild,
And I am black, but O! my soul is white;
White as an angel is the English child,
But I am black, as if bereav'd of light.[2]

People of colour can, of course, and do sometimes feel scorn towards pale white skin. A Mexican American, Richard Rodriguez, remembered the attitude of his relatives towards the appearance of *gringos,* or white Americans:

A *gringo's* skin resembled *masa* – baker's dough – someone remarked. Everyone laughed. Voices chuckled over the fact that the *gringos* spent so many hours in summer sunning themselves. (Amit-Talai and Knowles, 1996)

As is to be expected, the literature shows, for example, Oddou and Mendenhall (1992b: 210-21), that if we do not know people personally, we are far more likely to form inaccurate stereotypes.

Until a relationship exists, people rely heavily on stereotypes. As Langer (1989) says, 'If we think we know how to handle a situation, we don't feel a need to pay attention', and we may easily lapse into unfounded stereotyping. When people we meet disclose differences, these add to or replace the original stereotype. The best way of avoiding stereotyping is to get to know individuals, so insulating ourselves from the danger. We then see a friend not just as an Asian but as someone from a particular Asian culture, of a certain status, education, age and gender with a particular personality.

Problems with stereotyping include the way it can deny diversity within a culture and also can deny complexity. Stereotyping so easily becomes dogma and dogma becomes prejudice. Allport in his now classic work, *The Nature of Prejudice,* (1959) defines prejudice as thinking ill of others without sufficient warrant. No one admits to prejudice. People want to locate it outside

---

[2]   From *Songs of Innocence and Experience.*

themselves, hedging, expressing reluctance for and qualifying what they say: 'I'm not prejudiced but you must admit that … .'

When an individual behaves in a way that does not conform to the culture, for instance a bride wearing red to a western wedding or a widow wearing red to a western funeral, the person may be seen as rebellious or uncouth. Either the person or the circumstances are blamed. But if the person who disturbs our sense of what is right comes from another culture, the culture is held responsible. In some cases, as with a red wedding dress, the unfamiliar behaviour may be a cultural choice. Many cultures consider red or deep pink the appropriate colour for a wedding dress. In other cases, as with the widow's red dress, cultures might be considered responsible but the choice might be entirely the individual's, as unacceptable in that person's culture as in another.

Adverse stereotyping is particularly likely to happen in periods of stress. It can lead to behaviour which would be unthinkable at other times. The stories of German and Japanese atrocities during the 1939-45 war are legion in the west but need to be balanced by accounts of what happened in the United States, Australia, New Zealand and Canada during the same war. For example, in her autobiographical novel, *Obasan*, Joy Kogawa (1989) gives a harrowing portrayal of victimisation. In Canada during the 1940s, full Canadian citizens of Japanese heritage had their business licences revoked, their radios and boats, some built by their owners lovingly over years in home garages, confiscated, their cars sold for a minute fraction of their worth, and were forced to leave their homes. They were called spies and saboteurs and confronted with signs saying 'Japs keep out'. The men were separated from the families and sent to work camps in the north, with three metres of snow, no heating, no latrines, no work, little food if any. If they were ill, their illness was not attended to. Right through the war and for some time afterwards, they were kept as prisoners or war hostages.

Perception

In times of great stress, as during a war or in periods of acute unemployment, people think and act in ways that are extreme. We notice some things and are blind to others. Our perception of the situation is likely to be biased. In Edward Hall's (1976: 14) words: 'In its simplest sense, perception is the internal process by which we select, evaluate, and organise stimuli from the external environment.'

Our propensity to see certain aspects of a situation selectively becomes dangerous when jealousy and personal frustration are involved. Zak (1996) wrote of the anger of 'the growing number of workers who feel their livelihood is threatened', in California where Mexicans are doing much of the work previously available. In 1980, when women were beginning to enter the New Zealand work force in significant numbers, a male member of a university economics department reported the danger male employment faced from women in an article entitled "Stealing Jobs" published in *The Listener*, then the journal with the largest circulation in New Zealand. In Australia, New Zealand and California, the rest of the community notices when Chinese and Vietnamese students win a disproportionate number of scholarships and scarce places in university faculties teaching subjects like medicine and engineering. The spectacular economic growth rate of the 'five dragons' of South-east Asia – Hong Kong, Japan, Singapore, Taiwan and South Korea – compounds the sense of seeming injustice. Why, think those whose children cannot get the advanced training they want because the places go to the best academic students, many of whom are new immigrants, should the institutions we have paid for benefit others and not us?

There are problems of other kinds as well. One is the self-fulfilling prophecy that people who are thought to be poorly educated, or confused or even just worried, become so. Hamilton, Sherman and Ruvolo (1990) explain just what happens:

> Because each person in an interaction is a perceiver, each has the ability to 'create' the behavior that he or she expects from the other. However, each person is also the target of the other's expectancies, and his or her behavior will be affected by the expectancies held by the other. Thus, two people can interact in such a way as to bring to reality the mental image that each one has of the other.
>
> One particularly important characteristic of biases is their confirmatory nature. In virtually all cases these processes serve to maintain the status quo. That is, they preserve the beliefs or expectancies that generated the effects. To the extent that stereotypes are simplified, overgeneralized, and/or inaccurate characteristics of these groups, then this aspect of expectancy-based effects would contribute to the persistence of stereotypes, the conviction with which they are held, and their resistance to change.

The danger lies only partly with the stereotypes themselves; it also lies with lack of recognition that stereotyping is occurring at all and with lack of recognition of the reasons that lie behind whatever it is we object to. These reasons may be internal, such as food or water supply, or external, such as fighting or oppression from neighbouring countries. Or they may not be physical at all but political or philosophical. To develop an understanding of multiple perspectives we need to be able to distance ourselves from our own situation in order to understand and value the behaviour and beliefs of others.

Notions of Politeness

The assumption that manners are a sign of being well brought up is a common one, a symptom of ethnocentrism which is hard to overcome. Table customs and manners illustrate the very different perceptions of what is polite. In some cultures, especially those where time is considered of monetary value, lunch, dinner and even breakfast business meetings are arranged. In others talking business at the meal is considered crass.

In cultures like that of Mexico, it is common for the main meal of the day to be eaten at around 2 pm and to take up to two hours. In countries such as China, the midday meal is followed by a sleep; in countries like Spain the main meal of the day is eaten very late at night, at perhaps ten or eleven; in some places, as in New Zealand, it is polite to finish all the food you are given if you can; in others, like China, it is rude to do so. In parts of Asia belching during or after a meal, and noisy 'zooping' up of soup show appreciation. In Britain, and indeed in most western cultures, eating should be as silent as possible. In some countries like Malaysia, many people eat with their right hand only, especially at Malay banquets; in others, table implements are usually used.

Understanding Self and Others

To understand and appreciate the culture of others, we must first recognise our own culture, the norms and assumptions which colour all we see and hear and do. To discover how we see ourselves and our own culture, we need to consider our views on matters like these:

gender	age
ethnicity	nationality
religion	education
work	authority
interests	sports
family position	home
marital status	sexuality
other people	different animals

Once we know who we are and what our cultural assumptions are we can more easily understand others. Immersion in another culture is an excellent way to overcome ethnocentrism, at the same time learning what another culture is like. Beeby (1992: 65) tells us that as long ago as 1925 a New Zealand clinical psychologist got permission to serve a sentence of seven days' hard labour in a prison to get inside experience of the prison system, and we learn from Pedersen (1990: 7-8) that in one training programme in the United States to teach social workers to be helpful to prisoners, the entire training staff were locked up with the prisoners for 48 hours before the programme began so that they could learn to understand the prisoners' viewpoint. However, such experience is rarely practicable, especially when the educator needs to understand individuals from many cultures.

Seelye and Seelye (1995), using the western way of seeing things in terms of polarisation, call the opposite of ethnocentrism 'cultural relativism'. They describe that as judging others on the basis of their geographic, historical, and social context. This may go some way towards understanding others, especially when combined with, or followed by, cultural immersion.

Issues to Think About

Consider which of the following statements are ethnocentric, and why.

(1)   When you eat out with a group of friends, you should pay your share of the cost.

(2)   When a friend accepts an invitation to dinner, he or she should either come or else explain absence to the host beforehand.

(3)   It is acceptable to ask a person you have known for several months his or her first name.

(4)   An adult who is not a parent and has not specifically been given charge of a child should not reprimand that child for noisy or rude behaviour.

(5)   An employer has the right, in front of others, to praise staff for outstanding work or to reprimand staff for making mistakes.

The passage on the following page tells of the experiences of a Japanese when as a young man he went to work in Iran. When you have read it, consider the questions which follow.

A Japanese Man in Iran
by Yasuhiro Yoshioka

Twenty years ago, as a young graduate with a Bachelor of Arts with a specialism in English language and literature from Kitakyushu University, I was one of many young Japanese men who travelled to Iran. I became an administrative officer. My employer was Chiyodo Company, a joint venture in petrochemical engineering set up by Japanese and Iranian businesses, acting under licence from the United States. The project was at the time the biggest of its kind in the world. The location was Bandar Khomeini, near the city of Abadan. The attraction was twofold: I wanted to go overseas and I also hoped to make money to set me up for my marriage.

I found the Iranian way of life was very, very different from that in Japan. The food, the drink, the clothes, the customs, the manners, the climate, the language, the landscape were all very different. Everywhere the people crowded in the dirty bazaars. Most of all, from the time when we disembarked at the airport in Teheran, I felt the Islamic presence. The reading of the Koran, the mosques everywhere, the people praying five times a day, all that was so different.

All the people believed in Mohammed. The praying and the religion affected everything. The women had many taboos. They wore clothes which concealed their whole body, including a veil which left only their eyes showing. Because we were foreigners we were not allowed to talk to the women ever. If we had, we would have been punished. No one was allowed to eat pork or to drink alcohol. Some of my friends minded that very much. I did not mind not having alcohol but I missed the pork.

I had a vivid impression of great poverty and much crime, especially theft but not only theft. When a crime occurred, if five people said they had seen the crime, whether they had or not, the person they claimed had committed it was found guilty and punished in both the local and the Muslim court. On one occasion a Japanese man was in a taxi which hit a small child. The driver jumped out of the taxi and ran away. Five people said they had seen the Japanese man drive the car and hit the child so the foreigner was severely punished. After that I kept well away from the local people and the other Japanese people in Bandar Khomeini did also.

Penalties for crime were severe. A murderer could be stoned to death in public by the family of the dead person.

My only local friend was one of the Iranian supervisors. He took me to his lovely home. He was very rich.

At work I found many things hard to understand. I had a little Farsi because I had studied the language for six months before I went, but most of the Japanese did not have any. The Iranian workers seemed very lazy. They didn't work, they didn't know the way for working, they were uneducated and uncultured. I was perplexed at the laziness. I wondered if it came from the hot, humid weather or the religious sanctions or something else. In summer the temperature exceeded 50 degrees Celsius, the hottest in the world. It was unbearable. And the water was terrible. It could not be drunk, it was dirty and impure. Only mineral water could be drunk. In winter it was cold, with much rain and heavy hailstones. But the rain came only in the day time, never at night. The workers lived in tents, even in the hot summer and wet winter.

The people were very stubborn and not faithful. They were very easy going, and idle, even in working time. When the time for prayer came, even when the crane was shifting heavy, dangerous equipment they would stop to pray. It was confusing to the Japanese bosses and seemed a waste of time and a waste of money. The equipment and material were shipped from Japan and needed maintenance but did not get it unless extra under-the-table money, called *bakshis*, was paid. It also had to be paid to expedite the work when contracts were due. If the Iranian workers were hurt and given bandages and other medical aids they were very pleased, not expecting anything. Money and other rewards, as they saw the bandages, were the only things that talked.

Although the people were very poor they would never do overtime. They had no idea of being on time, were selfish, impolite and did not keep promises. They often did not do the work well and when asked about their work they were evasive and told many lies. They stole many things, even the propane gas and oxygen tanks. And they talked all the time while they worked. They wore no shoes, even in the hot summer, and their clothing was very poor. They would not wear safety helmets and safety shoes. They just did not have a safety mind. They were easily angered, arrogant and very quarrelsome, both among themselves and with the Japanese. We wrote many warning letters to them, up to five times. After five warnings we would dismiss them and then we would have to get a local contractor to hire more labour.

There were very few skilled workers. In Iran very few went to university then and very few had technical training. The few who were educated were very gentle and were good supervisors.

Most of the workers did not know how to handle the machines. We needed technicians – welders, pipe fitters, riggers, iron workers, and painters. They had to be trained on the job. Though there was a training centre it took a long time to train them. When there was pipe fitting to be done, one Japanese worker would supervise fifteen workers. They had to be taught everything – how to cut the pipe, to fit it, to assemble it and to install the completed pipe.

(1)   Do you think the writer ethnocentric? What information from the passage led you to your opinion?

(2)   How could the Iranian work force have been kept more productive?

(3)   What do you think of the system of giving five warnings and then dismissing workers?

(4)   Would it have helped to plan regular breaks for prayers?

(5)   Do you think the *bakshis* should have been paid? Why or why not?

(6)   How did you react to the stereotyping contained in the passage? Would a different approach have made it just as possible for you to learn about the writer's experience and about the behaviour of the Iranian workers?

(7)   To what extent do you think your own answers to these questions were ethnocentric?

4 VALUES

'The good we never miss we rarely prize.'

Cowper

Values, Milton Rokeach (1973: 48) explains, are 'standards that we learn to employ transcendentally across subjects and situations in a variety of ways'. Understanding values helps us to understand how people behave, and to predict how they might behave in future. The ideas behind values – protection of the weak, protection of the environment and many others – are widely accepted[1] but in different ways and to different degrees by different people. And people may have two sets of values, those they say are important and those they actually hold as important. Everybody would probably say that those who cannot look after themselves should be looked after by others, but some will gladly look after those close to them, while others are unlikely to do so and may even resent paying taxes to ensure that the state does it.

The values people hold, both theoretically and personally, depend heavily on their culture. To quote Rokeach (1979: 6) again, 'Gradually, through experience and a process of maturation we all learn to integrate the isolated absolute values we have been taught into a hierarchically organised system.' People who move from one culture to another cannot replace such values quickly, if at all. Nor should they have to do so.

Three aspects of culture particularly influence values: world view, religion and ethnocentrism. However, every aspect of culture impinges in some way on values. Both the overt manifestations like language, food and dress, and the underlying aspects like attitudes to hierarchy or education also affect values to such an extent that scholars often use one term to explain the other. So Varner and Beamer (1995: 4) call values 'cultural priorities'. The Chinese, for example, value people, hierarchy, relationships and form. These values, or cultural priorities, would mean that certain decisions, such as terminating the

---

[1] *The 1994 Year book of the United Nations*, page 1059, lists 143 nation states as party to the Convention for the Protection of World Cultural and Natural Heritage.

contract of a university staff member because his or her subject was no longer to be taught, or because he or she was a poor teacher, would simply not be an option. Some other work would have to be found within the organisation.

Our value system, or our sense of what is preferable in particular situations, is learned consciously and subconsciously. It represents what Rokeach (1968: 161) called 'a learned organization of rules for making choices and for resolving conflicts'. The choices people make may affect their behaviour when they have to give evidence in a court of law or submit work for a degree. Some cultures – those based on Christianity and Judaism – tend to view truth as absolute. However, where relationships are considered to matter above all else, truth may be seen as relative and harmony as all-important. Problems are sorted out personally, not in the adversarial way of western law.

If our values do not coincide with those prevalent in our culture, we offend others or even break the law. Value, Spradley and McCurdy (1990: 7) tell us, is 'an arbitrary conception of what is *desirable*[2] in human experience'. But it is not so arbitrary that each person can choose what to value, regardless of others. A man in whose culture it is acceptable to pinch the bottom of a young girl he does not know but finds attractive will find himself in serious trouble if he behaves that way in a culture with 'rules' about sexual harassment. Similarly, a woman who dresses scantily in an Islamic country may find she is quickly arrested or in serious personal danger.

Intercultural communication trains people to be tolerant but even tolerance involves value judgments. Stories abound about judges in western cultures who dismiss charges of assault on women and sometimes children on the grounds that the particular behaviour is appropriate in the defendant's culture. Similarly in Asian cultures there are stories about westerners who flout local laws about such matters as carrying drugs and are – or are not – judged more kindly because the crime is considered less heinous in the defendant's culture. Such decisions are much criticised either by some members of the host society or by some from the perpetrator's culture. Values are not stable, either for individuals or societies. As children grow into adults and their experience widens, they develop their own sense of values, sometimes in a priority order very different from that usual in the culture they grew up in. Many of them learn they have some choice over what they value, but the degree of choice will differ according to individual training, personality and intelligence. In the words of Hofstede (1986: 305):

---

[2]   Emphasis is theirs.

Values are broad tendencies to prefer certain states of affairs over others … they lead to feelings of good and evil, right and wrong, rational and irrational, proper and improper; feelings of which we seldom recognise the cultural relativity. Which means that cross-cultural learning situations are rife with premature judgments.

Vincent Crapanzano (1988) used an incident from his childhood to illustrate his own changed values. He described his uncle, a Vortrekker, or Boer pioneer in the Transvaal, catching a black man stealing one of his water melons:

> He forced him down and punched him. Then he started pulling out his hair – his eyebrows even, every bit of hair on his body. And when he ran out of hair, he pulled out his pocket knife and began stabbing him, just little stabs, on the inside of his thighs. The man couldn't walk for weeks.

He told this to show that as a child he was very impressed, but he continued:

> We've got to teach our children to question why they do the things they do. But when I was in school we just sat there like a lot of little birds with our mouths open and the worms were stuck down. That was that. We never asked questions.

Another Afrikaaner, Carl Niehaus, who later spent eight years in a South African jail because he refused to disassociate himself from the African National Congress, described a situation in which African and Afrikaans children, but not the adults, were members of a common group.

> There was a wide gulf between whites and blacks, them and us. As children we had played together but at a certain age, around puberty, this automatically ceased. Suddenly, and as naturally as the games played as children we began to play the same rules as our parents: master and madam, labourer in the field and maid in the kitchen. My mother tried to explain this: 'It's not that we reject or look down on them, it's just they're different from us.' Always 'us' and 'them'. (1993: 17)

Clearly, for these two writers, values did change. What was acceptable and unchallenged to the child had become totally unacceptable with maturation and experience.

World View

Values grow out of the world view of each individual. The belief that illness is caused by evil spirits, that certain colours are lucky, that logic is linear, or that natural resources are lent to a generation in trust and not for financial gain, will be held by people in particular cultures, according to the prevailing perceptual assumptions.

World view has been variously defined. Hoebel and Frost (1976: 324) see it as 'the human being's inside view of the way things are colored, shaped, and arranged according to personal cultural perceptions'. Samovar and Porter (1991) describe it as 'orientation towards God, humanity, the universe and ... concepts of being'. Later they call it 'the way people view themselves, each other and their places in the universe, and ... an underlying pattern for interaction within a culture'. They give as an example a dog seen as a pet in the United States and a food delicacy in China.[3] Jacques Maquet (1970) adds: 'The world view of a people refers to a kind of reality which is not directly observable. We can observe things and behaviour, but not ideas or mental attitudes.' We can, of course, infer them from what we observe.

These definitions explain how world view can affect values of an individual and also of many individuals who share a culture. For centuries Europeans have seen the main perceptual division between cultures as that between east and west. The basic difference has been isolated by Elgin (1981: 225) in these words:

> Where the western view is dualistic (viewing mind and body as separate, as well as God and humankind as separate) the eastern view is profoundly nondualistic.

The same idea expressed from an eastern view point has been put forward by Young Yun Kim (1991):

> The western view of the universe is characteristically dualistic, materialist, lifeless. Assuming a relatively barren universe, it seems only rational that humans exploit the lifeless material universe ...

> On the other hand, the eastern view is profoundly holistic, dynamic and spiritual ...

---

[3]   By 1996 dogs were not an uncommon pet in south China. Beautiful pedigree animals were being sold in the streets of cities like Shenzhen.

This idea will be expanded in the chapter on religion but is relevant here also, especially in the sections on high and low context and on power distance. But no single division works for all issues. Some western cultures such as those of Spain or Italy are, for example, high-context, although, as the table on page 64 shows, most western cultures tend to be low-context.

Cultures overlap and separate out in so many ways that any division is of limited use and needs to be considered carefully, but the division into east and west is certainly more acceptable than one which sees the world as divided into developed and underdeveloped cultures. As was mentioned earlier, 'developed' is taken to mean liable to contribute to financial help for needy cultures through World Bank projects and 'undeveloped' means eligible to receive financial help through such projects. This distinction seems to twist the meaning of the word 'developed' to something like 'with a high average income'.

Edward Hall: high and low contexts

One theorist who contributed significantly to the understanding of inter-cultural value systems was Edward Hall (1976) whose work on high and low contexts was introduced in Chapter 2 and whose work on space and silence will be considered in Chapter 7.

Significant differences exist between low and high context cultures, differences aligned closely with the east-west dichotomy seen by Elgin (1981).

(1) In a high-context culture like China, Japan or Korea, the information resides in the person. People are expected to know what to do in specific situations. The situation and the role of the teacher make a course outline unnecessary and unexpected.

In contrast, in a low culture like Germany, Switzerland or North America, most or all the information resides in the message. Messages are expected to be full and clear. A class would expect to receive a course outline as or before they began a university course of study.

(2) To a high-context person social and group characteristics are especially important. The Japanese term *nemawashi* (working together: literally 'root-binding') has the connotation of being a very desirable process. Consensus is always aimed at, not a majority vote. *Ringi* (the Japanese style of circulating documents right through an organisation till everyone is happy with them) is common. When anything new or potentially difficult is planned, go-

betweens are used to ease the transitional stage.

In a low-context culture, a person has individual rights and opportunities. Wife-beating, for example, violates the individual right of a woman to full protection of her person, whatever the circumstances. People in low-context cultures tend not to like things they cannot understand. They want to know everything. Tact and extreme politeness are less important than the full truth.

To a high-context person harmony and face-saving are what really matter.

To people in high-context cultures, the doer and the deed are one. Criticism of a deed is criticism of the doer, a personal attack which involves a loss of face for both attacked and attacker. Giving acknowledgment of assistance through gifts or money is courteous recognition of a personal favour. Sometimes in a business deal it is even a regular fee, one to three per cent of the value of the contract. To westerners, this smacks of corruption but in a high-context culture no stigma attaches to the practice.

In low-context cultures people tend to separate the issue from the person, to 'hate the deed but love the doer'. Bribery is dishonest, shameful both to the person bribing and the person being bribed.

(3)   People in low-context cultures tend to prefer a direct style of communication; high-context people prefer an indirect style.

(4)   People in low-context cultures tend towards analytic, linear logic in negotiation, a characteristic which will be discussed more fully in Chapter 8. To a high-context person a softer approach, incorporating feelings and intuition, is more appropriate.

(5)   People in low-context cultures seek personal information stressing individual characteristics. People in high contexts seek general information about the group.

(6)   People in high-context cultures respond holistically to people and situations but people in low-context cultures respond specifically. For instance, the waiter in a low-context culture is there to wait on the customers. In a high-context culture some sort of relationship has to be developed, perhaps by asking where the waiter comes from or by wishing the waiter a pleasant weekend. In a low-context culture a doctor will try to isolate and treat a patient's symptoms; a doctor in a high-context culture will be concerned with restoring full general health to the patient by both spiritual and physical means.

Notice that neither kind of culture is inherently more concerned with ceremony or ritual. In France, rules, rituals and social codes are strictly observed. The hand shaking in Germany and the changing of the guard in Britain, are just as important as the bowing in Japan or the court functions in Thailand.

In a high-context culture, however, formality is not for special occasions but for every day. In Japan, for instance, the traditional format for writing a letter, personal or professional, is well established. The salutation is followed by a remark about the season or weather, an inquiry about the receiver's health (in personal letters) or congratulations (in business letters) and thanks for a gift, patronage of some sort or some kindness recently received. Only after all this can the writer move into the main part of the letter, the reason for writing it. The letter should end with good wishes for the receiver's health or prosperity, the complimentary close, the date, the sender's name and the receiver's name, complete with appropriate title.[4]

Is it to be wondered then, that those brought up to respect such stylism want and expect to be told the exact format an assignment is to follow? Similarly, when contracts are finalised or qualifications completed, a formal ceremony is of great importance. When a new shop opens in China, the potted flowers and other decorations outside are impressive. If an international student graduates after he or she has returned home, all members of the family will contribute towards the vast expense of travelling back for graduation. Values are not restricted to ethical issues.

The distinction between low and high context cultures is not always sharp. In low-context cultures, deception and white lies are not uncommon. Conversely, in high-context cultures, there will be some who reject tradition. Jung Chang, brought up entirely in the high-context Chinese way, could write *Wild Swans*, a crisp and clearly documented personal history, which power-fully decries much that the Chinese hold dear.

Francis Schaefer: sacred versus secular cultures

Francis Schaefer (1968) divided the world into those cultures which pre-suppose natural causes for everything and those which consider there is always a spiritual dimension. The former are sometimes said to have a scientific approach, the latter an holistic approach.

The scientific approach may be religious and the holistic approach is not necessarily religious though it usually involves some recognition of *mana*, the belief in a supernatural force in some persons or objects (Dodd, 1991: 81).

---

[4]   Adapted from Haneda, Saburo and Shima, Hirosuke (1981: 21-32).

Although the western tradition is founded on a religion with a divine creator, Young Yun Kim (1991) points out that the Judaeo-Christian creator or God is seen as set apart from the reality of the material world, 'having created it and set it in motion'. Most Christians would assert that there are more things in heaven and earth than we can understand, yet still try to work out decisions logically, and books such as Albert Ross's *Who Moved the Stone?* (1981) methodically analyse what historical and scientific evidence there is that Jesus Christ returned from the dead for a set time.

Despite the fact that western civilisation is based on Judaeo-Christian thought, theories like Darwin's evolution of the species, which explains how human and animal diversity has emerged as a process of natural selection, are inherently secular. Some writers, for example Claude Levi-Straus in *The Savage Mind* (1991), have argued that thought itself is scientific, or explainable on entirely empirical findings. This kind of thinking goes back to the medieval scientist, Roger Bacon, and the Scots economist, Adam Smith who in 1776 held that pursuit of self-interest constitutes an 'invisible hand' guiding society as a whole towards prosperity. Individualism is the expected, the norm.

Sacred societies, on the other hand, do not seek to prove everything on scientific grounds. They depend on inspired sources by religious leaders. These inspired sources, including the Christian *Bible,* have influenced one another. Both the old and new testaments of the *Bible* have influenced the *Qur'an* and through it the Islamic faith. The Hindu *Bhagavad-Gita* has influenced Buddhism. But however much is common among religions, a faith like Hinduism, which teaches that complete effacement of the ego is essential for understanding truth, will inevitably produce a different set of values from a religion like Christianity which elevates the human person above all else save God, and teaches that human beings are responsible for their actions since they have free will.

A sacred society in Schaefer's terms is not necessarily religious. Most Chinese would say they do not believe in religion yet take enormous notice of supernatural beliefs. Ancestor respect, already discussed in Chapter 2 is extremely important.

In both sacred and secular societies value systems link with the environment. Jewish dietary laws, Hindu beliefs about avoiding animal products and treating cows as sacred, even nineteenth century Polynesian beliefs about cannibalism and human sacrifices, were all grounded in complex physical behaviour necessary in the particular society.

Geert Hofstede: the value dimensions of culture

In 1980 Geert Hofstede published the first major study of four underlying value dimensions: power distance, individualism and collectivism, uncertainty avoidance and masculinity and femininity. These four dimensions had been previously studied by two Americans: the sociologist, Alex Inkeles, and the psychologist, David Levinson. Hofstede's study analysed 116,000 written answers from 40 countries on 32 value statements. The study has been repeatedly updated. In 1991 Hofstede added a fifth dimension – long and short-term orientation. Hofstede (1986) correlates the first two dimensions – individualism versus collectivism and power distance – positively with economic prosperity but Japan, which came midway in both sets of calculations yet is one of the leading economic powers of the world, seems to contradict his assessment.

Even the quantitative results Hofstede presented have been criticised, partly on the grounds that an objective survey cannot truly measure subjective phenomena and partly because the sample, IBM middle-management employees, may not have truly represented the populations of the countries in the study. Particularly in the early sampling begun in the seventies, women and indigenous people may have been under-represented. And Hofstede (1991) himself acknowledged that all the countries in which the questionnaire was tested and developed were western. All the same, because of the size of the study, because it has been re-done several times, and because so many intercultural researchers have used it as a yard stick, it must be taken seriously.

Those who want to understand the five dimensions fully should not rely on the information provided here but should read Hofstede's own published work, in particular the authoritative intercultural study, *Culture and Organizations : Software of the Mind* (1991).

Power Distance

Hofstede (1991) defines power distance as 'the extent to which the less powerful members of institutions and organisations within a country expect and accept that power is distributed unequally'. It is rooted in attitudes of parent to child, ruler to ruled, employer to employed, man to woman; it permeates the whole society, changing as society changes. If a student moves from a culture with a very different sense of power distance from that in his or her own culture, difficulties are likely to occur.

From Plato to Foucault, many outstanding western thinkers have discussed the issue of power in the communication process. The Athenians, at the same time as they expounded equality, still assumed the existence of two classes: the élite and the others. The Romans similarly had their patricians and plebeians.

Machievelli turned attention to political power, the ruler and the ruled. Karl Marx wanted power to be given to the powerless. But underneath all is the conviction, introduced though not developed[5] by the Greeks, that each person in the community, however that community is defined, should have an equal say in the political process.

[handwritten margin note: Same society that promotes individualism to better one self]

Not so in the east. In many parts of Asia, the sense of hierarchy is deep-rooted, deriving from Confucius. According to him, scholars have the highest status, then farmers, then artisans and last, business people – the parasites on the community (Zhi Lin, 1994: 43). In some eastern cultures, this hierarchy is fixed, as with the now illegal Indian caste system. If people are born poor and powerless that is assumed to be somehow deserved, and there is little anyone can do about it except accumulate merit in this life to enhance the chance of a better future existence. In others, as with Thai Buddhism, people believe that they can overcome their bad *karma* (or social state of poverty and helplessness) in this life by personal goodness or by luck, and so rise socially, or become more financially secure.

From China this aspect of Confucianism has spread to other Asian countries in various ways. In Japan, a sense of hierarchy is particularly important, perhaps because there has been only one dynasty in the whole history of the country. It shows itself in a host of ways such as degrees of bows, degrees of gifts, and in different words of address according to seniority and gender.

A Korean student in New Zealand gave his lecturer a graphic account of power relationships at work in the military training which is compulsory for all young Korean men. The student explained that on the parade ground, when the newest recruit does something considered against military etiquette it is the responsibility of the adjutant to discipline the junior, but not directly. The whole company of forty must line up in descending order of rank. The most senior will administer one blow to the next in line. The next in line will administer two blows to the next in line, who in turn hits the next man three times. The punishment is passed along the line of forty men to the least important who receives a full forty blows. After the beating the junior is usually, in the words of the student, 'very sick'.[6] It is not uncommon to die

---

5   There was no suggestion that women, non-Athenians or slaves should share in the political process.

6   Jennifer Dobson (1993) in a master's paper in intercultural communication at the University of Waikato, reporting what one of her Korean students had previously told her.

from the beating. At the time such incidents had seemed normal, but at a distance the student naively commented: 'Military training makes you stupid.'

Other incidents of barbaric bullying have been narrated in novels like Alex Haley's *Roots* (1976) with its grim accounts of maltreatment of slaves from the eighteenth century onwards in southern states of the United States, in tales of schools, especially nineteenth century boys' public schools in Britain, and even today in accounts of incidents in military academies in many countries. However, the norm in contemporary low-context cultures is for independence and equality to be valued and for status primarily to come from doing, from achieving, and not from position in the society. Power is an abstraction which can and does move from one person to another, sometimes suddenly.

In high-context cultures, obedience and directed supervision are valued. Power comes from being or ascription. Ascription involves birth, social connections, age, gender and education. Power is much more likely to be tied to its possessor and to depend on status. It is constantly reflected in the language used by superiors and subordinates. Terms like *taa* (Kymer for 'grandfather') and *baowng bor* and *baowng srey* (Kymer for 'younger brother' and 'younger sister') are used when no kinship ties exist. The same happens in Mäoridom in New Zealand. An older person who is in what might be called a mentor role is aunt, uncle or even 'Mum' or 'Dad' to a young Mäori. Power can come from several sources:

- Status in a particular culture
- Expert competence
- Personal charisma

In hierarchical societies it is appropriate to say where you are in relation to others, to convey your status. People are concerned with the good of the group as a whole. In egalitarian societies, improving yourself, achieving expert competence becomes the goal. People are concerned with developing their own potential and that of members of the small family unit to which they belong, and with enjoying themselves.

In South-east Asian cultures a system of patronage, involving an asymmetrical relationship between patron and servant, is the norm, keeping in mind that the Kymer word for 'servant' means 'one who is told', not one who serves. The patron has power and influence which is used to assist and protect those who expect personal help and who give loyalty in return. Responsibilities go both ways. Status is an important part of the communication process. If the status of a person is not known, relating to him or her becomes very difficult.

Hofstede's research (1994: 26) showed that power distance, or the extent to which a person can influence another's behaviour, is substantially influenced by national culture. Here are his results. The higher the score, the greater the power distance.

Malaysia	104	Turkey	66	Jamaica	45
Guatemala	95	Belgium	65	USA	40
Panama	95	East Africa	64	Canada	39
Philippines	94	Peru	64	Netherlands	38
Mexico	81	Thailand	64	Australia	36
Venezuela	81	Chile	63	Costa Rica	35
Arab countries	80	Portugal	63	Germany FR	35
Ecuador	78	Uruguay	61	Great Britain	35
Indonesia	78	Greece	60	Switzerland	34
India	77	South Korea	60	Finland	33
West Africa	77	Iran	58	Norway	31
Yugoslavia	76	Taiwan	58	Sweden	31
Singapore	74	Spain	57	Ireland (Republic of)	28
Brazil	69	Pakistan	55	New Zealand	22
France	68	Japan	54	Denmark	18
Hong Kong	68	Italy	50	Israel	13
Columbia	67	Argentina	49	Austria	11
Salvador	66	South Africa	49		

The situation is changing all the time. Malaysia was not one of the countries surveyed but if it had been, the three main cultures – Malay, Chinese and Indian – might all be thought of as having high power distance. Yet in late 1996 the National Union of Bank Employees in Malaysia was publicly urging banks not to differentiate between management and lower level staff in medical and transport benefits (*New Sunday Times*, Kuala Lumpur, September 1996).

Democracy purports to have as its base the idea that all are equal and so should have an equal say in the way society is run. Because of the greater power of some in western communities, we all know this 'equality' is something of a sham, but it remains the declared system. Some western organisations keep becoming flatter, as layers of authority are stripped away.

In contrast, hierarchy is recognised as all-important in the eastern way. Age and rank, down-played in contemporary western society, are made much of. This sense of hierarchy is long-term, overlaps into work and personal life, and shows itself publicly. Students remember and keep contact with their teachers, and young employees with their early managers. The senior person has authority but the authority carries with it responsibility for such matters as health care,[7] meals, and family occasions such as weddings and funerals. When a person is cheated, he or she can rely on the senior person in an organisation to get it put right. Often this redress is sought indirectly, through others or through a patron of some kind. The punishment is open and public.

March (1996: 73), speaking of the way Japanese managers use the office as their own property, a place they have full right to treat as their home, comments:

> The Japanese take their shoes off, walk around in slippers, pare their nails, read the latest sports and general news from home … and go to sleep on the couch … Some play golf so often that their staff cynically refer to the golf course as the 'green office'.

The sense of hierarchy includes the family. If asked if I had any brothers I would answer that I have three brothers. A Chinese person in the same situation would say she had three younger brothers, or she had one older and two younger brothers or whatever the situation was. A much younger brother would become a 'little brother'. General terms like 'brother, 'sister', 'uncle' are unusual. Specific relationships are everything. Triandis (1991) and others point out that it is likely that even small differences in age (for example, one day older) will result in more respect for the older person in some cultures.

Similarly Korean has a special vocabulary for the two sexes, for different degrees of social status, for different degrees of intimacy, and for different formal occasions. The words used will be discussed more fully in Chapter 6. But even without considering the language, it is worth noticing how the principles of deference to elders and male-female segregation affect the structures in society. Almost all relationships in Korea are vertical, so people can only make friends with others of the same age and sex (Kim, Tae Woo, 1997). Others are considered either too senior or too junior.

North American and European films, television programmes and advertising are having a profound influence on values, both eastern and western, especially those held by the young. But every now and then, especially in the

---

[7]   On one occasion in New Zealand, a Chinese masters student, bleeding profusely, turned up at my home at 6.30 am to tell me that a ladder had fallen on her and that she had to go to hospital to have her lip stitched. When I offered to take her to hospital she told me her husband was there, waiting in the car to take her, but that she realised she must let me know!

east when relationships are concerned, the influence is challenged in major and minor ways. At the time this book goes to press, access to the Internet is still very restricted in China. And the Prime Minister of Singapore, Goh Chok Tong, slammed an advertising agency for showing a toddler with raised fist and baseball cap saying: 'Come on, Dad. If you can play golf five times a week, I can have Sustagen once a day.' Goh Chok Tong considered the casual familiarity of the child's words undermined the traditional politeness and deference Asian children should have for their parents. The advertising agency withdrew the advertisement promptly.

Whether in the family, the educational institution or in the community, hierarchy does not mean always attention to those at the top. In Thailand royalty are revered but no such distance occurs in Communist China. Deng Xiaoping said leaders must not 'stand above the masses, but in their midst; not above the party, but within it' (Evans, 1993). Even Mao Zedong, the Great Helmsman as he was sometimes called, who can be seen in statues all over China, prohibited birthday celebrations for party leaders, including himself. However, it must not be forgotten that attitudes to power are not fixed in place, in time or even in religions. Dickens' novels set in nineteenth England like *Hard Times* and Theodore Dreiser's novels set in early twentieth century United States like *Sister Carrie* portray wide class differences. The television series *Upstairs, Downstairs* showed the world the pronounced class barriers in the United Kingdom in the early years of the twentieth century. Half in fun and half in earnest, elementary schoolchildren in England would chant:

> God bless the squire and his relations
> and keep us in our proper stations.

And in English-speaking countries until recently, and perhaps in places even now, the pious would sing:

> The rich man in his castle,
> The poor man at his gate
> God made them high and lowly,
> And ordered their estate.

And although racism and sexism are publicly disapproved of in western countries, a comparatively recent (1986) British novel by Fay Weldon[8] has this

---

[8]   Weldon was born in New Zealand, went to university in Scotland, and lives and writes in England.

refrain running through it:

> White men
> Black men
> White women
> Black women
> Animals

She is implying that an unacknowledged and objectionable hierarchy exists in contemporary British society.

Individualism and Collectivism

In an individualist society 'I' comes before 'we' and 'we' before 'they'. In a collectivist society, 'we' comes before 'I': the self is subordinate to the group. Hofstede (1991: 51) explains:

> Individualism pertains to societies in which the ties between individuals are loose: everyone is expected to look after himself or herself and his or her immediate family. Collectivism as its opposite pertains to societies in which people from birth onwards are integrated into strong, cohesive ingroups, which throughout people's lifetime continue to protect them in exchange for unquestioning loyalty.

Triandis (1988) and others outline the difference between collectivist and individualist values in a clear cut way:

> The top collectivist values are: Harmony, Face saving, Filial piety (duty towards parents) Modesty, Moderation, Thrift, Equality in the distribution of rewards among peers, and Fulfillment of others' needs. The top individualist values are: Freedom, Honesty, Social recognition, Comfort, Hedonism, and Equity (to each according to his/her contribution to group performance) ... Professors in individualist cultures complain how hard it is to form work groups and to give one grade for the completed project.

In individualist cultures parents want their children to do the work which gives them most satisfaction in life wherever that satisfaction comes from. In collectivist societies the children are expected to do what is most needed by the group.

Those from collectivist cultures are more comfortable with vertical than horizontal relationships with those they have not grown up with, so in a collectivist culture some sort of hierarchical position will need to be established as early in a relationship as possible. The people are likely to be uncomfortable in competitive situations and to feel embarrassed when attention is called to them within a group, so educators need to be particularly careful with criticisms. And students from collectivist cultures will be constantly aware of the opinions of authorities back home and of responsibility to their families; failure of any kind has repercussions felt far beyond the individual.

Gift-giving is important in collectivist cultures. The importance of this will be discussed later in this chapter and again in Chapter 7. For the moment it is enough to notice that in collectivist cultures gift-giving is part of the inter-dependence that people learn to rely on. Gifts do not need to be reciprocated in kind or at the time of giving.

Hofstede's table (1994: 53) shows the relative individualism and collectivism he found in the countries he and his team surveyed. The highest numbers are those for the countries which the survey showed were most individualist; the lowest, for those which were most collectivist:

USA	91	Israel	54	Hong Kong	25
Australia	90	Spain	51	Chile	23
Great Britain	89	India	48	West Africa	20
Canada	80	Japan	46	Singapore	20
Netherlands	80	Argentina	46	Thailand	20
New Zealand	79	Iran	41	Salvador	19
Italy	76	Jamaica	39	South Korea	18
Belgium	75	Brazil	38	Taiwan	17
Denmark	74	Arab countries	38	Peru	16
Sweden	71	Turkey	37	Costa Rica	15
France	71	Uruguay	36	Pakistan	14
Ireland (Republic of)	70	Greece	35	Indonesia	14
Norway	69	Philippines	32	Colombia	13
Switzerland	68	Mexico	30	Venezuela	12
German FR	67	East Africa	27	Panama	11
South Africa	65	Yugoslavia	27	Ecuador	8
Finland	63	Portugal	27	Guatemala	6
Austria	55	Malaysia	26		

only as long as it benefits the indiv. In an individualist culture, people may and almost always do belong to groups, but the groups are not fixed and permanent as in a collectivist society. People join and leave at will. In a collectivist society a person is a member of few groups, but the attachment is strong and long lasting.

Educational situations have their own sets of groups, which in collectivist cultures are extremely important. In China, for example, a class tends to stay together for the whole time, all students taking all subjects together. This might happen in the west in a professional school training, say, mechanical engineers, but is not likely to happen in many faculties. Consequently, in individualist cultures students who have left university keep in touch with their classmates only if it suits them, sometimes irregularly and sometimes not at all. In contrast, in collectivist cultures like China and Japan students from the same class have lifelong relationships with each other and with their teachers.

In either type of culture students will belong to several groups, whether or not they take much part in them. The group will depend on whether the student is male or female, leading the class or struggling, poor or wealthy, living at home or in a hostel or in an apartment and so on.

When teacher and student belong to the same group, the relationship is very different in western and eastern cultures. I once taught my own sister Latin in a New Zealand secondary school. During the whole year she worked hard and did well but never spoke to me in class, nor I to her. Our behaviour was conscious and pre-planned. The only alternative was for me to ask to be given another class.

Hofstede (1991: 62) describes the very different recognition of group ties in a collectivist culture:

> [In collectivist cultures] students from the same ethnic or family background as the teacher or other official will expect preferential treatment on this basis. In an individualist society this would be considered nepotism and intensely immoral, but in a collectivist environment it is immoral *not* to treat one's ingroup members better than others.

For those brought up on Maslow's hierarchy of needs, with self-actualisation as the pinnacle of personal and educational achievement, the strong positive aspects of collectivism may come as a surprise. The first six of the seven principal values which Vander Zanden (1965)[9] presents as operating in the United States, and which could equally be said to operate in most western countries – materialism, success, work and activity, progress, rationality, democracy, humanitarianism – may seem self-serving.

---

[9]   Cited in Gudykunst and Kim (1992a: 55).

Gudykunst and Kim (1992a) contrast enjoyment, achievement and self-direction which serve individual interests with the values of an extreme collective culture, the Bedouin desert dwellers for whom the five predominating values are hospitality, generosity, courage, honour and self-respect. To people in a collective culture, individualism is selfishness. To them, in the words of Hutton (1995: 15), 'Altruism and the civilising values of an inclusive society have been sacrificed on the altar of self-interest, of choice, of opting out and of individualism.'

Not of course, that collectivist values operate only in collectivist societies. Australia ranks second only to the United States as an individualist country, yet within Australia there is a considerable proportion of the population from collectivist cultures. And even those very much from a British background behave in collective ways under certain conditions. In Colleen McCullough's great Australian novel *An Indecent Obsession* (1981) a group of soldiers successfully work together to convince the army authorities that a murder was a suicide in order to protect one of their group.

Uncertainty Avoidance

Uncertainty reduction theory was originally developed by Berger and Calabrese (1975). They studied uncertainty-avoidance and risk-taking, comparing them with tolerance for ambiguity, noticing that newcomers are uncertain how to behave in an unfamiliar culture and so are anxious. By extending their knowledge, understanding their own feelings and developing skills, the newcomers can reduce this uncertainty, and so the anxiety. Gudykunst and Hammer (1987) show that uncertainty and anxiety are separate but often occur together, and that if they are worked on together by both newcomers and hosts, the result will be improved communication.

Hofstede (1991) developed his work on uncertainty-avoidance as a by-product of some of his questions on power distance. He could not see why people who felt under stress should also feel strongly that rules should be respected and that careers should be long-term, yet the answers, country by country, to questions on stress, rules and the length of careers formed a clear pattern which he called an uncertainty-avoidance index.

Uncertainty-avoidance itself he defined variously as 'the extent to which the members of a culture feel threatened by uncertain or unknown conditions' and 'the degree to which the members of a society feel uncomfortable with uncertainty and ambiguity. This feeling leads them to beliefs promising certainty and maintaining institutions protecting conformity.'

Hofstede found, as with the other dimensions, clear differences in the countries studied, as the following table shows. People from countries with high scores do not willingly accept risk. They like to know exactly where they stand in work as in daily life. They expect long-term employment, and they assume they can rely on others to look after them in old age or illness. Those from countries with low scores like Singapore accept risk more easily. They tend to take each day as it comes, willingly changing the rules they live by whenever it suits. Here is the list:

Greece	112	Israel	81	Australia	51
Portugal	104	Colombia	80	Norway	50
Guatemala	101	Venezuela	76	South Africa	48
Uruguay	100	Brazil	76	New Zealand	49
Belgium	94	Italy	75	Indonesia	48
Salvador	94	Pakistan	70	Canada	48
Japan	92	Austria	70	USA	46
Yugoslavia	88	Taiwan	69	Philippines	44
Peru	87	Arab countries	68	India	40
France	86	Ecuador	67	Malaysia	36
Chile	86	German FR	65	Great Britain	35
Spain	86	Thailand	64	Ireland (Republic of)	35
Costa Rica	86	Iran	59	Hong Kong	29
Panama	86	Finland	59	Sweden	29
Argentina	86	Switzerland	58	Denmark	23
Turkey	86	West Africa	54	Jamaica	13
South Korea	85	Netherlands	53	Singapore	8
Mexico	82	East Africa	52		

Like all the other dimensions, this one takes no account of differences within the culture, and in addition, has some unexpected findings. For instance, India, a sacred society in Schaefer's terms, ranks surprisingly low on the list, while Pakistan is fairly high. However, some other research does validate Hofstede's findings. Bochner, for example, found that Hungarian and Japanese children showed greater anxiety than Swedish children (O'Sullivan, 1994).

In cultures where people are uncomfortable with uncertainty, they will be perpetually anxious, and wary, even intolerant, of those with deviant ideas or behaviour. Whatever they do is likely to be rigidly prescribed either by written rules or by unwritten social codes. These rules help people feel a sense of order, of control, of safety in the future. But it may be that this sense of order, control and safety can be deliberately achieved in other ways.

Gudykunst and Hammer (1987: 112) cite eight important variables which can help reduce uncertainty and so improve intercultural competence. They are 'knowledge of the host culture, shared networks, intergroup attitudes, favorable contact, stereotypes, cultural identity, cultural similarity, and second language competence.' Stereotypes seems a strange item in the list. A better variable than stereotypes might be the ability to make reliable predictions. Stereotypes too often tend to be narrow, inaccurate and self-fulfilling as Chapter 3 showed.

People react to uncertainty through laws and regulations, and through their religious beliefs as well as through their behaviour. Tolerance for ambiguity is the ability to handle situations you do not understand at the time, remaining confident without being arrogant.

In those cultures with a low uncertainty-avoidance index people tend to believe in fate and luck. They have lucky numbers and lucky colours (like eight and red in Chinese) and enjoy gambling and games of chance.

Of all the dimensions, though change will always be gradual, uncertainty-avoidance may be the one most likely to change. For instance, New Zealand, being the first country in the world to have a full social security system, used to have only a small proportion of people who insured themselves heavily for their retirement. Now that government pensions are more firmly controlled, the proportion of those who invest in forms of private superannuation has increased markedly. People have now become aware they have to plan for their financial security in the future.

In contrast, the Thai economy used to be largely dependent on its main crop, rice, and so was vulnerable to harvest variations and to changes in world prices. Now the Thai government has established a number of development projects to diversify and strengthen the economy. And China, which was formerly a country with extensive poverty and a huge, poor population, now has little extreme poverty, a substantial middle class and a very high savings ratio, bordering on 40 per cent. This gives it the resources to finance a very high level of investment.[10] Risk-taking in business has to be thought through carefully. The implications of uncertainty-avoidance in the learning process will be discussed in more detail in Chapter 8.

Masculinity versus Femininity Orientation
The masculinity-femininity dimension has little to do with the relative standing of men and women in a culture, already discussed in Chapter 2, or with the sexual mores in a culture before and during marriage, discussed in Chapters 6 and 7 on verbal and nonverbal communication. Rather it is a matter

---

[10]   Speech given by Pieter Bottelier, the World Bank's Chief of Mission to China, reported in *Asia 2000*, no. 8, May-June 1996.

of the link between the social roles and the biological facts of the men and women in a community. The masculinity versus femininity dimension is concerned with the extent to which men and women are constrained in their respective roles. It is also concerned with what Hofstede calls the 'tougher' values which are associated with masculinity and the more 'tender' values associated with femininity.

Geert Hofstede (1991) sees his own Dutch culture as extremely feminine. For example, Dutch women, although the proportion of them who work outside the home is not as high as in, say, Russia, consider household tasks and shopping are a man's work as much as a woman's. At the other extreme of the table is Austria, a near European neighbour but second only to Japan in the masculinity-femininity index his 1980 research provided:

Japan	95	Hong Kong	57	Spain	42
Austria	79	Argentina	56	Peru	42
Venezuela	73	India	56	East Africa	41
Italy	70	Belgium	54	Salvador	40
Switzerland	70	Arab countries	53	South Korea	39
Mexico	69	Canada	52	Uruguay	38
Ireland (Republic of)	68	Malaysia	50	Guatemala	37
Jamaica	68	Pakistan	50	Thailand	34
Great Britain	66	Brazil	49	Portugal	31
German FR	66	Singapore	48	Chile	28
Philippines	64	Israel	47	Finland	26
Colombia	64	Indonesia	46	Yugoslavia	21
South Africa	63	West Africa	46	Costa Rica	21
Ecuador	63	Turkey	45	Denmark	16
USA	62	Taiwan	45	Netherlands	14
Australia	61	Panama	44	Norway	8
New Zealand	58	Iran	43	Sweden	5
Greece	57	France	43		

In what Hofstede calls a masculine society, most people, male and female, assume men will be more assertive than women, that their place is primarily in the workforce while women's is primarily at home, that specific jobs will be primarily for men or women, that higher earnings will go to 'masculine' jobs, that those who do a good job will be publicly recognised, and that a substantial proportion of taxes should be spent on defence.

In a feminine society, men and women are seen to have equal right to be assertive, to work outside the home or at home, to take on any kinds of work at any level and to be paid equally for what they do. High personal praise is unusual and may be embarrassing to the recipient. A substantial proportion of taxes is assigned to helping the weak, the poor and the underprivileged. Social welfare systems are seen as essential, not as burdens the community is saddled with.

The implications for both staff and students away from their own cultures may be considerable. In feminine societies, both men and women teach at any level. In masculine societies, women usually teach the younger children, and have low status in the community. Men teach at institutions for boys only, and have senior positions in schools for girls and boys. When they teach at universities, they hold most of the senior administrative and academic posts there. In feminine cultures the brighter children do not want to be recognised as exceptional, whereas in masculine societies they want and expect to be singled out. A male doctoral student from a masculine culture may be uncomfortable about, and may even resent, having a woman as his chief supervisor. A senior woman academic from a feminine culture may be annoyed to find at a meeting she has arranged in a masculine culture that all questions and discussion are directed to her spouse who just happens to have accompanied her.

Even the fields of study chosen at university will be different in masculine and feminine societies. In the more masculine societies men will predominate in engineering, medicine, law and the higher roles in education while women predominate in the support roles of nursing, teaching at lower levels and doing secretarial work. In feminine societies roles will be more evenly distributed.

The masculinity-femininity dimension must not be overplayed. It can easily be over-ridden when other dimensions comes into play. For example, although Hofstede ranks Japan as one of the most masculine societies of all, the influence of collectivism and power distance mean that individuals tend not to like to be singled out, even for praise.

Long and Short-term Orientation

The research for the fifth dimension, long and short-term orientation which Hofstede added in his 1991 book, *Culture and Organisations,* shows an interesting correlation between collectivism and long-term orientation. He attributed the fact that this dimension had been missed previously to the predominantly western bias of most of those studying intercultural communication, including himself. Hofstede thanks Michael Bond, an American psychologist with twenty years' experience with Chinese people, mostly in the Chinese University of Hong Kong, for the insight that led him to include the new dimension and for much of the material collected.

[handwritten: Japan is long-term orientated.]

The fifth dimension is to some degree Confucian and has been said to explain the unprecedented and unexpected economic success of the 'five dragons' (Japan, South Korea, Taiwan, Singapore and Hong Kong).[11] China and Indonesia have been slower to move but estimates for their economic growth long-term are breathtaking. Hofstede sorts out several important differences between people from short-term oriented cultures and those from long-term oriented cultures:

- People from short-term oriented cultures respect tradition but see it as past and distant, whereas those from long-term oriented cultures continually adapt it to the current environment.
- Those from short-term oriented cultures notice social and status obligations within limits but those from long-term oriented cultures treat them as limitless. As discussed in Chapter 8 the Korean student who said 'I dare not walk even in the shadow of my teacher' was very much in earnest.
- Thrift and being sparing with resources are values in the long-term orientation. Although lip service is given to them in some western cultures, they are prized only where they are indispensable, and are not even included as values in surveys such as Hofstede's own, or the also famous Rokeach value survey.
- Those from short-term oriented cultures tend to have small savings and little for investment, while those from long-term oriented cultures tend to have large savings.
- People in short-term oriented cultures look for quick results, whereas those from long-term oriented cultures persevere, looking for eventual results.
- People in short-term oriented cultures insist on uncovering the truth, while people in long-term oriented cultures are concerned with 'respecting the demands of virtue'. (Adapted from Hofstede, 1991)

The short and long-term orientation will to some extent overlap with the masculine and feminine orientation. For example, in cultures where women are expected to be responsible primarily for the home and are not expected to occupy senior positions in business or academia, few women will be willing

---

[11] The list and the label vary slightly according to the writer or speaker. Some consider Japan separately and include Malaysia as one of the five; others label the group 'the five tigers'. The economic downturn of 1998 may mean that neither 'dragon' nor 'tiger' is appropriate for any of the group.

to undertake long courses of study leading to promotion to positions requiring them to spend much of their time outside the home.

In business also the length of time a relationship has existed is of major importance. A New Zealand firm found that it took more than three years to develop the necessary relationship with its counterparts in a Korean company before significant contracts were arranged and that even then third parties who had a still longer relationship with both companies had to be involved (Kim, Tae Woo, 1997).

Kluckhohn and Strodtbeck: value orientations

Every culture has its own preferred value orientations. Kluckhohn and Strodtbeck (1960) isolate five sets of assumptions which may differ according to the culture: those on human nature, on nature, on time (which has already been discussed as Hofstede's long and short-term orientation but will be considered in a different framework), on activity and on other people. These value orientations are not fixed but differ in degree depending on the individual and the culture. Samovar and Porter suggest a framework for these differences in a helpful table:

Orientation	Values and Behaviours		
Human nature	Basically evil	Mixture of good	Basically good
Relationship of humankind to nature	People subject to nature	People in harmony with nature	People the master of nature
Sense of time	Past oriented	Present oriented	Future oriented
Activity	Being	Being in becoming	Doing
Social relationships	Authoritarian	Group oriented	Individualistic

Samovar, L.A. & Porter R.E. (1995). This table is adapted from one in Kluckhohn and Strodtbeck (1961: 12).

Human Nature Orientation

Human nature orientation will come up in more depth in Chapter 5. It depends on whether human nature is seen as intrinsically evil, as in the Judaeo-Christian *Bible*, where, in the Book of Genesis, Eve tempted Adam to break divine law by eating the forbidden fruit. People can only counter this orientation by hard work, intense self-control or by seeking divine forgiveness. This theory of original sin was developed to its extreme by some denominations in the Puritan tradition. The Islamic tradition has a similar underlying principle.

In contrast, the Buddhist view is that people are born pure and that fate and their selfish wants in the physical world damage this purity. The aim is to reject this world and return to a state of innocence (Samovar and Porter, 1995). Western poets like William Blake and William Butler Yeats, both of whom both read and thought extensively about eastern philosophy, put these ideas into English poetry. Consider Blake's *Songs of Innocence and Experience* or Yeats' *Sailing to Byzantium*. But for many westerners this sense of the innate goodness of people is hard to understand, let alone accept.

The implications of different orientations to human nature show themselves in many ways, some of which are important in education. Clinical depression, for example, is a major health problem, one not infrequently experienced by people living outside their own culture, and without their familiar support systems. Psychologists have suggested that in the west, depression has guilt as a 'pivotal element' but that in the east, where the self is so much less important, guilt may not be a factor at all (Bond, 1994). In situations such as marital conflict, whereas westerners would exhibit the symptoms of depression, people from the east would react either by persevering or by overt behaviour.

People and Nature

People within different cultures can relate in very different ways to their environment. Some believe people should control nature, others that they should work in harmony with it, changing little and then only with great respect for nature. Yet others try to fit in with nature as best they can, changing nothing.

Those from the Judaeo-Christian culture tend to believe people are all important. Since in their view people should have mastery over nature damming rivers and raising or lowering lakes for electricity are acceptable projects. In contrast, those who believe people should work in harmony with nature will work with nature as it exists, treating the natural state with great respect. In Polynesia, for instance, fishing is perfectly acceptable normally but if there has been a drowning or a shipwreck, the sea, lake or river where the tragedy occurred would be regarded as *tapu* or sacred for some time. No fishing would be allowed, out of respect for the people who drowned, the place where they drowned, and the health of others who might otherwise eat contaminated fish. The Mäori people of New Zealand, like those from other cultures where this view is held, see water, land and air as lent, not owned.

Finally, those who believe that nature is the controlling force will simply accept what is there, moving on if the goodness of the soil is depleted, or building without special reinforcing even where earthquakes have occurred, sure that whatever will be will be, and there is nothing that can alter what is pre-ordained.

Attitudes to space and privacy certainly involve people's attitudes to nature but will be discussed in the chapter on nonverbal communication.

People Relating to Each Other

In the west personal relationships are usually separate from work relationships. The family tends to be small (often now even smaller than the nuclear family). At work employers are treated deferentially not because of their status but because of their power to hire, fire and promote. Education and business are conducted by rules established by the democratically elected government. In France, companies have pyramid-shaped power structures and managers rarely mix with their subordinates. In the British work place, the old school ties of Eton and Harrow, Oxford and Cambridge are never forgotten. In the United States graduates of some of the universities, particularly private universities like Stanford and Harvard, operate a similar system. In Australia schools like Scotch College in Melbourne, an independent boys' secondary school, have special status. In such cultures, people speak about 'networking' but they see it as a deliberate and conscious ploy, not as something inevitable.

The concept of role differs in every culture. In a study of role perceptions in Java and the United States, Setiadi (1984) found that the most important factor in Java was obedience, whereas in the United States it was having fun together.

In the east, in contrast, relationships control everything. Whether Confucianism is believed in or not, the Confucian stress on the harmony of social relationships permeates every society. Confucius specified the five most important relationships, the *wu lun,* and delineated the proper attitude governing those relationships and the obligations involved in them throughout a community:

between ruler and subject —   loyalty

between father and son —	filial piety
between husband and wife —	obedience
between elder and younger —	respect
between friends —	trust

As has already been shown in the section on power distance, this kind of hierarchical relationship runs through the whole of Asian society, including home life, education and business. Each member of the society must give the proper respect to the other. People are addressed by position and family name, not personal names unless permission has expressly been given. Contracts are often oral, since business is only done after rapport is firmly established and the assumption is that those involved can trust one another. Visitors are accorded hospitality which means both time and refreshments. Each member of society is tuned to what the Koreans call *kibun* or the mood, current feeling and state of mind of everyone else.[12]

Gift giving, sometimes viewed as bribery in the west, is the norm, part of the process, in many cultures. In Korea, for instance, relationships are built and maintained largely through gifts. Because gifts can symbolise the status of both giver and receiver, gifts may be large. Trivial gifts may mean both the giver and receiver lose face. To ensure this does not happen, Koreans are reluctant to open gifts in front of others, and will only do so if asked.

Even when gift-giving involves a breach of the law, as in giving money to persuade an official to provide an entry permit, in some cultures it may be acceptable behaviour. Triandis (1988) and others point out that the official may regard it as a legitimate part of his or her salary, possibly needed to support an extended family of, say, fifteen people.

Attitudes to age, already discussed in earlier sections, affect the way people behave in different circumstances. Fons Trompenaars (1993) gives the probable insulted reaction to those organisations who send 'whiz-kids' to deal with people many years their senior: 'Do these people think they have reached our own level of experience in half the time? That a thirty-year-old American is good enough to negotiate with a fifty-year-old Greek?' But the 'fuddy-duddy' scorned in achievement-oriented cultures, who is liable to be forgetful and may not always react quickly to suggestions, may be earnestly respected in ascriptive cultures.

As John Condon (1980) has pointed out in a comparison of Americans and Mexicans, it is not just that some societies have a different attitude to, say, age.

---

12   Noh, Mei-Young "The Republic of Korea". Master's paper written at the University of Waikato, October 1996.

Rather it is that some societies may want to maximise differences of age, status and gender, while others want to minimise them. ~~The doctorate and the position spelt out in great detail on a business card will be appreciated in an Asian culture~~. Greying hair, both men's and women's but especially women's, may be dyed to conjure a belief in the youth and therefore the attractiveness and the competence of the person in western cultures.

The collective wish for harmony inherent in Confucianism leads people to work comfortably together. In education throughout collective cultures, as in the Japanese workplace, people are thought of as one united family. The feeling is epitomised in the Filipino word *pakikisama* which means 'smooth interpersonal relations' and is the common ideal.

Both insistence on truth and insistence on harmony can lead to complications. In the west where truth and achievement are valued, smoothing over difficulties may cause trouble. The child who goes to the door and says, 'Mother says to say she's out,' is likely to find him or herself in trouble. Remember George Washington, 'I cannot tell a lie'. But in a collective culture, visualise a visitor asking the way to some place. The person questioned does not know but thinks it important to make the asker happy, and so gives information which is totally wrong. Telling the truth is so important in western society that the questioner may simply assume the answer is based on fact and spend a long time, perhaps in exhausting heat, trying to follow the directions.

The individualist concept of open debate, confrontation, standing up for one's rights leads to a very different ideal from that in a collectivist culture, an emphasis on truth rather than relationships. People from the Middle East can be especially assertive and can enjoy differences of opinion on many matters. A Yiddish proverb says: 'Where there are two Jews, there are three arguments.' And even primary classrooms in an Israeli kibbutz are highly informal. Students move around the room to get what they want, they talk among themselves and they readily criticise the teachers if they feel they are wrong (Anderson and Powell, 1991).

Sense of Time
Different attitudes to time have already been discussed, both in relation to culture and in relation to planning. Here the emphasis is on the very different attitudes to past, present and future prevalent in different cultures. This difference is to some degree reflected in the way a language treats time. In western languages, tense, the major indicator of time in English, is extremely important; in many Asian languages and in languages like Mäori and Hopi Indian tenses do not even exist.

Most people in countries like Great Britain, Greece, China and Japan are past-oriented, with a strong sense of history. Continuity is cherished. Others, like those in Latin America and the Pacific Islands, are present-oriented. People savour the day; life is to be enjoyed whenever possible. Tomorrow is another day. A Tongan student wrote about a large wedding she had attended for which the invitation gave 2 pm as the time for the reception. When the guests arrived, they were asked to return in the evening, as the *umu* (or oven in the earth) had not yet been put down and the food would take at least four hours to cook. The guests went away, singing and happy.[13]

People in yet other countries, like those in the United States, Canada, and perhaps New Zealand and Australia, look to the future. Being prompt is important. Change is admired; technological advances are seen to make life better and better.

The attitude to time is often complex. Koreans, for example, (Kim, Tae Woo, 1997) may give the sense of being in a hurry 'to gain a result; to get a point; to get off aircraft or a bus; and to be serviced'. Yet when it comes to business or study they tend not to be hurried in the initial steps but to rush in the final stages. One expatriate sales manager reported:

> [Once] they know you will stay for ten days in Korea, no business will be conducted in the first nine days. All business hopefully takes place on the last day, quite often negotiating in the airport. People like the last minute.

For students, the short or long-term orientation will have many implications, even in planning how they study. A student used to thinking long-term may obtain and read all set texts before a course begins. A student not used to thinking ahead may be late with every assignment or turn in work which shows that insufficient time has been spent on it. Workshops on time planning may be an indispensable part of the orientation of such students, and regular sessions to discuss progress may be necessary also.

Activity Orientation
People can be inclined to *do* things expecting a measurable outcome, simply to *exist*, enjoying spontaneous pleasure as children do when they play among themselves or to *be-in-becoming*, which means they contemplate and meditate to improve themselves. Some have suggested that the activity orientation is climate-linked, and to some extent it may be. However, in many cultures

---

13   Keung, Manu Kiwa Chantel (1997). Student assignment written at the University of Waikato.

tradition is more influential than climate. In South China, hot and humid as the summers are, the people are extremely industrious.

The western way is usually to be concerned with *doing*. People ask, 'How are you doing?' or 'Keeping busy?' When a young person becomes engaged to be married, the first question about the partner may be 'What does he [or she] do?' The industry of, for instance, the Dutch, is legendary, but the same attitude is held in some eastern cultures, like those of the Chinese and Vietnamese. Effort, optimism, achievement, competition are all admirable. If work is not available some governments may make a determined effort to find work – any work – for the unemployed, before giving them a living allowance. A thoughtful, reasoned answer is sought for every problem.

In *being*-oriented cultures people enjoy themselves spontaneously. Responses from the heart are thought to be the most trustworthy. Kluckhohn and Strodtbeck (1960) illustrate the concept by citing the Mexican fiesta in which all throw themselves into the celebrations with abandon. Latin cultures particularly display this orientation, as do South Pacific cultures. A Fijian student, although admitting difficulty in scheduling assignments ahead, told a classmate that Pacific Islanders were not slow to organise social events. 'When people from the Islands decide to have a party, the grapevine is like a fire and news spreads quickly' (Cameron, 1993: 23). In New Zealand the Mäori people love to sing and dance, enjoying the moment. The Thai word *ngan* means both work and party. In rural Thailand, when seasonal labour is to be done, large groups of people come together for *tham ngan* (work) with plenty of opportunity for social activity at the same time. [14]

In *being-in-becoming* oriented cultures, people are concerned with who they are, not with what they are doing. When someone makes a mistake, Thai people like to say *mai pen rai,* which means something like 'Never mind. You are not responsible.'[15] The contemplative *Chan* form of Buddhism and Hinduism with its emphasis on withdrawal from earthly life and on the cycle of birth-life-death-rebirth fosters this view. The height of perfection in such cultures will be the self-induced trance or the meditations of such groups as the Zen Buddhist monks. Both thought and feeling are sublimated. The Tibetan self-exiled ruler, the Dalai Lama, is a living incarnation of this cultural viewpoint.

---

[14]   Kusolsinchai, Orapin (1996). Master's paper written at the University of Waikato.

[15]   Campbell, Nittaya (1997). Master's paper written at the University of Waikato.

Other Differences

Three other sets of value differences need special mention: psychologists have given them the labels affectivity, universalism and instrumentalism.

Affectivity This is the term given to the tendency in some cultures to respond emotionally and personally rather than cognitively and impersonally to situations. We would, for instance, expect an overt show of feeling if a decision were made which a Latin American representative did not like. In the United States or the United Kingdom we would expect the response to be neutral or at least restrained and challenged only on reasoned grounds. When Diana, Princess of Wales publicly supported the Red Cross appeal to stop land mines being planted, she was reprimanded by senior British government officials and called 'naïve' and 'uninformed'. Her answer, that those who lost limbs through land mines were just as likely to be naïve and uninformed, was personal but also logical.

Universalism This is the tendency to follow a standardised pattern. In spite of the name, it tends to be favoured in individualist cultures while particularism is favoured in collective cultures as in Asia.

Instrumentalism This is the tendency common in the United States to treat things as a means to something else. Its converse, expressiveness, popular in Arab and Latin American countries, is the tendency to treat things as of value in themselves.

Issues to Consider

(1)   You are a lecturer, looking for the best possible assistant trained in your particular field to help with course preparation and research, doing a semi-clerical, semi-technical job. Several applicants have the academic qualifications you need so you have to make a decision on personal considerations. Which of the values listed below would you place first? What values would you add to the list? Which five would you place last?

Status	Justice
Glory	Obedience
Courage	Self-respect

Power	Respect for parents
Wealth	Friendship
Serenity	Loyalty
Aesthetic satisfaction	Independence
Love	Health

(2)   Choose a specific culture very different from your own. If you were planning to spend a year in that culture, which of the following concerns do you think you would have? Which would worry you most? Why?

Danger	Punishment
Ignorance (your own)	Ignorance (others')
Deviation	Loneliness
Arrogance	Theft
Accidents	Ill health
Bribery	Tipping
Eating and drinking	Face-saving
Nepotism[16]	

(3)   Remembering that business cannot be rushed in some cultures, consider the kind of orientation that would be most helpful for new students from cultures different from your own.

(4)   Consider the different levels of formality in different cultures. How would you decide how formal to be if, say, you had a position as a teacher in a culture with very different teacher-student relationships from those in your own culture?

(5)   Read some books which bring foreign culture alive such as Tehmina Durrani's *My Feudal Lord* and Betty Mahmoody's *Not Without My Daughter,* Jung Chang's *Wild Swans,* and Achebe's *Things Fall Apart.* Consider the ways in which the particular novels and biographies you choose help and hinder intercultural understanding.

(6)   If a student comes from a culture with a high power distance, how likely is it that he or she will contribute if asked to share in setting objectives for a course?

(7)   How do staff formally address students and students staff in your institution? Are some international students uncomfortable with this. If they are, what do you and they do about it?

---

16   Argyle (1982) called it 'the local equivalent of social welfare'.

(8) If an educational institution which has previously required six-monthly reports from all thesis students decides to require monthly reports, how should the information be conveyed to students? Should international students be told the same way? Why or why not?

(9) Do most people in your culture think a work group has the right to collective action, such as going on strike, if they are unsatisfied with pay or conditions?

(10) Do people in your culture openly use terms which imply levels in society, like 'lower' or 'upper' class? Think of examples.

(11) How do students from different cultures feel about addressing their teachers by their given names?

(12) Do matters like surrogacy, cloning, and the protection of children, the elderly and those with disabilities transcend the values of individual cultures? Is the stitching up of infant female genitals the business of those outside a given culture or not? Can you think of examples of matters which a culture should be able to decide on for its members and others which are universal and no culture should be able to decide alone? If such matters do exist, how can they be distinguished from specifically local concerns?

5 THE ROLE OF RELIGION

by Douglas Pratt

*'The faiths of others all deserved to be honoured for one reason or
another. By honouring them one exalts one's own faith and at the
same time performs a service to the faith of others. If we extol our
own faith and disparage another because of devotion to our own
and because we want to glorify it, we seriously injure our own
faith.'*

Asoka, Emperor of India ca.25 BC[1]

Asoka was a famous Indian emperor, a mighty warrior and ruler, born a
Hindu, who became a convert to Buddhism. His words stand as a beacon of
light shining through centuries of religious intolerance and rivalry. Religion
is about communication: all religions seek to communicate a message – about
life, about the gods, about human destiny. Indeed, whereas messages of *belief*
may differ, for the most part messages of *value and ethics* (in other words,
what it is to be human) are surprisingly similar across most religions. When
clashes between religions and cultures occur it is primarily because of a
breakdown in communication: essential religious messages that are life-
affirming have become blurred, confused, dominated by political agendas and
the lust for power and control.

Religion serves as a shorthand for culture. When we learn something of
another person's religious outlook, when we learn about a people's faith, we
gain direct access to cultural understanding. Religion is both the bedrock of,
and the window on to, almost any culture. Therefore, when we consider the
role of religion in respect of communication and culture it is important to have

---

[1]   In the chapter and throughout this text BCE, meaning 'Before Common Era', and CE,
    meaning 'Common Era', are used instead of the more familiar BC and AD since the
    former two are less ethnocentric than the latter two.

at least a cursory grasp of the major religious traditions which have impact, to a greater or lesser degree, upon world affairs and the lives of millions. This chapter contains a review of the five so-called major traditions – from the east, Hinduism and Buddhism; and from the near-east Judaism, Christianity and Islam, and touches on the prominent traditions of the far east, Confucianism, Taoism and Shinto.

Hinduism

To be a Hindu means to accept and respect the ancient religious traditions of India. Hinduism may be best thought of as an emergent religion, for it has emerged over time – beginning some 4,500 years ago with early Vedic religion. There are two categories of scripture in Hinduism: the Vedas, which are the ancient Sanskrit scriptures from the preceding Vedic religion; and a range of texts which have since emerged throughout the development of Hinduism, including the great epics of the *Mahabharata* (which itself includes the *Bhagavad-Gita*) and the *Ramayana* – both grand stories packed with communication from the gods and the wisdom of the ancients. The basic caste structure which also emerged with the development of the religion consists of the fourfold classification of Priests (*Brahmins*), Warriors (*Kshatriyas*), Merchants (*Vaishyas*) and Servants (*Shudras*). Those thought to be outside this structure were, by definition, outcastes or 'untouchables'. Within each of the four castes (*varna*), and in respect of each of the four stages of life (*ashrama*), there are appropriate life duties (*dharma*). The combination of these produces one of Hinduism's main undergirding concepts, *varnashramadharma*, meaning that individual identity at any particular time is made up of a matrix of factors: caste, stage and relevant duties or requirements.

Furthermore, life is governed by four goals. *Dharma,* as has just been noted, is the pre-eminent goal that applies, with appropriate variation in terms of content, to all life-stages and castes. It means the right way of living. *Artha* is the goal of worldly prosperity and material well-being appropriate to the middle or 'householder' stage of life. It represents the whole range of activities associated with the gaining and protection of material wealth. *Kama*, the pursuit of love and pleasure, both sensual and aesthetic is also a goal proper to the stage of the householder. *Moksha* is the ultimate goal of liberation or salvation. It consists, broadly speaking, of a spiritual release which is the final transcending of mortal existence. There is more than one way to arrive at this goal: the 'Way of Works' (*Karma-marga*); the 'Way of Knowledge'(*Jnana-*

marga); and the 'Way of Devotion' (*Bhakti-marga*).

Sometimes referred to as a 'family' of religions, Hinduism, for all its diversity, has a number of further distinguishing features and concepts that provide an undergirding cohesion. These include *Brahman*, the impersonal absolute; *samsara* meaning the 'wheel' of time and existence; *karma* meaning both action and the effect of action; and *moksha,* the final liberation from mortal existence as determined by karma and samsara. A triadic idea of deity is also central: *Brahma*, the god who created the world; *Vishnu* who preserves and protects the world and who appears in the form of a number of incarnations, or *avatars* – for example as *Rama* and *Krishna*; and *Shiva* who in the end destroys the world. However, the female principal deity, *Shakti*, came to occupy a prominent place such that, in effect, Hinduism has a double triad: the intellectual construct of Brahma-Shiva-Vishnu, and the broad devotional focus on Shiva, Vishnu, and Shakti yielding the threefold sectarian division of *Shaivism, Vaishnavism*, and *Shaktism*.

Buddhism

A clear grasp of the life-story of the Buddha is critical for understanding the religion he founded. He was born as Siddhartha Gautama in north India in the sixth century before the birth of Christ (BCE). There are six key features to his life story: the *Great Awakening* in which he gained his foundational insight into the nature of existence as *dukkha* (unsatisfactoriness, suffering); the *Great Renunciation* when Gautama left his life of luxury in pursuit of enlightenment and which symbolises the need to 'let go' of attachments and desires and so on; the *Six-year Quest* to realise personal salvation by pursuing the two extreme options of Hinduism – philosophic meditation and bodily asceticism – neither of which satisfied him; the *Great Enlightenment* in which Gautama attained his goal and became the Buddha, or 'awakened one' and from there formulated his teachings; the *ministry* or life-path which saw him preaching, teaching, and forming a community (*Sangha*) of converts (from Hinduism); and finally the *parinibbana* referring to his death in which he 'crossed over' to the final transcendental, or end-state, of *nibbana.*

Although there are some basic beliefs that bind Buddhists into their religious community, there is no dogmatic demand to believe a set creed or confession. Also, although there is a core scripture, namely the *Pali Canon* called the *Tipitaka* (meaning 'three baskets') which comes from the oldest (*Theravada*) tradition of Buddhism, there is no overriding sense of there needing to be a closed canon of scripture. For these reasons a great diversity and voluminous development of Buddhist texts and teachings has evolved, most often out of the *Mahayana* tradition which emerged as a reaction to the narrow and more austere way of the earlier Theravada tradition. A significant further development was that of the *Vajrayana*, or 'Diamond Way'. This was a relatively early development of Mahayana and refers in particular to Tibetan Buddhism. Theravada Buddhism is in effect today the Buddhism of Southeast Asia; Mahayana the Buddhism of northern lands such as China and Japan.

Buddhist teaching and belief is primarily pragmatic. However, there is an underlying and unifying belief-structure or worldview. A key concept, suffering, is due to the desire for permanence in a world which is fundamentally impermanent: it is this 'clinging-to-the-impermanent' which lies at the base of human suffering. *Samsara* is the concept of cyclicity or existence as a round of birth, life, death and rebirth; and *karma* is the notion that it is the actions and deeds which accumulate during a lifetime that determine human destiny. As well as the more philosophic – or metaphysical – dimensions of Buddhist belief, there are also sets of moral commands and ethical guidelines.

Religion is expressed not just through beliefs but also, and in particular, through its various practices. Homage is variously shown to the Buddha and to those who have seniority and are further advanced in a spiritual sense. There is for Buddhists, as well as a devotional focus, the task of cultivating right wisdom and insight – seeing things as they really are – as a necessary precursor to attaining enlightenment. Thus meditation (*samadhi*) is both the key element to the practice of the religion and a singular distinctive feature. There are also some significant pilgrimage and festival rituals that Buddhists, with some regional variations, tend to observe. For example, *Wesak* is a main Theravada festival comprising the three-fold celebration of the birth, enlightenment, and death of the Buddha. It is also known as 'Buddha day'.

Judaism

The Judaism of today is *not* the same religion as that of the ancient Hebrew people. Ancient Hebrew religion spans the period beginning with Abraham (around 2000 BCE) through to the Babylonian exile (586 BCE). Then followed a 600 year period in which a new – Rabbinic – Judaism emerged at about the same time as the beginning of Christianity. Hebrew religion and religious understanding is grounded in the idea of covenant. It was the key component in the making of ancient nomadic tribes into a people and a nation 'under God'. Over time the Hebrews became enslaved by the Egyptians, but around 1300 BCE a new leader, Moses, led an escape, or *exodus*. The forty years of wandering back to the homeland forged a closer sense of community identity, and a new covenant between God and People was forged: Moses was given the *Torah*, the Word of God. This spelled out the divine commandments (*mitzvot*). So, from out of the covenants the essential divine message was issued and the basis of Judaism as a religion, which one Jewish scholar has described as itself a 'system of communications', was laid.

The grounding communication, the *Torah*, is in two forms, written and oral. The written form is the Hebrew Bible, called the *Tanakh*. The oral *Torah*, believed to have accompanied the emergence of the written *Torah*, then later, with the development of rabbinic Judaism, codified and written up, comprises a vast array of interpretation, narrative, and commentary. It forms an excellent example of the development of a system of communication.

Jewish identity in biblical times was tribal. This gave way, during the development of rabbinic Judaism, to the two great geographic and cultural blocks: *Ashkenazim* (European) and *Sephardic* (Spanish) Judaism. Today there are several branches of the religion. *Orthodox* Judaism regards itself as the 'true' Judaism. Zionism and support of the state of Israel tend to be a predominant feature. *Reform* Judaism, a liberalising development, began in Germany in the eighteenth century with the emancipation of Jews. *Conservative* Judaism emerged as a European reaction to the Reform movement: it sought to adopt a centrist position. Within and to the 'right' wing of orthodoxy lie various groups that together constitute the ultra-orthodox dimension, for example the *Hasidic* (saintly, pious) groups.

Judaism is above all a religion of tradition. Jews adhere or belong to a way, a history, a people. Historical identity is reinforced as tradition is lived out; past is made present through ritual events; the future is faced from a perspective of historical groundedness and an acute awareness of what has been. There are two primary settings for Jewish worship and ritual observance, the home and the synagogue. The sense of the sacred in Judaism is not so much to be found in the creation of holy place or space, but in the honouring of a sanctuary created in time: the *Sabbath*. This begins at sunset on each Friday and concludes at sunset on the Saturday.

The celebration of religious festivals is important. Very often the remembrance of joyful events is tinged with the recall of tragedy and pain in the life of the people. The new year of the Jewish lunar calendar is called *Rosh Hashanah*. Ten days into a new year sees the festival of *Yom Kippur* – the day of atonement. Repentance and forgiveness are the underlying religious themes. In recent times two new festival occasions have been added to those which are based on the biblical traditions and events. These are *Yom*

HaSho'ah and *Yom HaAtzma'ut,* respectively commemorations of the Nazi Holocaust and Israel's Independence day. While there is much that takes place at a communal level, at the level of the individual and family there are traditions, or rites of passage, which mark life and define relationships and responsibilities.

Christianity

Christianity, like Buddhism, is a founder religion. The life-story of Jesus is the starting point. The details of conception and birth are, of course, surrounded by legend. But whatever is made of them, the significant religious issue so far as Christianity is concerned is that Jesus is deemed to be both *human* and *divine*: 'born of woman' and 'Son of God'. The Christian view of Jesus as 'God incarnate' is the basis of a religious mystery and much controversy. The ministry, or life-work, of Jesus begins with his submission to the act of baptism which involved immersion into, and the arising out of, water. This may be viewed as a symbolic act of spiritual and moral 'cleansing'– the dying to an old life and the rising to a new one. Immediately following this he began gathering a group of twelve followers, or disciples. They became the nucleus of a continuing community.

After his death, Jesus becomes, at the very least, an enigmatic figure. To the believer he is the 'Risen Lord', an ever-present divine reality. The 'crisis of continuance' that a founder-religion faces upon the demise of its founding figure was met, in the case of Christianity, by the institution and development of the community of Christians as 'Church', or *ecclesia*. The earliest Christians did not reject Judaism; they saw their 'faith' as the fulfilment of Jewish messianic expectation. But Christianity soon moved away from its founding Jewish orbit. The outwardly expanding missionary activity of the first Christians meant, in the end, that Jewish Christianity waned in favour of Gentile Christianity. Then came the formulation of beliefs and doctrines into a sophisticated summary creed, together with the emergence of a canon of scripture, *The New Testament*. All this took place over several centuries.

Against competing claims from without, and counter-claims from within, the question of what precisely constituted the correct and true faith, and how this was to be expressed and lived out in daily life and worship, lay behind the need for an orthodox self-definition of the religion. At two great councils of leaders convened early in the Common Era the classic resolutions defining Christian orthodoxy were arrived at. The matter of correct Christian practice, 'orthopraxis', is something which also came to the fore as the institutional structures of the Christian Church gradually took shape. A variety of worship practices had emerged during the first two centuries which established norms and defined dimensions of orthopraxis that have been held ever since. The two primary sacraments which quickly emerged were baptism and the eucharist (Mass or Holy Communion).

For the Christian religion, worship is a phenomenon that is expressed through many different forms and modes. In general terms it has to do with acknowledging 'worth'. It is both an individual act and a group activity. Variety of expression notwithstanding, it is still the case that the broad patterns of Christian worship are universally recognisable. So far as festivals are concerned, there are three major celebrations of foundational events: Christmas celebrates the birth of Christ, Easter celebrates the birth of Christian faith, and Pentecost celebrates the birth of the Christian church. Although pilgrimages are by no means an essential element in Christianity today, many do undertake them still and, for many centuries – particularly in the west before the Reformation – pilgrimages were, indeed, an important aspect in the spiritual life of the Christian church, as well as playing a significant role in terms of the social and economic dimensions of religion.

Islam

Islam is a founder-religion to the extent that it begins, historically speaking, with a man who became a messenger, or prophet, of God. Muhammad was born in Mecca in 570 CE. From the year 610 CE until his death in 632, Muhammad uttered recitations which he, and his followers then and since, believed were given directly by God (Allah). These were to become the text of the *Qur'an*. In 622 CE Muhammad migrated to the town of Medina. This event – the *hijra* – marks the beginning of the Islamic calendar. At Medina Muhammad laid down the basis for Islamic religious belief and practice, and the formation of a community under God, a theocracy, called the *Ummah*.

Within some thirty years of Muhammad's death Islam had an impact on the surrounding countries of the near eastern world and expansion out of Arabia was well under way. Immediately following his death leadership of the community was in the hands of a series of four caliphs. Then a ruling dynastic era, based away from Arabia, held sway for several centuries. Alongside the religious ideal of a single united Islamic community, the political reality was one of diversity and difference. Until relatively recent times the Islamic community was to be found in a variety of kingdoms and caliphates. And in the modern world, Islam is found in a diversity of nation-states.

Although the apparent resurgence of Islam in the late twentieth century reflects an element of religious extremism and fanaticism from some quarters, for the most part Muslims are politically, if not religiously, moderate. But they are very intentional about their faith. Islam cannot be ignored. Worse yet is the response that dismisses or otherwise tries to negate it. Struggle with unbelief from within, or threats to belief from without – the essential meaning of *jihad* – has steeled this religion through the centuries. Islam, the religion of peaceful submission (the root meaning of the word *Islam*) to the will of the all-merciful and all-compassionate God, is not so much a religion to be feared as a faith to be understood, a religion inviting dialogue and respectful recognition.

Islam is divided into two main groups whose origins derive from a difference in view on the question of the right line of succession from Muhammad, an issue that is both religious and political. The majority (approximately 85 per cent) of Muslims belong to the *Sunni* group which traditionally holds that the political successor to the Prophet Muhammad is no more than a guardian of the prophetic legacy. *Shi'ite* Muslims hold that the principal religious figure for the ongoing community is the *Imam*, believed to be one invested with the qualities of inspired and infallible interpretation of the *Qur'an* in the mode of spiritual succession directly from Muhammad himself. The other major movement within Islam, *Sufism*, originated in pious asceticism and cut across the other more politically oriented divisions within Islam. It gives expression to mysticism and the contemplative ideal.

The belief that God is One; that Muhammad is the last of the divinely sent messengers or prophets of God; and that the *Qur'an* is the final Word of God, are fundamental tenets of Muslim faith. Daily life is a matter of living in accordance with the *Shariah* or Divine Law based on the *Qur'an.* The essence of Islam is conveyed in both belief and law. There is not one without the other. Muslims everywhere practise the Five Pillars – *arkan* – of religious duty: the utterance of the declaratory creed (*shahada*); obligatory prayers (*salat*) – five times daily for Sunnis, three for Shi'is; the annual almsgiving (*zakat*) which is a form of social taxation; the fast (*sawm*) from sunrise to sunset daily during the lunar month of Ramadan; and the pilgrimage to *Mecca* which all Muslims are meant to undertake at least once in their life-time, health and wealth permitting. Of these the most likely to affect Muslim staff and students are the obligatory prayers and the need to worship from Friday noon, demands which could easily clash with scheduled classes or field trips. The religious requirements must take precedence over all other commitments. Special exemption can be sought but only for specific occasions, such as an examination.

The Far East: Confucianism, Taoism and Shinto

Confucianism

Confucius was a great Chinese sage and teacher. He was born in obscure circumstances in 551 BCE and during his life-time received little recognition. He excelled as a scholar and teacher and his sayings have subsequently been collected to become *The Analects*. In essence he taught a system of cultured humanity, venerating the principles and virtues of an earlier period in Chinese history, promoting a life of peace and harmony in accordance with the 'Mandate of Heaven' as a counter to the rule of law and punishment with its response in violence and hatred. For Confucius the goal of humane goodness (*jen*) is represented as harmonious interaction. Such a goal requires cultivation through an educational process that involved the study of Classics which Confucius himself collected and edited.

In the religio-cultural system of Confucianism the key principle is *li* meaning 'propriety', 'respectful ritual', at the heart of which is filial piety directed towards ancestors and parents. *Li* is the outward form enabling the cultivation of *jen* within. For Confucius the discipline of study and the practice of ritual was a self-transformative activity the foundation of which lay in sacred power. Confucius was primarily concerned for human life in family and society, not with the invocation of gods and spirits as such. The essence of religion is found in Confucius' placement of the Mandate of Heaven (that is, the belief in a transcendent reference point for mundane life) as the corner-stone of his world-view.

The strong focus on ritual that developed over the centuries goes back to the ritual sacrifices offered to the ancestors. In its primal sense, the perform-ance of ritual effects the maintenance of the universe, communion with the ancestors, and the harmony of human society. For traditional Confucian society, government officials were required to perform rituals for the harmony and happiness of the community which they served and which they represented.

Taoism

Taoism is both a philosophy and a primal religious tradition. The legendary 'founder' is one Lao Tzu, born 604 BCE, an older contemporary of Confucius. His written work, the *Tao Te Ching* (Classic of the Tao and its Power), propounds the view of the sacred principle immanent in nature which is the source of all and to which all returns. Together with its philosophical foundations and proponents, Taoism over time evolved a religious mode and practice complete with sacred writings, priests and various sects. There emerged a common concern for long life and immortality and a central focus on obtaining harmony with the eternal Tao by actions aimed at getting in tune with the spiritual forces of the universe. In general terms, Taoism produced an abundance of scriptures, rituals and organisations as an expression of the religious development of a philosophical perspective on life.

Lao Tzu and later Taoist thinkers identified primeval chaos with the Tao: the Tao is both the origin and inner source of continual transformation (*viz*, the process of generation and evolving-forth; also devolving and return-to-source). From out of a primordial dualism that the Tao effected, there evolved the polarities of Heaven/Earth or *Yang/Yin*. The Tao is the functioning principle of the interaction of *Yang* and *Yin*. Human welfare is a matter of harmonious balance and interaction both directly with, and indirectly modelled on, the functioning of Tao in respect of *Yang* and *Yin*. The pursuit of human welfare may be via the philosophical route involving meditation and withdrawal from society, or religiously through engaging in practices and rituals aimed at accessing divine powers and promoting the balance of Yang and Yin forces. Both are ways of the Taoist path.

Shinto

Shinto meaning 'Way of the *Kami* (transcendent spirits)' is the name given to the ancient primal religious tradition of Japan. The 'Way of the *Kami*' signifies understanding life in accordance with the will of *kami,* a kind of animistic fatalism as the term 'kami', basically, denotes animated existence in all its multifarious manifestations. For Shintoism the multiplicity of *kami* does not equate with the apparent fragmentation of polytheism: kamic collegiality undergirds the kamic dynamism of the holistic Shinto world view. As with all other forms of life and matter, humans are deemed to have originated from creative *kami* and are defined as having *kami* essence within.

The origins of Shinto are lost in the mists of time, but its textual source is found in the writings known as the *Kojiki* and *Nihongi* – compilations of cosmological myth and mythic chronicles. These earliest recorded forms of Shinto reflect both the political and religious motifs for unifying Japan. There is no single set of scriptures, nor a sole foundational myth. Nonetheless there is one major and pervasive mythological theme, namely the descent of the sun goddess *Amatesaru* from whom came the imperial family line.

Shinto religious activity involves ritual required to maintain the cosmic order and to effect communication, via priestly intermediaries, between the human realm and the 'divine' realm of the kami. The Shinto shrine is the locus for much ritual and spiritual activity. The location of a shrine is often a sacred precinct such as the dwelling place of ancestral spirits. Shinto allows for the existence of malevolent kami who are evil and violent – the Kami of Great Evils. There are also the Kami of Great Good. So, just as there are forces for badness in life, there are forces for the good. The original purity of human creation is defiled through wrongdoing or contact with malevolent kami. Such pollution interrupts contact with beneficent kami thus restricting and reducing access to the sources of goodness and beauty. Set rituals are required to be followed in order to restore purity and ameliorate pollution. The values, which attach to this as well as the actions, form a pervasive sub-theme to Japanese religious and cultural life.

Other Supernatural Beliefs

A whole range of other genuinely-held supernatural beliefs, folk and popular religions and superstitions exists. Some of these are linked to formal religions and others are not. Often they operate only at a local level but still affect culture and so behaviour significantly.

Though diffuse they are widespread and traditional. They may take many forms, such as space reserved for altars and for spirits within and near buildings, or, like *feng shui,* involve the way a building is sited or a room laid out. Insistence on good or bad luck may be closely linked with such beliefs and can defy any logical explanation.

Not having a row number 13 in an aeroplane, or deciding red or the number eight is lucky is similarly irrational but still pervasive in particular cultures. Sometimes some reason does exist, such as that the number four in Mandarin sounds ominously similar to the word for death, or a ladder may collapse on someone walking under it. But whether there is or ever was a reason or not, to mock such beliefs is to separate ourselves from those who hold them earnestly and sincerely. It is possible, indeed interculturally sound, to accept and respect such views without necessarily holding them personally.

In Korea it is considered normal before an important decision is made to consult *Shaman* or a fortune teller, because there seem to be too many factors to work any problem out with only scientific analysis in the changeable and competitive environment of today. In Tae Woo Kim's (1997) words: 'Koreans tend to accept that personal feelings or superstitions are sometimes more effective to predict their business future than the analyses of hard facts.'

6 LANGUAGE

'Absolutely nothing is so important for a nation's culture as its language.'

Wilhelm von Humboldt, 1799

The Nature of Language

Language is the means through which we send and receive messages. The Greek proverb tells us: 'Nothing done with intelligence is done without speech.'

The language process, whether the message is oral, nonverbal or written, works well when the intended message is conveyed. However, if speakers and listeners come from different cultures this may not happen. As Kameda (1996: 62) says:

> Words do not 'mean' at all. Only people 'mean'. And people give entirely different meanings to words, meanings they have acquired through experience.

Slips can occur either when the sender puts the message into language or encodes it, when the receiver interprets the message from language or decodes it, or at both stages.

To increase the likelihood that a message will be understood in the way intended, the speaker can re-phrase it or ask the listener to give his or her understanding. Alternatively the listener can ask for it to be repeated, put in other words or explained. Or else the listener can repeat what seems to be the gist of the message and ask if it has been correctly understood. Either speaker or listener, if a meaning seems to be wrong, can then suggest what was intended. In an intercultural interchange, this kind of checking might be indispensable if an exact meaning is to be conveyed. Irony, humour, the accompanying nonverbal communication, the vocabulary itself, or a range of other matters that differ between cultures might have tripped the recipient. But how often is understanding checked, especially in an educational setting?

Victor (1992: 15) points out the importance of a mutual language in the communication process. 'Without a shared language, direct communication is at best filtered through a third party and at worst altogether impossible.' Even when a language is shared, it is usually the first language of one party but not the other. When the first language of two communicators is different, as so often happens when staff or students move to another culture, problems occur. Some of these will be discussed in more detail later in this chapter.

The misunderstandings mentioned are bound to arise. No people can expect all others to share their culture, let alone speak their language. If members of two cultures do speak the same language, one group as a first language and the other as a second language, those in the first group have no right to assume the others will be able to speak the shared language with equal facility. When students go abroad to study or staff to become 'foreign experts', it is essential for those who are using their own first language at least to help by careful, empathetic listening.

The greater our cultural and linguistic knowledge, the more success we are likely to have in intercultural communication. Culture and language impinge heavily on one another. Even saying or hearing 'yes' or 'no' can depend on the culture of the speaker and listener, so that closed questions, to which a one-word answer is expected, are best avoided. Even when the answers given follow up the ' yes' or 'no' with an explanation, understanding what is meant by those answers in particular circumstances can depend on the depth and range of cultural and linguistic awareness of both speaker and listener, as the later section on answering questions will show. Problems may come from vocabulary, grammar, pronunciation, expectations, knowledge of the environment, knowledge of the subject, relationship with the speaker, or from some combination of these.

Metacommunication, or messages about communication like 'I know you won't like this but ...', reinforce messages. They can give a useful indication of the speaker's expectation, an expectation that the listener can accept or reject.

Language Processes

People use language to make sense of their world. Their culture will determine which language (or languages) they use, and the ways they use it. But does culture shape language or language shape culture – or both at once?

In the 1960s Edward Sapir developed the theory which has become known as the Sapir-Whorf hypothesis after Sapir and his outstanding student, Benjamin Whorf. The Sapir-Whorf hypothesis implies that language controls culture through shaping thought patterns. According to it, people are almost controlled by whatever language they have been brought up to speak. In Sapir's (ed. Mandelbaum, 1960) own words:

> Human beings do not live in the objective world alone but are very much at the mercy of the particular language which has become the medium of expression for their society.

Whorf (1962: 249) adds to this:

> Every language is a vast pattern-system, distinct from others, in which are culturally ordained the forms and categories by which the personality not only communicates, but also analyzes nature, notices or neglects types of relationship and phenomena, channels his reasoning and builds the house of his consciousness.

Many later linguists, while accepting that language does affect the way people think, believe each language is only what it is because of the culture of the people who transmitted it to their children. In other words, if time is considered much less important than people, as it undoubtedly is in many cultures, the concept of lateness and therefore a word for lateness may not exist.[1] In many languages – Māori, Mandarin, Bahasa Malaysia and Bahasa Indonesia – tenses simply do not exist. On the other hand, European languages make time, in the form of tense, a part of every single sentence. Is this because Europeans are time-conscious, or does the existence of tenses make the people in the culture time-conscious?

Similarly, if seniority is extremely important in a culture, that may need to be shown in the words used to speak to, or even to speak about, particular people. The section on cultural differences later in this chapter will give a selection of instances in which language reflects a culture in this way, and especially the relationships within a culture.

The Sapir-Whorf hypothesis, so useful in understanding the psychological underpinnings of language, has given way to a descriptive approach to language. Michael Halliday (1978) developed a systematic theory of the way languages work. He and others since have produced a theory of systemic

---

[1] In *The Silent Language*, Hall (1959) points out that there is no word for lateness in the Navajo language.

grammar which explains both what language is and the dynamic ways in which languages can and do change.

Two other approaches to language processes demand mention: the theory of relevance and the theory of semiotics. The first was developed by Sperber and Wilson (1990) who pointed out that what is relevant to the speaker dictates both language design and practice, often unconsciously. It is tempting in education to favour this approach since it enables teachers to narrow their focus on to the particular genre which interests them. The danger is that the allusiveness and subtlety of language may be swept away as irrelevant. Linguists like Raymond Cohen see this as a very real loss. The second dates back to Wittgenstein (1958) and Eco (1979) who showed that any language is a code with all its signs defined by other signs so that there is no possibility of any definition being absolute. Language is seen as a series of 'verbal habits' (Nida, 1991: 21).

These 'habits' are not owned by anyone, though people behave as though they are. This is particularly true of names. People resent having their names misspelt or mispronounced, and often dislike discovering other people with their own name, though in languages like Welsh or Korean with restricted pools of names this happens frequently.

Family names in South Korea illustrate the kind of power language can exert. For centuries there has been a law barring couples with the same name and same ancestral village from marrying. Since 22 per cent of South Korea's 44 million people are named *Kim*, this restriction is heavy. It is heavier still, climbing to 55 per cent, when the names *Park, Lee, Choi* and *Chong* are added. Supporters of the ban say inter-marriage would stain the clan name.[2] About once in ten years the government relaxes the ban for the year, but ten years may seem a long wait for some!

In many languages names are associated with particular qualities. 'Lee', one of the most well-known Chinese names, means 'celestial dragon', a good name for a leader like the former long-term Singaporean Prime Minister, Lee Kuan Yew, or his eldest son, Lee Hsien Loong, Deputy Prime Minister of Singapore as this book goes to press.

In China it used to be considered improper to address someone in power by his or her given name. Mao Zedong was Chairman Mao. Now, however, Jiang Zemin and other leaders are given their full names openly in the Chinese press.

In business the sense of ownership and association extends to trade names.

---

[2]   'If you're a Kim, Lee, Park or Choi, finding a spouse will be tricky', *New Straits Times*, 13 September 1996: 24.

In Wellington, New Zealand, an Indian New Zealander whose family name was 'Harrod' had a small fabric shop in which he employed two members of his family, and no one else. He called his small shop 'Harrods'. By chance, the owners of the famous Harrods in London heard of this shop and asked the owner to change its name. He refused. The owners of Harrods, London, then sued the Indian New Zealander. Might is right. Or is it? The New Zealand reaction to the suit was, at first, disbelief. Then a small farming township called Otorohanga took the law into its own hands. Every business in the community changed its name to Harrods – Harrods Dairy, Harrods Cycles, Harrods Cinema, Harrods Fish and Chips and so on. Rather than make itself an international laughing stock the London firm withdrew its suit and the small fabric shop continued with its own name in Wellington. The Otorohanga businesses changed back to their earlier names.

But the fact remains that many people view names as of major importance. Shakespeare's Juliet could say:

That which we call
A rose, by any other name would smell as sweet

but few believe her.

Very often a student from Asia coming to a western country takes on a western given name to help the staff who might have trouble pronouncing the unfamiliar name, and to encourage classmates to accept him or her more easily. Even *within* countries like China and Japan when students have a foreign teacher, they sometimes take western names and even numbers for classroom use. The student who is learning a whole new language is saving the teacher from learning a single new name! Surnames can be changed too, so causing confusion. Students from Arab countries sometimes use one surname with one agency such as the university registry, and another with the accommodation office or the medical centre.

The student or teacher who simultaneously holds different sets of verbal habits in mind has a real advantage intellectually over the monolingual speaker. But monolingual speakers can at least try to acquire understanding of the culture. For example, in a culture where age is venerated, visitors can show respect for the elderly even without knowing the words with which to address them correctly.

Within any language words go through phases of acceptance. To me and to most readers now, words like 'nigger', even in novels written as long ago as *Huckleberry Finn*, are immediately disturbing but the word 'Negro' has no negative connotations. But some years ago many United States citizens more intimately concerned about the situation, finding the word 'Negro' had connotations they did not accept, decided to use the term 'Black' instead, proudly. 'Black' has since been replaced by the term 'African-American'.

The problem always is the layers of unconscious stereotypes that may lie behind the choice of particular words. In today's lecture room the implications of words and phrases like 'minorities' and 'third world countries' are beginning to be challenged, but the terms themselves are still common currency. Although in most countries women make up slightly more than 50 per cent of the population, they are sometimes considered a 'minority', perhaps because they are still in the minority in positions of power. More seriously, those who are a 'minority' in some places are very much a 'majority' in other parts of the world. Similarly some of those countries referred to in documents as 'third world', usually because of their economic dependence, are fast becoming leading economic powers. The use of such terms may establish inaccurate perceptions in the minds of students who hear them.

Even the choice of a language may produce different ways of thinking in the students. Hofstede (1986: 315) gives a practical example of the way different languages affected education, an example all the more telling because the languages used, French and English, are cognate. In an international business school he was teaching the same executive course in French each morning to one internationally-mixed half of a class and in English in the afternoon to the other half:

> It was remarkable that the discussion of the same case studies in French would regularly lead to highly stimulating intellectual discussions, but few practical conclusions; in English it would not be long before somebody asked 'So what?' and the class tried to become pragmatic. Nobody in the French-speaking group even asked '*Et alors?*' (So what?); and the English language would hardly find the words to express the French intellectual speculations.

The Interpersonal Uses of Language

A major use of language is interpersonal, to sustain relationships with others. The problem is that relationships within some cultures have very different levels of formality from those in other cultures, even for similar situations. For instance, a student in a New Zealand university would call his or her supervisor by that person's given name, John or Brenda or whatever it was. In Britain a supervisor might be Dr Smith. In China, he might be Dr Peter, assuming Peter was the given and not the family name. In Germany a supervisor might be Frau Docteur Professeur Lieselotte Weidner, with all five names used, at least at an initial meeting. A person, whether teacher or student, used to one level of formality (or register, as a linguist would say) could be thrown off balance on hearing a different level used.

At one western university, students, asked why they did not tell staff at the international students office about their problems, had this to say:

> When I went, the staff member did not leave the computer to come to the counter. She was speaking to me while still looking at the computer screen. I found that action very offensive.

Another, from the same university but from a different culture, claimed:

> I once went to see someone concerning a grade that I had lost because I went to a funeral without proof. The woman carried on typing and without looking at me said, 'What do you want?' In my culture it is appropriate to inquire how you are before asking of a problem. I could not talk to her.

In each incident it was not what was said that the student minded, but the absence of a friendly opening, as well as the absence of the kind of nonverbal support which will be discussed in the next chapter. In an academic situation you might assume that most language would be used to give or receive information. It has, however, been suggested that the information function of language probably does not amount to more than 20 per cent of all uses of language (Nida, 1991), and there is no reason to think that an academic setting would be different from other settings.

For informative language to achieve its purpose, speaker and listener or writer and reader must have similar knowledge, experience and feelings. When sender and receiver come from different cultures, the chance of similarity is less likely to be high.

The very attitude to language itself may differ. In some cultures a contract is not secure until it is in writing. In others, the oral contract is the one that matters, the written one being dependent on changing factors and so variable, whereas the underlying spirit of the spoken agreement is sacrosanct.

Even the language itself changes. Technological advances spawn new types of technical language. Spin doctors are a phenomenon of the 1990s and so is the language associated with them. E-mail has its own conventions which scholars in organisations like the Association for Business Communication are carefully studying.

Literature is only fully accessible through language. What Scot would accept a translation into Hindi of "Auld Lang Syne" as the real song? Creative literature, whether novels, poetry or plays, tells imaginatively how people felt and behaved in specific situations; it humanises a language, challenges stereotypes and shows up empty generalisations for what they are.

Language Universals

Heather Bowe and Margaret a'Beckett (1994) have pointed out that concentrating on differences between languages may be an over-reaction and may prejudice understanding of the processes used by speakers of various languages.

All cultures, for example, use greetings for strangers, other greetings for acquaintances and yet other greetings for close friends. And all cultures use both verbal and nonverbal greetings. However, differences exist in the kinds of greeting used.

Some languages focus on the time of day as in the Greek *Kalimera* ('Good morning') or well wishing, as in the French *Ça va*. Others involve family relationships, as in the Vietnamese 'Greetings, older sister'. Yet others use veneration of age or status as in the Mandarin *Ni hao* and *Nin hao* ('you are well'), *Ni* when speaking to someone of the same status or lower and *Nin* to someone of greater age or status.

Bowe and a'Beckett show that after the initial greetings, conventions may go beyond the word level, so that in some cultures newcomers will be barraged with questions whereas in others they may be ignored. In either case we may feel uncomfortable if our expectations are not fulfilled.

Again, convergence exists in sounds, rhythm, pronunciation, syntax and grammar across all languages. Divergence exists as well, but this can usefully be seen as part of a pattern rather than as a set of differences.

To understand these divergencies we need to understand why, for instance, English uses embedding[3] frequently, while Indonesian uses the passive widely, why some languages have elaborate pronoun codes and others do not, why some languages use the subjunctive mood and others do not, even if they once did.

If we accept the definition of the linguist, Finegan (1994), communicative competence is the 'ability to produce and interpret utterances appropriate to

---

[3]   'Embedding' is inserting a word, phrase or clause inside another construction. For example, 'because she worked hard' is embedded in the sentence 'Joan, because she worked hard, succeeded.'

their context of use'. However these contexts differ, the purposes will be the same. Just as all languages have systems of greetings, so they all have ways of conveying other meanings such as balancing politeness and efficiency. To be able to understand, say, the system of politeness in Japanese, we need consciously to recognise our own system of politeness. English, for example, uses the terms 'Please' and 'Thank you' often whereas most Asian languages have no real equivalent. As intercultural theorists like Gudykunst and Kim (1992a) point out, to interact well with people of other cultures, people must first understand their own culture.

In many – perhaps in all languages – shades of meaning exist which newcomers do not catch. Thai, for instance, has a language game called *kham phuan* or 'twisted words', which is used as a secret code of a group or as a private way of sharing what those outside the group would see as a socially unacceptable joke.[4]

Cultural Differences in Language

Because language and experience are so interrelated, knowing a language is important in knowing a culture, and knowing the culture is important in knowing a language.

A corollary of the Sapir-Whorf hypothesis mentioned earlier is that people will tend to live and believe it best to live in the way their language predisposes them. If the magic words in the society are 'finance', 'success', 'computing', 'science', 'latest', 'newest' and 'research', they will tend to test and experiment all the time, trying to raise the standards of living and even of dying. If the magic words are 'song' and 'dance', 'festival' and 'pleasure', they will celebrate all they can in the ways they enjoy most.

If, as can happen so often with both education and business, speakers feel that the words must convey a sense of harmony, courtesy will take 'precedence over truthfulness, which is consistent with the cultural emphasis on the maintenance of social harmony as the primary function of speech' (Gudykunst and Kim, 1992a).

Some traditions, especially Latin, Arab and Islamic traditions, are male-oriented, and based on a strong authority figure. The assumption that the world is male carries over into language. It is not only the choice of the word 'man' but the underlying thought that makes the Arab proverb 'A man's tongue is his sword' a good example. In English, too, the number of words and phrases with positive associations that come from masculinity or predominantly male

---

[4] Kusolsinchai, Orapin, assignment submitted at the University of Waikato, May 1997.

occupations like war and organised sport is significant. Consider terms like 'vigour', 'powerful', 'mighty', 'indomitable', 'chivalrous', 'operation', 'drive home', 'briefing', 'field day' and 'outvie'. The connotations of 'weaker vessel', 'distaff side', 'housewife', 'bustling' and 'matronly' are surely less positive.

Even the uses of language differ. In some cultures, as has been discussed in Chapter 2, staff expect the senior executive to help with advice concerning difficulties with children, marriage, accommodation, finance and other personal matters.

Day-to-day chat will be whatever the people involved want it to be, and will probably lack any pattern of organisation. But for formal spoken or written work the organisation will be very different according to the culture. People from low context cultures are likely to try to follow a direct plan and will regard clarity and conciseness as very important. Those from high context cultures, which include most of Asia and some parts of the rest of the world like South America and some Mediterranean cultures, will favour an indirect approach and will value richness and allusions.

Hall (1976) reminds us that any verbal or nonverbal transaction can be high, low or middle context. Usually high context communication is 'economical, fast, efficient and satisfying; however time must be taken in programming'.

The elaborate endings of a letter in French, or the calls for Allah to bless the reader and the reader's family (Varner and Beamer, 1995) in both books and letters illustrate this kind of embellishment. Arabic is full of terms like *inshalla,* which means 'God willing'. Similarly those who speak Bahasa Indonesia use *Insya Allah* in the same way in what seems to outsiders an exaggerated speaking style. Whatever has already occurred is precious. As Hall (1976) put it: 'HC [High context] actions are by definition rooted in the past, slow to change, and highly stable.'

Languages themselves are very different. In English a rising tone at the end of a sentence may be the only indication that a question is being asked. And in English as in other western languages tones indicate feelings such as anger or delight, an extra which the speaker uses at will. But in many languages tones are an essential part of the language itself. The tone of a word dictates its meaning.

Consider, for example, Mandarin, the language of China's largest nationality, the Han, the official language of China, and the only written language throughout almost all China. The script has around 50,000 characters or pictographs, of which 5,000 to 8,000 are in common use. *Practical Chinese Reader, Elementary Course Book 1,* a widely used elementary Chinese textbook, to comfort the new learner, comments: 'Of these merely 3,000 are used for everyday purposes' (1997: 18).

All originally represented their meaning pictorially, with for instance, a cross through a rectangle meaning a person standing in a field and so a man, since men did the outdoor work. Now only a few are linked in any recognisable way. A pictograph stands for one syllable. That syllable can have any one of four tones: the flat tone '-', the rising tone ' '', the dip and rise tone ' ˇ', and the falling tone ' ''. The meaning will differ accordingly. Consider, for example, the word *shi*. It can mean 'lion' or 'wet' if it has the first long flat tone; 'stone' or 'true' if it has the second rising tone; 'history' or 'beginning' if it has the third tone which falls and then rises; and finally, 'oath' or 'yes' if it has a sharp falling tone.

The tonal complexities of Mandarin pale in significance beside those present in the unwritten language of millions of people living in south China. Their language, Cantonese, has nine tones! Even fluent speakers of Mandarin not familiar with Cantonese have difficulty conversing with a Cantonese speaker. Tones, so easy to master for those used to them, can be extremely difficult for those who are not.

When the Japanese took Mandarin as the base of Japanese, they rejected tones altogether. And certainly the fact that Bahasa Malaysia is not a tonal language may be one of the reasons that the Indonesians took Bahasa Malaysia as the base of their national language. Another reason is the script, Roman letters, so much easier to learn than, for instance, Mandarin script. The situation in Indonesia may surprise those outside the country. Bahasa Indonesia, now the official language of Indonesia, is the second language for most of those who speak it. Though there are over three hundred languages in Indonesia, one language, Bahasa Indonesia, which is the first language of only a small minority of Indonesians, is spoken and understood by 70 per cent of the 200 million people. There are, of course, historical and political reasons for the choice also, but the linguistic reasons cannot be overlooked (Sanjaya, 1996).

Turn Taking

For those who by dedication and industry or chance of birth do speak second and other languages, there are still conventions to become familiar with. Consider turn taking. In western countries people are supposed to speak one at a time, although, of course, in families and other intimate situations this does not always happen. In some cultures a person will begin to speak just before the other has finished. In other cultures people speak in the order of rank. In yet others a spell of a few seconds is expected between each utterance to give members time to think. Successful communication will depend on observing the other person's conventions.

Introductions

In individualist cultures, a person or a group can approach any other person or group if circumstances warrant. Not so in collectivist cultures in which an introduction, oral or written, almost invariably requires an intermediary. Usually the intermediary knows both parties and may write letters of introduction, may arrange meetings or interviews, may suggest suitable gifts, or may telephone or write ahead. Whatever is done helps establish credibility for both parties.

Initiating Relationships

Dodd (1971) makes suggestions which go beyond word choice on ways to initiate relationships.

(1)   Take responsibility for communicating with those from different cultures.
(2)   Try to look beyond surface differences such as appearance and dress.
(3)   Develop a curiosity about the internals of culture, such as thought patterns.
(4)   Look for a wide range of sources about [other] cultural groups, so our stereotypes are not too narrow.
(5)   Discover ways that feelings affect messages and messages affect relationships.
(6)   When you have negative stereotypes about any group, work on discovering positive attributes to balance your view.[5]

Greetings and Leave Taking

Although in every culture people use greetings and leave-takings, they are so very different that it is hard to generalise about them. In China, though few if any go hungry now, the greeting is likely to be: 'Have you eaten yet?' or,

---

[5]   Adapted from a set in Dodd (1971).

'Have you had lunch?' In parts of Scotland, though the mist may be thick, the greeting could well be 'Fine day today.' In many countries, western and eastern, a greeting is likely to be about health, though only the closest family and friends would expect a real answer to 'How are you?' or *Ni hao?*

In a small country like New Zealand it often seems as if everyone knows, or is likely soon to know, something about the background of everyone else, so unless the streets are busy it is normal to greet anyone you see with a 'Hello', 'Good morning', 'Gidday' or a smile or a nod.

In many other cultures, however, people can fairly safely assume they can slide into a crowd unnoticed. The 'Hello' becomes, not a friendly greeting but a polite means of avoiding communication. In contrast, *Bonjour* or *Salut* supported by a handshake or a kiss *(la bise)*, is both more formal and more sociable.

'In my culture', wrote a Malaysian student in New Zealand, 'we do not say, "Hi" or "please" or "thank you" whenever we do something like make a purchase or use a laundrette. Here people think you are rude if you don't. And if you don't have the habit of queuing, you seem really ill mannered. I am often mortified.'[6]

To Elizabeth Ochobi from the foothills of the Kisii Highlands in Kenya the New Zealand greeting habits seemed rude, curt and interfering. She explained the greeting ritual she was used to:

> For us, when you meet some one, the first thing you did was to shake their hands and enquire after their health. It went like 'Are you all right?' 'How have you woken up?' and then you proceed to enquire after the household and how they were doing and then the names. There was no question of being in a hurry – that part had to be fulfilled.[7]

For a student conditioned to expect a courteous unhurried greeting, a visit to a western doctor can be a harrowing experience. A quick diagnosis, linked exactly to the symptoms described, with no preliminaries to establish trust, may be more upsetting than the illness itself. When an institution has its own medical service, the doctors should be alerted to the expectations of students from collectivist cultures.

In a task-oriented culture the doctor and the teacher alike are expected to prove themselves by their work. Not so in an ascriptive culture, where those

---

[6] Lim, Ee Hean, assignment submitted at the University of Waikato, October 1996.

[7] Ochobi, Elizabeth, assignment submitted at the University of Waikato, September 1996.

qualified would be expected to spell out their qualifications, and to earn credibility by explaining what they have done and what they can do.

In a formal setting, including an international conference, the common practice is to present a business card. Ideally the card will be in the recipient's language. A Dutch author would travel with cards of three different kinds for different purposes (Trompenaars, 1993). Many travellers have their card in one language on one side and another on the reverse, as in the example below.

Professor Peter H. Oettli
Dekan der Geisteswissenschaften
Tel.: +64 (7) 838 4114
Telefax: + 64 (7) 838 4636
Email: gem0067@waikato.ac.nz

Universitat des Waikato
Te Whare Wānanga o Waikato
Private Bag 3105, Hamilton, New Zealand. Tel. +64 (7) 856 2889

Professor Peter H. Oettli
Dean of Humanities
Phone: +64 (7) 838 4114
Fax: +64 (7) 838 4636
Email: gem0067@waikato.ac.nz

The University of Waikato
Te Whare Wānanga o Waikato
Private Bag 3105, Hamilton, New Zealand. Phone +64 (7) 856 2889

Titles are important on cards, at meetings, in course outlines, and even on the telephone. Whatever the locals choose to call themselves, they can expect their students from ascriptive cultures to be more comfortable openly acknowledging the status of the teacher. Indeed in China *Laoshi Yang,* literally *Teacher Yang,* would be the usual form of address. The convention quickly becomes automatic.

On the telephone, different conventions may not be so easy to assimilate. Marcus and Slansky (1994) describe Singapore-Malaysian leave-taking on the telephone:

In Singapore and Malaysia, leave taking on the phone when speaking in English is quite abrupt; there are no softening statements such as 'Get back to you soon', or 'I'll talk to you later'. Often, the caller finishes what he or she has to say and simply hangs up. There are no discourse markers to alert the American, Australian, or British person listening on the other end that the conversation is coming to a close. Misunderstandings may occur until the newcomer figures out that even though English is being used, the rules for telephone leave taking in this culture are different.

Leave-taking, like so many other conventions, depends both on the individual and the culture. However, in a western culture it is usual to lead up to saying goodbye and to take time over it. Some tend to dawdle endlessly. In an Asian culture leave-taking tends to be abrupt. It takes westerners some time to realise nothing dreadful has happened when visitors they are entertaining rise suddenly and announce 'let's go'. Probably some quiet understanding had been reached earlier by those leaving but it can be bewildering to those not used to it. In parts of Asia the same pattern can be seen with diners at any restaurant.

Compliments

Compliments are given in different ways and accepted in different ways, both according to the culture and according to the personality of the receiver. In some cultures people are encouraged to accept them graciously. In others, they are accepted but belittled, with some phrase like 'not really'. In others they are strenuously denied and in yet others they are turned round to flatter the receiver. Valdes (1986) gives an example of a conversation between two Iranian friends:

A: Your shoes are very nice.
B: It is your eyes which can see them that are very nice.

Apologies

Apologies similarly will differ for the same reasons. In some cultures apologies for something like not attending a party after earlier accepting the invitation are essential and profuse. In others they are acceptable but not necessary. In yet others they are simply not needed. If the habit of the person expecting an apology is different from that of the person from whom one might come, extreme rudeness might be read into a situation, rudeness that was not intended. Assignments, for example, may be handed in late without any explanation by a Pacific Islander who will feel deeply guilty but will say nothing. If the assignment is rejected, that may heighten the stress in an already stressful situation. Thoughtful training of both lecturer and student is needed.

Offering and Accepting Food

In some cultures such as those of China, Korea, Thailand and Indonesia, when a person is offered food, and especially a second helping of food, the immediate response is to refuse. The host then presses the guest and eventually the food is accepted. But in a western culture a refusal is taken as a refusal. No further offer would be made. Meanwhile the person offered might be waiting, hoping for a second offer, an offer that need not be refused. International students quickly learn to accept if they want more, but other visitors might not ever learn.

Answering Questions

Questions, especially those questions requiring the answer 'Yes' or 'No' can cause much trouble. In some cultures saying 'No' is considered rude and people will avoid it to save face both of the person who is asking and of themselves, even if so doing means misleading the questioner. The Japanese 'No' if given at all, is a deep sigh, expelled with a sound like 'Sssaahh'. The Chinese 'No' is more likely to be worded 'That may be difficult' (Varner and Beamer, 1995) or 'I will need to find out.'

Conversely, saying 'yes' may be a way of furthering harmony – nothing more. Cohen (1991: 22) calls it 'the social affirmative'. 'Yes' can mean 'Yes, I'm listening', 'Yes, I agree', or 'Yes, I understand what you are saying.' Japanese *hai* is likely to mean, 'Yes, I hear what you are saying' rather than 'Yes, I agree'. When students – or others – say, 'I don't understand' they can mean:

(1)   I don't understand the words you use.
(2)   My interpretation of what you say is not what I expected and makes me wonder if this is actually what you wanted to say.
(3)   In my perception, your words and nonverbal behaviour do not complement each other and I am puzzled.

In one experiment in which directions to a non-existent place were sought, 20 per cent of Iranian people gave directions to a foreigner when asked. No English people did (Hofstede, 1980).

The problem is caused not by the language but by the failure to recognise the context fully. In his study of business communication between New Zealanders and Koreans, Tae Woo Kim (1997) stresses the importance of being able to read implicit meanings in the communication context. Very often the real meaning is not expressed but embedded in the context.

This especially occurs when Koreans feel uncomfortable about giving direct answers, especially refusals, because of the specific relationship, combined with the specific communication situation. For a young Korean girl to be able to tell an older male teacher that she would not be ready to give a presentation on a particular day would be almost impossible. In a culture in which students are expected to answer frankly and honestly, the context and so the impossibility of the situation might be overlooked and the 'yes' understood in a way that was never intended.

Concepts of Politeness

Concepts of politeness are universal but shown very differently. Thai and Indonesian people are extremely gracious but hardly ever use the word for 'please'. In other cultures the equivalent of 'please' and 'thank you' is sometimes used in what can seem a demanding manner. Apparent deference may be taken for servility, eagerness for brashness, unless the cultural norm of the other person is known.

The Challenge of Learning and Using Another Language

For students or staff who move from their own country to one where the medium of instruction is different from the one they are used to, there is little choice but to use the target language whatever their level of competence.

Communicating in another language is not easy for those who must do it. International students, when asked about the problems they face in their host institution, constantly put language first.[8] Their difficulties may be linguistic, cultural or both. Sometimes, to complicate the issue, blame for difficulties caused by cultural mismatch is laid on language incompetence.

In many cultures, both western and eastern, knowing only one language probably means that the person is poorly educated. In Europe where national boundaries have changed several times and especially now that free passage is available for nationals of all member countries throughout the European

---

[8]   Chinese staff who were studying at Staffordshire University surveyed by Sun Nian Hong at Foshan University in May 1995; Malaysian students surveyed by Colleen Mills at Lincoln University, New Zealand, and reported on at the HERDSA conference in Perth, July 1996; and Korean, Indonesian and Thai students surveyed by Margaret McLaren in October 1996 at the University of Waikato, New Zealand, asked what worried them most, all gave language as their main concern.

Union, it is common for people to know several languages. In the Mediterranean many people will know at least two languages, including one of French, English, Arabic or Farsi.

Similarly in Japan and China young, educated people will probably have some English. In China, if their first language is other than Mandarin they will learn both Mandarin and English so that three languages become the minimum. Similarly in India if their mother tongue is other than Hindi, educated people will know at least three languages: their mother tongue, Hindi and English.

Should those who go to work in other countries, and especially to teach in other countries, learn the local language? Ideally, yes. Good understanding is not possible without it. But learning a new language demands a great deal of time and effort. Kaplan (1990) cites Carroll in 1963 estimating that something like 1,000 hours of instruction are required to achieve any significant knowledge of a language. Further, this 1,000 hours has to be received during a time which is not so great that the rate of forgetting exceeds the rate of learning, nor so short that the learner is pushed into an identity crisis. The only consolation is that, unless intrinsic difficulties such as those with tone and script complicate the learning, a third language is then less time consuming, a fourth still less, and so on.

Demanding as language learning is, having the target language is of immense benefit to those who intend to spend much time communicating with those who use it. Western countries which used to limit language teaching in schools and universities to a small number of cognate languages taught to the brightest children only, now have ambitious schemes to increase language learning. In California and some other parts of the United States Spanish is taught in almost all schools and universities and some Asian languages are taught and studied seriously. In the United Kingdom there is now much greater emphasis on languages in secondary schools and, through the Pickup Scheme, centres have been set up where adults can acquire at least a minimum knowledge of languages they need for international business. The level of language acquired will differ greatly, depending on the quality of the teaching, the motivation of the students and the number of chances the learner has to use the target language in real situations.

Those brought up to be bilingual may have native skill in languages other than their mother tongue, or the first language they learnt as a baby. Those who did not learn a second language as children but subsequently learnt and used one for many years may acquire native ability but are more likely to be near native, that is, extremely competent but occasionally betrayed by pronunciation and odd usages. Those who spend a few years learning and using a language may never become fluent, but should certainly have language that is functional, conversational or merely at survival level, depending on their intrinsic and extrinsic motivation and perhaps also on their natural flair.

It is easy to be scornful of those who acquire a modicum of a language and think they can use it effectively. However, even a little verbal and nonverbal language is better than none. In the words of Samovar and Porter (1995): 'Our first piece of advice is this: If you spend time around people from other cultures, try to learn their language.' Their first language is important to every group. Even a few key terms such as those for 'Please', 'Thank you', 'It was no trouble', 'I'm sorry', and 'Hello' can be precious door openers. The numbers up to ten are invaluable also. As Cathie Draine and Barbara Hall (1986) put it: 'You have much to gain and little to lose in speaking the language.'

But just how much of a language is that happy minimum many people want? Though cultural fluency is as or more important than linguistic fluency, every thoughtful person should at least be able to express and pick up certain messages. These will differ according to the user's needs but should include the ability to greet, thank, apologise, and arrange meetings. Certainly, the more of a language a person who wants to understand a culture has, the better; to try to do without any is surely rash.

Problems with Second Languages

Dell Hymes (1962) has shown that culturally defined meanings can control language. Meanings reside in the minds of people and words bring out those meanings. A Chinese student will use the word 'activist' proudly on a *curriculum vitae* written in English for a scholarship overseas, being unaware that that word may have negative connotations outside The People's Republic of China.

Conversely, a person who knows nothing about the recent history of Taiwan may use the terms 'The Republic of China' and 'The People's Republic of China' interchangeably, with no realisation of the political implications of the terms in Beijing and Taipei, and sometimes with disastrous results.

Perhaps the most serious linguistic misinterpretation of all time came when the Allies demanded Japan's unconditional surrender near the end of World War Two. Japan's Premier replied that his government would *mokusatsu,* meaning 'consider'. But the Allies understood another meaning of the word, 'watch from a distance', interpreted as 'So what!' and the atomic bombs were dropped on Hiroshima and Nagasaki (Farb, 1974).

The words used may take on meanings that were never intended. Said (1979) in his disturbing challenge to the ways many British people view countries like Japan considered the very concept of 'Orientalism' itself a kind of clichéd study of the east by westerners. The language of Hollywood and various television programmes like *The Young and the Restless* may similarly present a stereotyped and severely biased picture of life in the west, especially in the United States.

Whereas discriminatory language is condemned in the west, perhaps because of the Judaeo-Christian declared, if not always practised, belief that all people are of equal value, many Asian cultures and languages, including Japanese, Mandarin and Korean, reflect the social status of the person addressed every time an utterance is made. The relationship within a group is likely to be important and lasting and to make everyone want the words used to be exactly right. Speakers use different verb endings when they speak to people of equal status, higher status or lower status so that the relationship is fixed and clear. In Japanese a senior person adds the suffix *san* when speaking to an equal or senior person, but *kun* when speaking to a subordinate. And there are at least fourteen different words for 'you'.

Indonesian languages are similar in their emphasis on status. Spoken Javanese, for example, uses nine levels reflecting rank, status, age and degree of acquaintance between speakers. Even family names reflect social importance (older, younger) rather than gender (sister, brother).

Thai has four kinds of language – royal, ecclesiastic, familiar and slang. Each of these has ways of showing the importance of relationships. Within them there are forty-seven pronouns, including seventeen forms of 'I' and nineteen forms of 'you'.

Hindi has four words for 'you', the respectful *aap* and *aaplog,* and the informal *tum* and *tumlog.* German still retains *du* and *Sie*, French *tu* and *vous*, Italian *tu* and *voi,* Russian *Bbl* and *TbI* . The fact that standard English now has only one word for 'you', 'thee' and 'thou' having become archaic, may account for the Australian and New Zealand colloquial plural, *yous,* and for the southern United States *You all* or *Y'all.*

In English the subject of a sentence is of great importance. Not so in collective languages. Neither Japanese nor Mandarin require a subject in a sentence.

English distinguishes between his, her or their horse. In Mandarin the words for 'his', her and 'their' sound the same, though they are written differently. And Hoijer (1954) tells readers that Navajo has no distinctions based on gender or number but does have a word, *bili* meaning the horse of one of our people as distinct from *hali,* meaning the horse belonging to someone who is not one of us. Personal possession is clearly of little importance.

Gender, even in such cognate languages as German, French and English, or Mandarin and Japanese, is not the same as sex. In some languages it is very much more important than in others. In French it is shown constantly. Consider the simple statement: 'The good teacher has arrived.' If the teacher were male that sentence would read: *Le beau professeur est venu.* However, if the teacher happened to be female the sentence would become: *La belle professeure est venue.* Four of the five words are feminine.

In German the word *fraulein*, a young woman, is neuter – an occurrence that would be unthinkable in French. Even within genders, conventions differ. In the eighteenth and nineteenth century 'Mrs' in British English simply denoted an older woman. Consider, for example, Mrs Slipslop in Fielding's *Tom Jones* or Mrs Grundy in Dickens's *Pickwick Papers,* neither of whom were, or had been, married. However, in the first three quarters of the twentieth century and still today for most people, 'Mrs' in English has come to denote a woman who is, or has been, married. Yet in French *Madame* denotes seniority but not marital status, and in German *Frau* is the same.

In British English women usually take on their husband's surname entirely when they marry, dropping their own. In the United States, the custom is to take the husband's name but to keep the father's name as a middle name. In Scotland a woman used to retain her *mother's* maiden name as a middle name. In many parts of the world, as in China, married women keep their own names.

Within the sexes there are differences, some of which have faded. In British English, a boy was always referred to as 'Master'. Seelye and Seelye-James (1995) tell us: 'One society in Africa even has a different form of address to differentiate boys who have not yet been circumcised.'

Differences in perception itself may be reflected in the language. Colours, for instance are referred to in different ways. Blue and green have the same name in Navajo, whereas black has different names according to the shade (Hoijer, 1954). Points of the compass are also seen differently. While in western languages we tend to refer to the points of the compass as north, south, east and west, in Asian languages the order tends to be east, south, west and north. Even geometric perceptions differ. African languages are short of words to describe geometric shapes (Berlin and Kay, 1969).

More about Vocabulary

Learners of new languages need to watch carefully for what the French call *faux amis* ('false friends'), words and phrases which seem to be easy because they are familiar in one's own language but have different meanings in the target language. This is especially likely to happen when the script is the same. For instance, the word 'gift' means poison in German. The French phrase *des coups de téléphone abusif* does not mean rude telephone calls but private calls made from an office telephone without paying. A *libre école* is not a free school but one free from state control so you do have to pay to attend.

Confusion can occur even within the same language used in different places. A 'sweet' is a dessert in the United States but confectionary in the United Kingdom. A 'biscuit' is a crisp sweet cake in the United Kingdom but a dinner roll in the United States. At a meeting an American suggesting something be 'tabled' would mean it should be set aside for the meantime. A visitor to the United States from the United Kingdom would assume the speaker wished to discuss a matter he or she had not duly informed the secretary about in advance.

Even within a culture, words have different meanings in subcultures. 'Partner' to some means business associate: to others permanent or at least long-term life companion, and to yet others a temporary arrangement with another. The first time my husband received a formal invitation from my university to attend a function 'with partner', I was startled, assuming the third meaning was intended. Had I known the urban Thai use of 'partner' to mean a person with whom a man can dance for a fee for one hour I would have been still more startled. The term now is far more common on written invitations than 'husband' or 'wife'.

Some English words are familiar to speakers of other languages. Germans use 'pollution' and 'marketing' rather than *Umweltverschmutzung* and *Marktwirtschaft*. Others are misleadingly similar. Ricks (1983) cites a student from Indonesia who translated 'software' as 'underwear'.

Within a language, very different meanings can be given to the same word. A British billion is a million million whereas an American billion is a thousand million. And Varner and Beamer (1995) point out that numbers are written in different ways. A number like $2,213.50 in the United States would be written $2.213,50 in Germany.

Acronyms can be especially difficult. When the British talk about the EU (European Union), they mean what the Germans call the EG (Europaische Gemeinschaft).

Speaking

Important as the word, or language, is in all cultures, this does not mean that the oral word is always valued more highly than the written word, although sometimes it is.

Haneda and Shima (1982) explain that even contracts are often oral in Japan. One reason, they suggest, is the extremely formal rules still expected in Japanese writing, and another is that, 'being a nation of virtually one race, one language, and one culture, the Japanese have felt little need to write down in black and white all the talks leading to a contract.'

Usually it is in high context cultures that people look on the spoken word as the one that counts for anything important. An oral contract can be worked through not only in detail but also at different times as circumstances change. The element of trust is important. In such cultures an hour – or a day or even a year – may need to be spent before any business can be transacted. The western habit of immediately raising the main purpose may be offensive in the extreme.

Members of high context cultures tend to use an indirect style of speech; low context, direct. When misunderstandings are due to different styles, the person who first realises this must 'try to accurately interpret the other person's messages, and then shift his or her style of speech' (Gudykunst and Kim, 1992a).

An oral language is not necessarily less complex than a written one. During the Second World War the American armed forces used Navajo as an unbreakable secret code very difficult for Europeans to learn partly because it is tonal, partly because it was only learnt orally and only came to be written as a result of this exercise, and also because its grammar is different from that of western languages (Taylor, 1980).

The amount of speech differs according to the culture. As the section on silence will show, absence of speech is valued in some cultures.

So too tolerance of speaking is different. In western countries it is assumed one person in a single group will speak at one time. That is not the practice everywhere. Teachers who go to China are surprised to find that even though the students treat them with great respect, chattering in class is common. The chattering will be hushed and occasional when the teacher is speaking but may be continuous and even noisy when a classmate asks a question or gives a talk. To a teacher used to full and easy control, this can need negotiation with the class.

A story is told of a famous western scientist asked to address a large Chinese audience:

[He was] disconcerted to find a number of children were playing and chattering in the aisles. His impatience increased when he realized no one was attempting to quieten them down as he was about to begin. He exploded angrily at the interpreter, 'Will you tell those little bastards to shut up!' With perfect aplomb the interpreter spoke quietly into the microphone, '*Xiao pengyoumen, qing nimen shao wei anjing yidian, hau bu hau,*' which roughly translates, 'Little friends, would you please be just a bit more quiet, if you don't mind.' (Berris, 1991: 265)

On 16 September 1995 a concert was given in Foshan, a city just south of Guangzhou (formerly Canton) in China, to celebrate fifty years of liberation from the Japanese. The large professional orchestra and choir were all in formal black or white evening dress. By Chinese standards the tickets were extremely expensive but the theatre was packed. Yet throughout the performance children chattered and people came and went, while attendants walked around handing out bottled water. There was little applause.

No disrespect was intended. The attitude to a live performance was simply not that westerners would expect. Even during acrobatic exhibitions, when dangerous acts far above the ground are being attempted, the chattering and crowd movement go on. Westerners seeing such performances on television are liable to be aghast.

Both the level of formality and the degree of exactness will differ. The level of formality may differ more from subculture to subculture than from culture to culture. In every language children come home from school with turns of phrase which shock their parents. And in every language words the equivalent of 'oldie' and 'nerd' in English, words not in themselves objectionable but sometimes used disparagingly, may be unfamiliar outside the peer group.

Exactness may depend on both the situation and the culture. The United States is usually considered a culture which favours an extremely direct style of communication, yet parents, at least in the Midwest, ask their children, 'Would you like to set the table?' The children understand that is a courteous order. In New Zealand it would be taken as a real question to which the children would probably answer, 'No' and not set the table. They would expect an order to be couched in some sentence like, 'Please set the table.'

The immediacy of speaking means that its value is inestimable. Its only drawback, impermanence, has now been overcome since any speech can be recorded.

Writing

In low context cultures the written word is viewed very seriously, as giving permanence to an arrangement of any kind. The value of writing is that it is permanent and can be easily checked at later times. In English, in spite of the widespread knowledge and use of tape recorders, the written word is taken as more dependable than the spoken word, both for content and form. 'Did you get it in writing?' is a common question to ask some one who feels unfairly treated. 'Put it in writing and I'll consider it' is a standard way of delaying an answer to a request.

Language can be a powerful unifying influence. Latin and Icelandic tie together many western cultures, so that a person who speaks a language derived from one or both can make some sense of any word in another language similarly derived. In an even more powerful way, the written form of Chinese ties together Chinese, Koreans, Japanese, and those Thai and Vietnamese people who speak Chinese. There are, of course, differences in the Chinese used in different places, just as there are differences among the types of English used in different places and in different situations. But writing gives a continuity to any language, and makes change a subject for prolonged debate.

In France the French Academy is the arbiter when people disagree about vocabulary or grammar. The language is kept more or less 'pure' since the French Academy imposes sanctions on the use of words from other languages like 'weekend', 'sandwich' and 'walkman', regularly publishes a current list of officially unacceptable neologisms and imposes heavy fines on companies which use them in their advertising. For English there is no such official watchdog. When people are in doubt they refer to dictionaries and handbooks of usage. The computer thesaurus and Internet reference sections are now part of any list of likely reference sources, but they, too, are written. Sydney Greenbaum (1988) expressed it this way: 'Notions of correctness in writing largely determine what is felt to be correct in speech'.

In style, in form, and in status, writing differs immensely, depending on the culture. The differences persist even when the medium of writing is the same. English, which has absorbed both words and structures from many other languages, is a remarkably elastic language. Linguists have written about the many reputable 'Englishes' which exist in different places. As Haneda and Shima (1982) remind readers, for most Japanese business people, 'their mother tongue, customs and manners concerning communication in general, and their cultural background are so different that they cannot get away from their native ways even when they communicate in English.' And, they could ask, why should they?

When the use of different languages on the same topic is compared, stylistic differences are marked. Collins *et al.* (1996) carried out a comparative study of styles of writing preferred by North American English, German, Arabic and Chinese readers. They prepared a professional document in several different versions. The first version was in English with the characteristics normally taught in the United States – and in most other English-speaking countries where business communication is taught – and included clarity, brevity and sincerity. It was then translated into German including digression and lack of transitional words and phrases, into Chinese, rich in ambiguity and honorifics, and into Arabic, with the associated embellishments of subordination and redundancy. The target document was then translated back into English and finally the original document was translated into the target languages. Because the project was small scale they reported their findings tentatively but did show that reader expectations can be very different.

Other differences may be even more obvious. Not only are the scripts different; even the direction of the writing may be different. This text moves from left to right and from top to bottom, but text can just as easily move from right to left and bottom to top. An American firm marketing in Saudi Arabia showed pictures on a washing powder packet of a pile of dirty clothes turning into a pile of clean clothes. But the agency did not realise that Arabs read from right to left. Similarly the position of the stamp and the order of information in an address on an envelope differ according to the culture.

Order for address in English-speaking countries	Order for address in Mandarin, Korean and Japanese
Name of person	Country
Organisation	(Province and post code)
Street (with apartment and building number if they exist)	City
	Suburb
Suburb	Street (with apartment and building number if they exist)
City	
(State if there is one)	Organisation
(Post code if there is one)	Name of Person
Country	
▼	▼
Dr Margaret McLaren	New Zealand
University of Waikato	Hamilton
Hillcrest Road	Hillcrest Road
Hamilton	University of Waikato
New Zealand	Dr Margaret McLaren

The order of a date may be different. The People's Republic of China puts the year first, then the month, then the day of the month – 1999/04/10. Some countries put the number of the month before the day of the month and others put the day of the month before the number. Does 1/8/1997 mean 1 August or January 8? In a 1997 printout of a list of international members whose subscriptions had expired, a professional organisation had printed after each name and address 'Expired 1996-02-01' (or whatever the date of expiry was) and then, after each entry the words 'year-month-day' in brackets. The purpose, to avoid ambiguity, was achieved. A simpler solution would have been to spell out the month each time.

Sometimes the status of the recipient relative to that of the writer is also part of the address. Visualise an applicant for a job writing to a potential employer and receiving a reply in Bahasa Indonesia. Even the envelope will include reference to honoured status.[9]

Kepada Yth
Bapak Santosa Sanjaya
DEPARTMENT PENDIDIKAN
DAN KEBUDAN
di
JAKARTA

▼

To the Respected
Honoured Santosa Sanjaya
Department Pendidikan dan
Kebudin
JAKARTA

Kepada Sdri Dewi Kurnia
Jl Gajah Mada 4444
JAKARTA

▼

To Miss Dewi Karnia
4444 Gajah Mada Street
JAKARTA

Appearance is always important. In some cultures writing is not only a permanent means of communication but also a visual art. Traditionally Chinese and Japanese calligraphy is done with a brush, black ink and a roll of paper. There is no paragraphing and no pagination either, since the paper is cut wherever the writing ends (Haneda and Shima, 1982).

Certain things remain the same in any writing. Correct titles and spelling of

---

9   Sanjaya, Santosa provided me with these examples.

names, for example, are always important. But in many cultures written communication, especially business communication, has a time-honoured history which has given the local form characteristics of its own, and an elaborate format. The formal style of writing Japanese business letters, with relationship-building coming at the beginning and remembered at the end, illustrates this:

> After the salutation a remark was made about the season or the weather, then a question was asked about the recipient's health, then thanks were given for a gift or some other kindness and only then did the main message begin. Similarly the close, instead of the western restatement of the central message and an indication of the hoped for response ended with good wishes for the receiver's health or prosperity. (Haneda and Shima, 1982)

Western business writing is likely to be much more straightforward, following the direct method mentioned earlier, but even within it there are many differences. Americans like purpose first. Canadians like recommendations at the beginning of a report. Germans like the background first. French take linguistic elegance very seriously.

English

Although Mandarin is spoken by more people as a first language than English, far more people speak English as a first, second or subsequent language than any other. In 1989 Brian McCallen estimated that between 700 million and one billion people worldwide were either native speakers of English or had some speaking ability in it. Now that English is taught in schools throughout China, and even in some kindergartens in large cities like Beijing, Shanghai and Guangzhou, the number will be greater than it then was. Other languages which are widely used as a second or subsequent language, like German, Swahili and Bahasa Indonesia have nothing like as many speakers, and are used regionally rather than world wide.

English is not always learnt formally. Children of immigrants to English speaking countries teach their parents. And in cities like Auckland in New Zealand, language corners can be found in city parks where Chinese can practise their English and New Zealanders can practise their Mandarin and Cantonese. These corners are probably derived from the speaking corners common in parks and cultural centres in China.

A survey by Naoki Kameda (1996: 42-50) showed that English is widespread as a *lingua franca* for business in Asia and that, except in China, where interpreters are still used frequently, the preferred method of communication is face-to-face, without an interpreter.

The fact that English is so widely used for business does not mean that people everywhere want to become western. Rather, as Naoki Kameda explains: 'English may be an inexpensive alternative to the use of interpreters when neither party knows the other's language.'

Nor is the fact that English is so widely used always something for those who speak English as a first language to be proud of. Hofstede (1991: 214) claimed that having English, the language of world trade, as one's mother tongue is a liability, not an asset, though native English speakers do not always realise it. Hofstede was well aware that many speakers of English, often those from the United Kingdom, the United States, Australia or New Zealand and sometimes from South Africa, speak no other language. Like many Europeans he could well have considered that those who spoke only one language were uneducated.

Some have suggested that English may have even been harmful in its effects. Phillipson (1992) has argued that through the dominance of English in developing countries some of the indigenous languages and cultures have been deliberately and successfully displaced. Culture has become undervalued and marginalised.

Yet English is often the choice of those who could use other languages. Joseph Conrad, the Polish ship captain who did not learn English till he was an adult and then wrote a series of some of the finest novels and works of non-fiction that exist in English, is reputed to have said that if he had not written in English he would not have written at all. In *A Personal Record* (1928: 281) he spoke of the language almost in awe:

English – the speech of my secret choice, of my future, of long friendships, of the deepest affections, of hours of toil and hours of ease, and of solitary hours too, of books read, of thoughts pursued, of remembered emotions – of my very dreams.

Even in the 1990s some writers think in a similar way. The African novelist, Bisong, (1995) considers the choice to write in English is pragmatic. It works for him. He cites Chinua Achebe who, literate and fluent in his own language, chose to write in English:

I feel that the English language will be able to carry the weight of my

African experience. But it will have to be a new English, still in full communion with its ancestral home but altered to suit the new African surroundings.

Bisong points out that other Africans, like Ngugi wa Thiong'o who achieved fame by writing in English, later chose to return to their mother tongue, in his case, Gikuyu.

In commerce as in literature it is a simple fact that English is international. It is the language of business, of much technology and of international air travel. Some countries rejected English at one stage but have now returned to it. Malaysia, for example, which for twenty years ruled that Bahasa Malaysia and not English was to be the language of commerce, decided in 1994 to allow English for scientific and technical instruction at universities since so much international science and business required it. In Singapore over 80 per cent of the population use English for shopping and banking, travelling on public transport and other activities (Kameda, 1996). English is taught as a compulsory subject throughout Japan and China, though this is much more recent in China than in Japan. China has decided to continue to use English in the courts in Hong Kong, since translating Hong Kong law into Chinese would be such a formidable task.

The Bank of Japan has made English its official language. Komatsu in Japan has laid down that employees even in the Japanese home office should communicate in English (Varner and Beamer, 1995). Usually the situation is different. What the linguist, Bernstein, has called the restricted code or the local language is used for the home, for the local office and for the in-group, and the elaborate code or the international language is used for dealings which include foreigners, whether in business, law or diplomacy. A shift in code is significant – keeping the language shows acceptance of the person spoken to, but moving outside it may imply distance, or at least talking down to one who is an outsider.

It may also be that English is as widely spoken as it is because of the inability or unwillingness – or both – of native English speakers to learn other languages. Or it may be that those who speak English have an arrogance from which speakers of other languages are free. Some English speakers assume, without themselves taking on the trauma of learning another language and using it for communicative purposes, that the English of those who speak it in a recognisably non-native way is sub-standard. These native speakers use labels like 'Chinglish', 'Japlish' and 'Spanglish' in a derogatory way without really considering the linguistic and cultural difficulties the speaker of other languages faces. Haneda and Shima (1982) emphasise that foreigners need 'to avoid making the mistake of taking modesty for inability, respect for lack of friendly feelings, and politeness for a downright lie'.

Native English speakers also need to realise that variations of English may be deliberate within a culture. Kameda (1993) cites new words from Singapore like *shink* (exceptional, beyond description) and words with different meanings like *alphabets* (meaning letters of the alphabet). Those who use such terms may be very proud of them. T.T.B. Koh, formerly Singapore's representative to the United Nations, explained:

> When one is abroad, in a bus or train or aeroplane and when one overhears some one speaking, one can immediately say, 'This is some one from Malaysia or Singapore.' And I should hope that when I'm speaking abroad my countrymen will have no problem recognising that I am Singaporean. (Kameda, 1993: 235)

In any language, including English, it is important to watch slang, colloquialisms and idioms especially carefully. At a meeting of the International Committee at the 1994 Association of Business Communication held in San Diego, the overseas members, many of whom were Japanese, specifically asked that speakers of English as a first language either avoid or explain idioms and slang they used. References to baseball, like ballpark figures, were especially puzzling. Buzz words from one culture like 'quality' and 'transparent' can perplex those from another. And some technical terms can be confusing. In Indonesia, for instance, where Bahasa Indonesia is the official language but the first language of a small minority only, does 'bilingual' mean 'in English and Bahasa Indonesia', 'in the local language (say, Javanese) and English' or 'in the local language and Bahasa Indonesia'? What Langer (1989) calls 'being mindful' is indispensable in word choice.

Irony and jokes are similarly dangerous, partly because the context is so often culture-specific and partly because what seems witty or amusing in one culture may not be so in another. Varner and Beamer (1995: 68) give a telling example:

> There was once a speaker who delivered his speech through a translator to a foreign audience. His audience laughed at the appropriate places. What he did not know was that the interpreter supplied his own jokes and asked the audience to laugh because the speaker had just told a joke and it would have been impolite not to laugh. Just imagine this situation if the speaker speaks to an audience of people from ten different countries who all have their own simultaneous translators. Jokes would be a nightmare in this environment.

Universal as English is, relying on knowledge of English alone is rash. A receiver going through the files of a British bankrupt company found a letter written in German. If someone had translated it, the firm would have had the largest order in its history and been saved from insolvency. An American car manufacturer tried to market its Nova car in South America, not realising that the name, roughly translated, means 'will not go'. And there is the story of the two British business people who got into a furious row in a restaurant in China over their astronomical bill as they tried to pay for the date.[10]

People whose travels have involved moving from aeroplanes to luxury hotels to tourist resorts may be surprised if they go to teach English in South East Asia how few people outside the academic and business world speak English. Given the fact that Hong Kong was British for so long, and Japan since 1945 and South Korea since 1951 have had so many Americans stationed there, many western visitors assume almost everyone will speak and understand English.

The assumption is unfounded. Even those who can read English well may not speak it easily or understand it when it is spoken. Stress and intonation make words familiar in print unrecognisable. People who have learnt a foreign language in the classroom without any immersion in a place where the target language is spoken will understand the difficulty communicating orally in a foreign language presents. The problem is compounded if people pretend to understand, as is appropriate in some cultures.

Translation

Translation is always inexact since words almost always mean something at least slightly different in different languages. Some ideas are untranslatable into some languages. Others have shades of difference.

The main thing always is to catch the spirit of the original. These words from Eugene Nida (1991: 3) were written to apply to the written word only but in fact they are equally or more true of the spoken comment: 'A few errors in the correspondences of lexical meaning are much more excusable than missing the spirit and aesthetic character of the source text.'

One of the problems is that languages are always changing, but two languages are unlikely to change in the same places and at the same rate. A translation that is right at one time may not convey the intended meaning at another. Armies used to retreat; now they re-group. Stock markets no longer fall; they consolidate instead.

---

[10]   "Language bloopers cost millions" (28 April 1996) *The Sunday Star Times,* Auckland.

To ensure that we convey and understand the intended message we need to be able to realise what cultural factors are involved, how they could interfere in the communication process, and how to repair misunderstanding caused by such interference.

If there are problems, they may be caused by different values, different assumptions, different beliefs, different communication styles, or different body language. Fortunately, they may be overcome by sensitive recognition of the sources of the problem and wise accommodation by both sender and recipient of the messages.

Suggestions

(1) Make certain you are addressing the other person by the name and in the way he or she prefers to be addressed.

(2) Use plain language. (If the language is English this will mean short average sentence length, low proportion of passives, familiar vocabulary, any technical terms explained, few foreign terms, no slang and few idioms.)

(3) Speak slowly with no hint of condescension. Speaking loudly, shouting or speeding up does not help people understand and may be upsetting to them.

(4) Check understanding in a friendly way.

(5) If understanding is incomplete, paraphrase (but explain that you are doing so, so that listeners do not think you are saying something new) and re-check.

(6) Summarise and ensure you agree on any decisions before closing the meeting.

(7) Listen for what is not said, as well as for what is said.

(8) Ensure you have listened to the whole message from the other person.

(9) Give both the other person and yourself time to think before answering.

Topics for Consideration

(1) Just how important is language? How do you feel when you have to look after a visitor who has:

    (a)   none of your language;

    (b)   survival words and phrases only, like 'Please', 'Thank you'. 'Do you have … ?', 'How much is … ?', 'Where is the toilet?'

    (c)   simple conversational skills but not enough for any business beyond making a simple purchase or booking accommodation or travel;

    (d)   a fair grasp of vocabulary and structure of your language but pronunciation that is difficult to follow;

    (e)   a good grasp of the language but strange pronunciation of a few words.

(2)   When they meet strangers, people of different cultures will tend to talk about very different subjects. Part of being communicatively competent is knowing which subjects are immediately welcome, which are acceptable even if not right at the beginning and which are taboo.

    (a)   In the first half hour, talking to some one you did not know at all but from your own culture, what subjects from the list below would you be likely to talk about, what would you save up to talk about if you met the person again, and what would you expect not to discuss at all, at least until you knew the person extremely well?

    (b)   If you are western, please be sure to find out the opinions of at least one person who is not. Similarly, if you come from a collective culture such as Malaysia, try to include at least one person from a western culture in your questions. Then share your findings with others in your group. To what extent do you agree with others in your own culture? To what extent did you find those from other cultures agree?

        (i)   Marital status.

        (ii)   The number of children the person has.

        (iii)   Politics of the person's country.

        (iv)   What the person earns.

        (v)   The weather.

        (vi)   The person's religious beliefs.

        (vii)   Sexism in the person's country.

        (ix)   Health.

(x) Your work.

(xi) Problems at your own workplace.

(xii) The private life of public figures in the other person's culture.

(xiii) The chances for promotion in your own field.

(xiv) Who you know in common.

(xv) The place the other person comes from.

(c) Imagine meeting a student with a very different cultural background from yours. Consider the kinds of common ground you think you might have or be able to generate.

(d) Consider what you appreciate – or think you would appreciate – when someone from another culture whose first language is different from yours is looking after you. And what do you think visitors in a similar position would appreciate from you? What about visitors with some conversational English and a good dictionary with them?

7 NONVERBAL COMMUNICATION

'There are no universal gestures. As far as we know, there is no single facial expression, stance or body position which conveys the same meaning in all societies.'

R.L. Birdwhistell, 1970

In a busy street in Kuala Lumpur I once saw a visiting European exploding with anger because he needed a taxi and none would stop for him although, close by, taxis were taking on passengers all the time. His beckoning became more and more demanding, less and less successful. All the time he remained unaware that his hand movements were different from those every other taxi hirer was making. It does not take a list of what to do and not do to see how culture-bound such nonverbal communication is, and how easily it can be misinterpreted at the very time the communicator needs it because he or she cannot speak the language.

Victor (1992) points out that nonverbal messages convey their meanings in subtle and covert ways, and that the silent character of nonverbal messages is both natural and continuous. Lustig and Koester (1996) see nonverbal communication as a 'multi-channelled process that is usually performed spontaneously and involves a subtle set of nonlinguistic behaviors that are often enacted outside a person's conscious awareness'.

Most of the time the division between verbal, or word-using, and nonverbal language is itself arbitrary. Very often words are used at the same time as gestures and other forms of unspoken language, so that they either reinforce or contradict each other. And anyway, what is a word? And where do the various forms of sign language, the language of the deaf, belong? Ruesch and Kees (1956) placed sign language firmly in the category of nonverbal language, but there is surely a difference between a single gesture, such as a hitchhiker making a sign with the thumb and a structured, complex system of signs as is used in the three languages taught to and used by the deaf.

Wherever the line between the two is drawn, nonverbal or unspoken language is unquestionably important in any communication, and particularly in intercultural communication. Different scholars have different views on how important it is, especially in different types of context. Gudykunst and Ting-Toomey (1988: 275) state: 'Researchers examining communication competence in individualistic, low-context cultures would place a higher value on *verbal* communication competence. Researchers analysing communication competence in collectivistic, high-context cultures would place a higher emphasis on the study of *nonverbal* competence.'[1]

Other researchers do not support this opinion for individualistic, low-context cultures. R.L. Birdwhistell (1970), in one of the earliest of the major studies, suggested that up to 65 per cent of a message may be conveyed nonverbally. Mehrabian and Wiener (1967: 109-14) had put the percentage even higher. They considered that as much as 90 per cent of the social content of a message may be transmitted paralinguistically or nonverbally. Even if we are silent or absent, we are communicating certain messages, messages that will be understood differently by people from different cultures. And it may go further than understanding. One study (see for example Collett, 1971: 209-15) showed that if people from one culture are trained to use the nonverbal signals (such as gaze or distance) of another culture they will be liked more by members of the second culture.

Certainly at initial meetings nonverbal behaviour, in particular appearance, eye contact, posture and gestures, are extremely important. When initial meetings are between people from different cultures so involving some degree of anxiety and uncertainty, the nonverbal behaviour may be particularly important. Gudykunst and Kim (1992: 186) sum up the position:

> When strangers violate our nonverbal expectation we tend to interpret those violations negatively. These negative interpretations decrease the effectiveness of our communication with strangers. To communicate effectively with strangers we must learn to accurately interpret their nonverbal behaviour and their violations of our expectations.

When time for such accurate interpretation is not available, it may help for strangers to suspend the emotional and value judgements they might usually make, choosing their words carefully and trying to elicit a verbal rather than a nonverbal response.

The problem is that nonverbal behaviour varies from culture to culture to such an extent that no one has been able to prove or disprove Birdwhistell: 'Although we have been working for fifteen years [1950-65] we have found

---

[1]   Emphasis added.

no gesture or body motion which has the same meaning in all cultures' (1970: 30-1). The most we can say is, as Eibl-Eibesfeldt (1975) has suggested but not conclusively proved, that some sequences of behaviour such as coyness, flirting, embarrassment and a lowered position for indicating submission may be similar across cultures.

The message sent, whether consciously or not, may have a very different meaning to sender and receiver. For example, a smile inviting friendship may be seen as an indication of stupidity to a Korean. Koreans consider it improper to smile in public. 'Smiling is something the mentally retarded do, or children before they are properly trained.'[2] For the Javanese, a smile, a deprecating laugh or even a giggle can also convey intense embarrassment, especially in times of grief, as when delivering bad news (Draine and Hall, 1986: 210). For the Thai, a laugh may convey embarrassment and discomfort. O'Sullivan (1994: 38) describes an incident in which a Thai driver accidentally bumped the rear of another car and then infuriated its American driver by laughing.

Within a country, subcultures may have their own nonverbal patterns. Draine and Hall cite a popular anecdote about the typical Indonesian man who has his toe trodden on.

> If he were Batak, he would scowl savagely and immediately vent his displeasure in loud, direct, abusive terms ... and do nothing; if Javanese, he would clear his throat politely, gesture vaguely in the direction of the offending digit, call a large group around him and arrive at a decision by consensus to possibly do something about it some time. If he were Balinese he would pray; if he were Buginese or Madurese, he would immediately beat the person up; if he were Padang, he would offer some money to make it all right. (1986: 211)

Even within a subculture, nonverbal behaviour may be misread. In a western culture, folding your arms in front of you may be submissively defensive; it may be arrogant, indicating a refusal to accept what another is trying to communicate; or it may simply be that you feel cold. Only when a cluster of behaviours occurs, such as folding your arms, shrugging your shoulders, raising your eyebrows and refusing to meet the eyes of the other person all at the same time, can nonverbal behaviour be interpreted with any degree of certainty.

Active nonverbal behaviour is deliberate. Triandis *et al.* (1991) give an example of a case in a high context culture in which a boy wanted to marry a

---

[2]   Kim, Tae Woo. Personal communication, 16 May 1996.

particular girl. The girl's mother signalled that she did not approve of the relationship by serving tea and bananas to the boy's mother who came to visit her. Since the combination was considered 'unsuitable' the behaviour told the boy's mother that the match was considered unsuitable. No words were spoken on the subject, so face was saved.

Passive nonverbal behaviour is not conscious, though it may still to some extent be controlled by the sender and interpreted by the receiver. A young woman may know when she is inviting attention, but may not know just what she is doing to get it nor may the recipient be aware of the methods she is using. Both coding and decoding, though initially learnt processes, are mostly unconscious. And both may differ significantly between cultures. A white wedding dress, symbol of purity in the west, may seem reminiscent of death to guests from another culture, an interpretation which will be discussed later in this chapter.

Aspects of Nonverbal Behaviour

Kinesics

Kinesics itself has been subdivided into five categories:

(1) Emblems
(2) Illustrators
(3) Affect displays
(4) Regulators
(5) Adaptors

Emblems are signals used instead of, or as well as, words to convey a message. The message can differ significantly according to culture. The western gesture of slitting your own throat to say 'I'm in real trouble' conveys the meaning, 'I love you' in Swaziland (Schnapper, 1979: 136). The 'V' sign which, according to the English scholar, Argyle (1982: 36), is rude in Britain, is used to show victory in the United States, Australia and New Zealand but simply means the number 2 in Greece.

The thumb-up sign used by any hitchhiker in Australia, New Zealand and the United States has to be a thumb-down sign in Europe if drivers are not to think the hitchhiker is signalling to them that they are utter scum. The 'OK' gesture with thumb and forefinger touching implies great success in western countries, money in Japan, worthlessness in Tunisia and a sexual insult in southern Europe and Latin America. Pointing at your own head with the index finger can mean you consider yourself highly intelligent or really stupid. One particularly risky gesture is the 'fig' (the thumb inserted between the index and the third finger) which Knapp and Hall (1992: 193) identify as an invitation to have sex in Germany, Holland and Denmark but a wish for good luck or protection in Portugal and Brazil.

Beckoning to summon a waiter or a friend at a party with fingers upturned and palm facing your own body is offensive to Filipinos, as they use it to beckon animals and prostitutes (Chaney and Martin, 1995: 55-6). Similarly in Ethiopia Melvin Schnapper (1979: 134) cites an instance of a peace volunteer causing trouble in a health centre by going into a waiting room and calling the next patient by pointing to the person and then beckoning with his upturned index finger – as would be done, there, with a dog. There a patient should be called by holding the whole hand out, palm down, and closing it repeatedly.

The French, a demonstrative nation, use many gestures, with meanings they all understand but others may have great difficulty with. For instance, the French, using the right hand with the palm facing down, trace an imaginary line from left to right, level with their eyebrows, to mean, 'I'm fed up, I'm utterly sick of all this!' A New Zealander or Australian is likely to think that the person is shading his or her eyes, trying to look into the far distance. The intended meaning would be totally missed.

Those who travel from their own culture to teach or study elsewhere may find themselves unable to understand non-verbal signals in the new place. Some signals are almost private, a secret handshake in a fraternity. Rapping gently with one or two or three fingers on the table in south China to say 'Thank you' when given tea or being served in a restaurant comes into this category.

The danger is always that gestures made with little thought may be interpreted very differently by others. For instance, many years ago the British Queen Mother patted my brother, then a young child, on the head and this incident is narrated in the family as an example of extreme graciousness. In Malaysia touching the head is regarded as *sayang*, or genuine sympathy.[3] However in a Pacific Island culture or in Thailand, both places where the head is regarded as sacred, the seat of the soul, such a gesture might be insulting.

On a still more practical level, passing something with your left hand in a culture where the left hand is reserved for toiletry ablutions, could be considered rude in the extreme. Even crossing the legs and in doing so

---

[3]   Kongmanwatana, Chomonad (1997: 2) student paper written at the University of Waikato. Chomanad, a Thai, was taught this by her Malaysian room mate.

pointing the foot at others can offend. So can sitting on a table, a casual and friendly move teachers often make, but likely to be interpreted as offensive in Polynesian societies, for the table is for refreshments, not for the human bottom.

Illustrators are gestures used at the same time as speaking to add to and reinforce spoken messages. They, too, differ from culture to culture. A speaker can draw attention to something by extending a hand palm upwards, by pointing with one finger or two, or by a rough kick in a particular direction. In a culture in which pointing with either the hand or the foot is insulting, like that of Korea, an outsider may use offensive illustrators unintentionally.

Similarly arm movements are used in different ways. Japanese women hardly use arm movements at all and men use few of them, partly because of the confined space and perhaps also to avoid being conspicuous and so interrupting the harmony of a situation. Arabs, on the other hand, use arms freely, in a way that might seem exaggerated to those unfamiliar with the culture.

Often greetings are accompanied by illustrators appropriate in the culture. A light, firm handshake is common in the United Kingdom, the United States, Canada, Australia and New Zealand among business people. In academic circles it is rare, occurring in those countries only when one person is a visitor or has been away for some time. In contrast, German academics, just like German business people, shake hands with each other and with visitors at every formal meeting, sometimes several times a day. In France, business people shake hands on both meeting and parting. Normally a handshake is brief but in some countries such as Spain it may be prolonged for several seconds. This does not show deep personal warmth as it might elsewhere. In Japan, a less demonstrative society, business people and academics alike bow whenever they meet. If the situation is a business one, or the people have not previously met, cards will be presented at the same time, with two hands. In any formal Asian situation courtesy is highly valued, so the card is looked at closely and often commented on before being put away carefully. The western habit of writing on someone's card as a reminder to do something later is considered rude in the extreme.

Affect displays show feeling – anger, happiness or any other kind of feeling. Although some, like the smile which may indicate pleasure in some countries but embarrassment in others, do differ depending on the culture, few of them have multiple meanings.

They do differ, though, in intensity. What would seem melodramatic in some cultures may seem normal in others. This is noticeable in expression of emotion. What may be expected in a woman, such as tears in time of stress, may seem uncontrolled in a man, especially in what Hofstede would call a 'masculine' society where male and female roles are strongly differentiated. Further, since individuals themselves differ in the degree to which they will show emotion, it is not always easy to tell whether affect behaviour is a personal or a cultural reaction.

Affect displays differ also in frequency. At Polynesian functions members of a group will move from their seats to go and stand behind every speaker in turn as he (it normally is he) finishes, and then break into a *waiata,* or ritual song to support him. A New Zealand rugby team will challenge its opponents with a *haka,* or Mäori war chant and dance. In contrast, in Britain it took the end of World War Two for Siegfried Sassoon to write 'Everyone suddenly burst out singing ...'

Tae Woo Kim (1997: 74) explains that in Korea, as in many Asian countries, a smile can have several meanings:

> Of course, Koreans smile when they are happy and pleased as anyone else in the world would do ... Yet the smile can also mean embarrassment, nervousness, unhappiness, a weak refusal or ... a sort of expression in which they want to hide their true feelings. Smiling at strangers may be seen as a mental disorder.

Koreans will detect the various meanings of a Korean smile. Others may not. Wedding portraits of a whole extended family with no one smiling, including the bride, look strange to western eyes. But in Korea smiling in a serious situation may imply that the participants are not serious, or not concentrating on the business in hand. There is a saying: 'If a bride smiles in a wedding ceremony she will see her first born a daughter,' which, says Tae Woo Kim, is a 'rather undesirable occasion' from a Korean perspective.

Displays of affection differ conspicuously according to the culture. Tongan women, for example, will embrace warmly on being introduced, but showing particular affection to a member of the other sex, even a fiancé or husband, is seen as inappropriate. Engaged couples do not hold hands in public, and still require someone to accompany them as chaperone when they go out. In contrast, young French couples in love may let the world know, to the embarrassment of people from other cultures. One New Zealand student wrote:

> Last year we had two students from New Caledonia in our tutorial who

were obviously involved in a relationship. They sat very close and were continually touching and kissing during the class. It was very distracting, and all of us commented that we thought it was inappropriate, and certainly not something New Zealand students would do.[4]

Regulators are the cues listeners give to encourage a speaker, to stop a speaker, to check a point or to get a turn to speak. They may be in different forms like silence, nodding, raising the eyebrows or leaning forward. The forms differ according to the culture and may easily be misinterpreted. A foreign student who says nothing except when directly invited to may be waiting for a break of, say, thirty seconds, in the conversation. Meanwhile the speaker, uncomfortable with silence, may never let such pauses occur.

Most people nod their heads to agree, and shake to disagree but Bulgarians shake their head to agree. Indians also move their heads from side to side to show interest and agreement rather than disagreement.

Again, while a shrug of the shoulders in a western culture may suggest arrogance and a refusal to pay attention, to a Mäori it may show ashamed recognition of the justice of a rebuke, as far from arrogance as it is possible to get.

Adaptors are reactions people make without realising they are doing so. They may involve imitating the behaviour of others, or they may involve modifying or correcting one's own behaviour, like flicking the hair when it seems in the way. In a television programme shown throughout New Zealand and Australia, Alan Pease, author of *Body Language*, showed Prince Charles preening his hair and stroking his tie, movements which now amuse watchers whenever they see him perform them on television.

In comedy programmes, one person often imitates the actions of another, crossing or uncrossing legs, touching the face, or sitting in a particular way. The same thing happens, usually unconsciously, every day when people meet. We all 'adapt' to those around us.

These five categories – emblems, illustrators, affect displays, regulators and adaptors – first labelled by Paul Ekman and Wallace Friesen (1969), do not cover all body movements. Some actions not intended as language at all may give offence. In some countries the only time men spit in public is on the sports field, and women do not even do so then. In other countries men and women spit almost unconsciously anywhere outside when the mood takes them, so possibly shocking some visitors. Those same visitors may in their

---

[4]   Burnett, Heather Jean (1997). Student assignment, written at the University of Waikato.

turn disgust the spitters by carrying around with them in their hands or their pockets handkerchiefs or used tissues.

Appearance

In some cultures, such as the British, there is enormous diversity of appearance. People are short or tall or somewhere in between. Their build, their complexion, their eyes, their hair can be very different. In other cultures this is less likely. In Asian countries the people are remarkably alike in stature and colouring.

Appearance can carry strong messages but is largely out of the individual's control. Cosmetics, wigs, hair dye and coloured lenses can superficially change appearance but height and body type are impossible to alter. Certainly some of those who would like to be jockeys and so need to stay light, and would-be models who want to be tall, try, but with limited success.

Dress, however, is in the individual's control. The advice of Polonius to the young Hamlet: 'Costly thy habit as thy purse can buy' has been varied countless ways in western countries. What is acceptable at one time or place may seem objectionable at others.

In a western society, jeans and bare feet indicate a relaxed way of life. The suit and the briefcase indicate professionalism. In New Zealand a student who is being interviewed for a job and does not own a suit may borrow a friend's formal clothes, sometimes with amusing results, though an employer would be unlikely to hold the odd appearance against the student, especially if he or she guessed the clothes were borrowed.

Flexibility with dress does not exist in all cultures. The turban worn by the Sikh man or the chador and long sleeved dress worn by the Ethiopian, Malay or Iranian woman is not optional at home and may not be for the student studying abroad. Both formal and informal rules operate within cultures and within subcultures. A woman from Cornell, one of the leading private universities in the United States, recently told a class of New Zealand students that she bought three high quality navy suits to teach in when she became a professor, a statement astounding to the students who had visualised the United States as the land of the free, and who certainly did not expect their own professors to dress so formally. She, in turn, may have been astonished to see bare-footed students and professors in jeans or shorts in the classroom.

In 1996 North Korean men studying at the Beijing University of Culture and Language were conspicuous by the pinstriped suits they all wore, supplied by their home government and in marked contrast with the casual trousers and jackets worn by other male students and staff. If the local students do not recognise unfamiliar dress as being culturally required for some international students, the newcomers may feel alienated and be still less inclined to ask questions or draw any attention to themselves than they would otherwise have been.

Notions of what is attractive differ according to the culture. One Tongan student commented that in Tonga it is desirable for a woman to be *sino,* or fat. It lets others know she enjoys food and will cook well for her family. In most western countries today it is considered attractive for young women to be slim, though this was not always so, as some Renaissance painters such as Botticelli show.

In some instances behaviour is influenced by beliefs about appearance. For example, a Japanese woman will often hold a hand in front of her mouth when she smiles, because she is not supposed to show her teeth. This link with appearance and behaviour is especially noticeable with eye behaviour, or what is technically known as oculesics.

Oculesics

Oculesics is the name given to communicating with the eyes. The most common form is eye contact, which can show attention and, sometimes, intimacy. If there is not enough, others may assume lack of interest or even lack of trust. If there is too much, people may assume rudeness, although in some cultures there is nothing rude about staring. Greeks are used to being stared at in public and feel ignored when they go to places like England where staring is considered objectionable.

In Korea, *nunchi,* or the art of communicating with the eyes, is specifically taught. With members of the opposite sex direct eye contact may be consider-ed 'too emotional' (Kim, Tae Woo, 1997: 78) and other ways to use the eyes to achieve the effect of paying attention are carefully studied. Children learn to show total concentration without looking directly at their teachers. In most cultures, however, communicating with the eyes is almost unconscious, a skill people learn from imitation without being aware they are learning it.

The trouble is that the amount of eye contact customary differs from culture to culture, so that what seems to indicate genuine interest in one culture may seem over-curious in another.

In an educational institution the intended message may be hard to read. Whereas open eye contact may be expected and even necessary in an exchange between teacher and student in a western culture, in the Pacific Island, parts of Africa and parts of Asia it would seem challenging and even impertinent. A student who graciously avoids eye contact to show respect may be seen as uncaring. Andersen and Powell (1991: 211), for example, tell readers that in Jamaica looking at teachers is a sign of disrespect, while not looking at them is a sign of respect.

What may be thoughtful interest on the part of a young girl of one culture may be taken as a sexual invitation by a young man from another culture. Conversely, avoiding eye contact at an interview, intended as a sign of deference, may be seen as evasive or even insolent by a supervisor or a potential employer.

Eye contact in the west may signify honesty, but in Asia intrusion, an invasion of privacy. Arabs use intense eye contact and may seem to overstate anger or annoyance as they fix their gaze on the listener. To hide their feelings they may wear dark glasses, a practice often seen on television. To them, short eye contact may seem discourteous, as though the recipient is not worthy of real attention. Japanese, on the other hand, rarely hold eye contact for more than a few seconds and simply avert their gaze to ensure they do not give away their feelings. Too long a gaze may seem rude.

Some eye movements signal culture-specific meanings. Dodd (1991: 206) tells us that winking, which connotes 'only joking' in the west, tells a Nigerian child to leave the room and in India may be taken as an insult.

Haptics

Haptics is the term for touching behaviour. People are conditioned by their culture to expect and accept a varying amount of touching and will find more or less than they expect embarrassing.

Hecht, Anderson and Ribeau (1989) labelled some cultures like Latin America, the Middle East, the Mediterranean and eastern Europe 'contact' cultures and others like those in northern Europe, Asia and North America 'distance' cultures. Victor (1992: 209) considers that 'in the United States touching behaviour is generally less common than in most other cultures'. Perhaps it is in Michigan where Victor teaches. But as a visiting professor in places as far apart in the United States as Illinois and California I have repeatedly had young male students pat me on the shoulder or slap me lightly on the back as thanks for helpful advice on some assignment – behaviour showing genuine gratitude but unimaginable in New Zealand. It may be that Knapp and Hall's (1992: 253) suggestion that the United States is changing from being a non-contact culture has some foundation. At the same time, awareness of the potential for sexual misinterpretation, an awareness which has sharpened considerably in the past few years, may stop people touching others as freely as they feel inclined to do, both in a business and an academic setting.

Touching behaviour does differ from culture to culture. In high contact cultures such as Latin America more touching during greetings can be expected than in low contact cultures such as Scotland.

As was mentioned earlier, the different attitudes towards embracing and kissing vary significantly from culture to culture, between women, between men and women and between men. In France women kiss women on greeting, men and women kiss each other and men kiss each other if they are close friends or family. As is often seen on television in countries like Iran and Iraq, Spain and Italy, the kiss on both cheeks can be a normal and perfectly acceptable greeting between two men. In Spain to show personal warmth and affection, the greeter would also clasp the arm of the other person. At Polynesian functions women will embrace men, men will embrace men, and women will embrace each other freely. However, Englishmen and Scotsmen embrace one another publicly only in moments of jubilation on the soccer field.

Touching to gain attention is rare in low contact cultures, except from children. Not so in high contact cultures. Older Koreans, for example, are reported to touch, push or grab people for attention, even those they are not intimate with such as air hostesses (Kim, Tae Woo, 1997).

In some cultures, Chinese, southern European and north African cultures for example, same sex hand holding in public is common. Men are openly affectionate with one another, and so are women. Similarly, in countries like China where homosexuality is simply not acknowledged to exist, male to male and female to female touching is common. It would, though, be rare to see a man and woman holding on to one another or embracing in a public place as happens without any embarrassment in western cultures. In China, touching a member of the opposite sex is considered sexual harassment.[5]

What is important in an academic context is *not* that an individual should behave in the way his or her students or teachers behave. Rather, each individual should do what seems right to him or her in the specific context, realising at the same time that adaptation may be necessary since not all people will react in the same way to different forms of touching. What may seem intrusive and even sinister may be intended as no more than friendliness.

Proxemics

Place attachment and its converse, the sense that a person is not where he or she belongs, are concepts which have recently received attention because of

---

[5] Zhang, You Ru, personal communication, 24 February 1997.

the emotional impact they may have on a person. Place attachment has been called 'environmental bonding' (Collins, 1996). New Zealand Mäori call it *türangawaewae* which roughly translates as 'belongingness'. Since both staff and students away from the place they feel most at home may suffer a sense of deprivation so severe that it affects their mental health and their sense of commitment to work, place attachment is certainly an issue to be understood and openly discussed.

Place signifies different things in different cultures. A senior British or American manager sits alone, usually facing the door but with a window to look out of. In France, offices are spatially organised around the manager who, as controller and observer of all that goes on, is at the centre. Every person takes it as his or her right to have natural light, and French people are shocked to find that in the United States even senior people may have offices which have no windows and only artificial light.

Although the culture is in most ways so different, like the French manager, the Japanese senior manager has a seat somewhere in the middle of a large room shared with his staff so that he (the term is used consciously) has easy access to them. The person who is not expected to contribute much, perhaps because of advanced age or because he is out of favour, has the window place at the edge of the room. Often this is a senior man who in a western culture would be retired whether he wished to be or not.

Proxemics is the use of space to communicate. It, like other aspects of nonverbal communication, differs from culture to culture. Hall (1966) proposed four spatial zones:

(1)   Intimate (=18 ins)
(2)   Personal (18 ins - 4 ft)
(3)   Social (4-12 ft)
(4)   Public (12-25 ft)

He suggested these as usual North American zones. They differ significantly according to the culture and the individual. In Japan, people greeting one another would bow from several feet away, and yet a bow is usually a personal rather than a social greeting. For a person who regarded two feet as within his or her intimate zone, a Latin-American who preferred a personal space of eight to twelve inches might seem offensive. A person who has shared a bed-cum-study room with seven others, as is not unusual for university students in south China, may feel utterly cut off when living alone.

Whatever the culture, people stand at a different distance from one another to greet and to converse, depending on whether the situation is intimate, personal social or public, to use Edward Hall's categories. Sometimes gender is significant. Varner and Beamer (1995: 149) express the idea perfectly: 'When women sit in an easy chair, they seem to borrow the space; men, on the other hand, seem to own the space.' That, too, may be culture-specific. In some Asian cultures it is rare for men ever to sprawl in a chair, especially in public.

The language of space, though probably picked up subconsciously, is marked. What is personal in one culture may seem intimate in another. English people queue, and they stand about three feet apart as they shake hands. Mediterranean people do not queue but move forward ruthlessly in groups. When introduced they like to be no more than one and a half to two feet away.

In countries with a high density of population, personal space is treasured, so accidental touch and arm movements are avoided. This control of space enables people to be crowded into a commuter train yet somehow to remain individually separate, denying the physical closeness which exists. Arabs and Latins sit close, by choice, whereas Finns require a great deal of personal space (Malmberg, 1992). Americans sit and stand face to face or at right angles. They like strangers to come no closer then 18 inches, about an arm's distance away and feel most comfortable when people are about five feet away (Murphy and Hildebrandt, 1991).

Westerners like to 'stand tall'. Arabs do business sitting on the floor. Japanese also sit low down, with legs tucked under. In China space connotes power so students tend to stand or sit well away from a lecturer but close to people of the same age and rank.

As with haptics, the important thing with proxemics is not that people should behave as others expect, but that they should recognise all different proxemic habits as the right of others to practise as they see fit, particularly within their own cultures.

The way houses are arranged is a proxemic matter. Condon and Yousef (1975) consider that, because of the cultural assumptions the home discloses, the home could well be considered a microcosm of society as a whole. For instance the light sliding doors, with no locks, usual inside a Japanese home make intimacy natural, and the heavy set of doors, always locked at night, entirely shut out the outside world. Since the same spaces are used day and night for different purposes, no person has his or her own room; this illustrates the lack of individualism in the Japanese home, separated as it is from the world outside. In contrast the mid-western American open plan home, with a large unfenced front lawn and curtains usually wide open, typifies the social-centred home where each member of a small family comes and goes at will. And the solid German home with locks on many inside doors but often a shared hall or yard for which tenants have legal responsibilities, typifies the formal, private life of many Germans.

The absence of space may in its own way affect the type of communication. Jews, for many centuries in Europe, could not own land so tended to do work which depended on communication like teaching and medicine rather than industry or building which required a fixed base.

Privacy and Territoriality

Both the times at which and the places where people can call on others vary from culture to culture. In China, where academic staff rarely have their own offices and the home accommodation is usually provided on campus by the institution, it is not uncommon for students to visit their lecturers in the evening or weekends without making any prior arrangements. If Chinese students do the same when studying in another culture, it might not occur to them, until they are told, that the lecturer might resent the intrusion into his or her privacy.

The Dutch author, Fons Trompenaars (1993: 75), whose book *Riding the Waves of Culture* contains many worthwhile insights, refers to this aspect of nonverbal communication as 'life spaces' and gives striking examples from his own experience.

> I remember arriving as a student at the Wharton School in Philadelphia, Pennsylvania. Bill, a new American friend, rushed to help me move in. In gratitude for his hard work on a hot summer day I asked him to stay for a while and have a beer. I went to wash up and came back to get him a beer out of the refrigerator. I did not need to, he had already opened the refrigerator and was helping himself. For him, a refrigerator was my public space into which I had invited him. To me and most of my Dutch compatriots, it was definitely private space. A few days later I was struck by a similar event. I was enquiring about transportation across town when Denise, a fellow student, tossed me her car keys and said to call her when I had finished with my errand. I could not believe it. To me, a car was certainly private space. Have you ever tried to borrrow a German acquaintance's Mercedes?

This kind of different attitude to possessions, common in a highly mobile society, will be discussed further in the section on objects later in this chapter.

Paralanguage

Paralanguage is the sound of language, the vocal characteristics like speed, resonance and shrillness. Although it is part of spoken language it is excluded from verbal language since it cannot be checked in any dictionary. Like other aspects of nonverbal language it is culture-related, and can add to or reduce the effectiveness of the message considerably.

One New Zealand academic avoided an American in the common room of her institution for two years before discovering how interesting he was. The reason for avoiding the American was his loud and strident voice. Whether the academic had become more tolerant or the voice had quietened in the two years is difficult to say. Hall (1966) even suggested that speaking loudly is part of American openness to show they have nothing to hide.

Some 'fillers', or sounds which do not have specific meanings like 'er', 'um', 'eh', 'sort of' and 'you know' are another form of paralanguage. They can be used unconsciously by speakers but can seem to some listeners, especially those from cultures where they are not common, uneducated and irritating.

Paralanguage can also include sounds whose meaning is established in a culture but could not be found even in a dictionary of slang. The sounds may have different meanings in different cultures. A hiss in Japan signifies approval, not rejection or contempt as it would in the west. A young New Zealand woman teaching in France could not work out why the children laughed every time she indicated they should be quiet. The 'shshsh' she used in her culture was not at all effective. One boy finally told her they were laughing because she sounded like a snake – a creature she, coming from a country where snakes do not exist, had never heard. She found that the 'tttttt' sound, made by pushing the tongue up against the front teeth, is what it takes to silence a class of French children.[6]

Grunts and wolf-whistles and oohs and ahs of delight are another form of paralanguage. So are moaning, groaning, sighing and giggling, and even physical sounds like belching and swallowing. All of these have meanings which differ according to culture.

Tones, touched on already in Chapter 6, are also part of paralanguage. Tone certainly exists in western languages but it affects the meaning of the structure rather than of the discrete word, and is part of the written language only in texts on phonetics. A rising tone may indicate a question in English: 'You are going to write a second essay?' It may also indicate self-doubt or

---

[6]   Kelly, Joanne. Personal communication on 21 August 1996.

uncertainty. In French almost all sentences will end on a high note. These patterns may seem very strange in a tonal language, in which the meaning of each word depends on the rise or fall of the voice as the word is spoken. For example, in Japanese and Korean the word order remains unchanged for statements and questions. The tone of a statement will be flat throughout. The tone in a question will rise towards the end, and the verb which completes the sentence will have a different ending. In Chinese, as was seen in Chapter 6, every word has its own tone which is an important part of the meaning.

Colour

Colours carry different meanings in different cultures as has been mentioned earlier. In some cultures white, symbolising purity, is the favoured colour for a wedding dress. In other countries brides wear red or pink, symbolising good fortune. In China brides wear red embroidered with dragons, carry a red parasol and at the ceremony red fire crackers are exploded, even in provinces where firecrackers are now illegal. In parts of the Middle East, yellow, symbolising fecundity, is chosen. In Hindu cultures brides wear old tattered yellow sandals six days before the wedding to drive away the evil spirits, and both bride and priest wear yellow robes for the marriage ceremony.

In western countries people wear black or dark clothes to funerals but in China and in some parts of South America white is the colour of mourning. In Mexico, family and friends give purple flowers to the dead. In Korea, red ink is used to record deaths but never to write about living people. In China a man who wears a green hat is telling others that his wife is unfaithful (Chaney and Martin, 1995: 68). In European cultures purple symbolises nobility but in Asian cultures yellow does.

In some cultures avoidance of colour is important. In their part of the United States, two Amish brothers refused to wear bright orange or yellow clothing while hunting although it is a safety law. To do so was against their religious belief, which prohibits the wearing of 'worldly' colours. They were standing by their principles and were willing to risk being shot at by other hunters or jailed by the authorities (*New Zealand Herald*, 24 March 1997).

Smell

Little published research has been done on smell. However, the many deodorants and breath sweeteners sold in the west make it clear that natural human smells are considered unpleasant. In contrast, in some African and Arabic countries human smell is considered desirable. Almaney and Alwan (1987: 17) put it this way:

Smelling is a way of being involved with another, and to deny a friend his breath would be to act ashamed. In some rural Middle Eastern areas, when Arab intermediaries call to inspect a prospective bride for a relative, they sometimes ask to smell her.

In cultures where human smells are considered undesirable, people, especially women, like to use scent, whether from flowers, bark or chemicals, to make themselves more attractive. Such use could be a bewildering interference to people from what are sometimes called 'olfactory cultures' in which smell showing fear or delight or other emotional responses is part of normal communication. The African American comedian, Richard Pryor, tells a story of his excitement about going to Africa to meet his 'brothers'. He picked up two Africans hitch hiking and was disgusted by their odour. Then he looked in the rear view mirror and saw each had his head out the window beside him. Apparently Pryor's cologne or deodorant had a similar effect on them!

Russell (1981) shows that there have been times when undesirable scents have been manufactured and used deliberately, as during World War Two when Chinese children were given tubes of a foul-smelling and unremovable liquid to squirt on the trousers of Japanese officers (Knapp and Hall, 1992).

Silence

One of the most intriguing forms of nonverbal language is silence. Some are comfortable with it; others are not. In low context cultures, silence is avoided; in high context cultures people use it as a deliberate strategy.

Buddhists value implicit communication and the ability to sense meaning without being told. The Buddhist attitude that people should distrust human communication because it is incomplete and limited, whether oral and written, has had a widespread effect.

For example, the Japanese believe silence is preferable to conversation. It is through silence that they believe they can discover the truth inside themselves and others. They process messages largely through interpretation of nonverbal behaviour and personal meaning. Contemplation and meditation take place in silence. While westerners typically view silence as a gap in conversation, the Japanese believe silence is part of conversation. Many Japanese sayings bear this out: 'He who speaks has no knowledge and he who has knowledge does not speak', 'By your mouth you shall perish', and 'A flower does not speak'. A Taoist saying is similar: 'He who knows, does not talk, he who talks does not know'. So is the Confucian advice: 'The superior man is diligent in duty but slow to speak.'

The silence which can last more than half an hour, is very unsettling to people from other cultures. Sessin in 1973 claimed it is an 'in joke' among the Japanese that if Americans are kept waiting long enough they will agree to do anything (Smith and Luce, 1979).

Respect for silence is not unknown in the west. Sayings like the British 'Empty vessels make the most sound', the Belgian 'The mouth maintains silence in order to hear the heart talk' and the Swiss 'Sometimes you have to be quiet to be heard' exist, but the attitude behind them does not control communication in the way that it does in many high context cultures. Although Hall (1983) has explained that silence is much more than pausing, that it is what makes 'interpersonal synchrony' possible, most westerners are uncomfortable with, even intolerant about, prolonged silence.

Asian cultures which do use silence as a useful tool do not all do so in the same way or to the same extent. Gudykunst and Kim (1992a) explain that Caucasian-Americans will initiate talk as a control strategy in situations where native-born Chinese would use silence. The African Gbeya can only eat in silence. Tae Woo Kim explained that in Korea visitors find silence can cause problems because they cannot tell when it implies dissent and when assent. Nor do they realise that Koreans are sometimes silent even when they have something to say because of a tendency to hide their real meanings.

Sometimes within a nation cultural groups can be distinguished by their different attitudes to silence. In New Zealand *Pakeha*[7] tend to be uncomfortable with silence, but Mäori use it as a control strategy. Similarly Basso (1970) found that silence was important in the Apache culture in the United States. It is appropriate whenever social relations are hard to ascertain, and especially when the role of the main participant is not fully understood (Gudykunst and Ting-Toomey, 1992b).

Dining

In cultures where it is imperative to establish rapport before any worthwhile communication can occur, meals and giving of food are an important part of the process, a part sometimes ignored by people in western cultures. A Chinese teacher abroad, for instance, who knows students at home take gifts of fruit and nuts and baking for teachers at any time and especially on teachers' day, may feel ignored when no such gestures ever occur.

At the table itself, practices can be diverse. The types of food will, of

---

[7]   *Pakeha*, the Mäori word for a European New Zealander, is commonly used by New Zealanders.

course, differ. Intestines, rodents, snakes, beetles and scorpions, dogs specially bred for the purpose, and cats are eaten, especially in south China. 'Thousand-year-old eggs', and chicken feet steamed in ginger are special treats. Similarly those from outside the west might be disconcerted by many western habits and food choices. Pork will upset some, beef others, any kind of animal meat yet others.

Even times for meals differ widely. In China lunch is 11.30 am or 12 noon, dinner around 6 pm. In Spain lunch could be 2 or 3 pm and dinner 10 or 11 pm.

In western countries people usually eat most meals with implements, though these are not always the same, nor used in the same ways. For instance what is called a 'tablespoon' in Great Britain is exactly twice the size of a tablespoon in North America, a fact which has resulted in many failed recipes. In parts of the United States, even in the finest of restaurants, diners are expected to keep their forks after eating their main course, a practice which astounds some visitors.

Mostly, though, table manners are fairly similar in the west. People eat as silently as they can, use knives, forks and spoons, eat bread, cakes and some fruit with their hands, and talk with each other during the meal. Compare this with the standard Korean practice:

> Belching, hawing and hiccupping is permissible at the dinner table although blowing the nose is not. Talking is usually avoided until the meal is finished, and food is not touched with the hands, only with chopsticks, spoons or forks. (Park and Kim, 1992)

In Malaysia too, belching during a meal can show appreciation of it. A formal meal may be eaten with the right hand and no implements; finger bowls will be provided for each person.

In Asian cultures chopsticks are used for almost all food except soup, with a dexterity amazing to the westerner. Rice, for instance, is almost swept into the mouth.

Alcohol, evil to some, is valued by others in both east and west. Liqueurs, snake wine and bamboo spirit will be kept for rare occasions, but at formal banquets, male visitors are expected to join in and to enjoy drinking alcohol. Women have more choice. For men who prefer not to drink alcohol, or at least not to drink alcohol they are not familiar with, health and personal preference are good excuses. Tea is an acceptable safe alternative almost anywhere in Asia.

Behaviour with Animals

Attitudes to animals can differ radically across both cultures and subcultures and can be expressed in very different forms of communication. One American told me she brought up a lamb with her own children, changing its napkins in the house without any revulsion just as she would those of a baby. New Zealanders spend hours watching sheep dog trials at shows and on television, a pastime which seems extraordinary to people from elsewhere. And, like English people, New Zealanders with dogs assume others will accept them as members of the family. Elizabeth Ochobi from Kenya recalled her terror at being greeted by a dog which stood up to its full height – taller than hers – and put his front paws on her shoulders. When almost out of her mind she begged the owner to call him off, the owner simply laughed and answered 'Oh, he just wants to say "Hi!" He is such a baby!'[8]

Favoured animals in the west tend to be creatures the owner can indulge, like a cat to be given cream or a pet poodle to be played with. In the east they tend to be creatures that the owner can use, like an ox.

Much interesting work has been done on the communication patterns of animals, ranging from the flight paths of bees to the sonic systems of dolphins, the mating calls and smell tracks of wild animals to the vocabulary intelligible to apes. The most interesting work is perhaps that done by sociologists in the United States who have spent many years observing chimpanzees to see how their communicative ability differs from that of humans.

Objects

Objects are sometimes used, consciously or unconsciously, to convey particular messages. Some university scholarships such as the celebrated Rhodes scholarship are given for all-round excellence. It has not been unknown in Australia and New Zealand, when interviews for such a scholarship are imminent, for candidates without sporting backgrounds to be seen around campus in sporting garb, complete with racket and towel, implying they are regular tennis or squash enthusiasts.

Conspicuous consumption, admired in some cultures, is despised in others. Occasionally personal possessions of famous people like Jacqueline Onassis are sold for great sums of money. This would be inconceivable in cultures in which personal possessions are supposed to be unobtrusive. Sometimes well-meaning parents who are new settlers in a foreign culture buy

---

[8]   Ochobi, Elizabeth (September 1996). Special release to the *Sunday Star Times*.

their children the smartest of clothes and even expensive cars thinking that by so doing they will ensure their children become accepted. In New Zealand or Australia the very opposite happens. The extravagant objects serve to alienate the children from their classmates who see the newcomers as thinking they are superior because they have more material possessions.

Gifts are an important part of life in cultures in which the people are constantly aware how inter-dependent they are. A gift sweetens a meeting and keeps an established relationship harmonious. What seems a bribe in some cultures is simply a part of the payment in others.

The gift, though, has to be chosen thoughtfully and with some knowledge of the recipient's culture. In Germany all the guests at a private party bring flowers or chocolate with the result that the venue can start to look like a florist's or confectionary shop. But the flowers must not include red roses except from a lover. In parts of China cut flowers imply a death wish; in other parts they are a warm gesture of appreciation.

The symbolism of a watch or clock varies greatly across cultures. In the west giving a time piece is often a way of honouring a person retiring after long and useful service. In some Asian cultures a clock can symbolise the ticking away of time and so be seen, like the cut flowers just mentioned, as a kind of death wish – not a suitable gift whatever the occasion.

Construing Nonverbal Differences

In the workplace, especially the educational workplace, differences in nonverbal communication can interfere with teaching and learning. Those from low context cultures, who do not easily reveal their thoughts and feelings either verbally or nonverbally, may be taken to be uninterested in everything going on by those who release their emotions effusively. Those who admire restraint and self-control may consider animated expression of the ordinary to be shallow, even empty. The quiet, sensitive observance of cues will help the intercultural communicator know what is intended.

Other forms of nonverbal communication, such as posture and art and music, differ across cultures. What sounds harmonious in one culture may seem a strange noise in another. A way of sitting or standing admired in one culture may be offensive in another. Like other aspects of intercultural communication anything unfamiliar can be a worry to those not sure of its meaning. A discussion of the nonverbal behaviour noticed by one sojourner working in a foreign country follows.

My Perceptions of the Differences between United States and New Zealand Nonverbal Behaviour

By Samuel Coad Dyer, Jr.

There are some interesting differences between the nonverbal communication behaviour of Midwesterners and New Zealanders. I refrain, of course, from generalising to the entire United States because there are many, many cultures flourishing among the 260 million people there. I come from a small town in the Midwestern part of the USA, a very conservative, agricultural region. My personal experience with Kiwis – as New Zealanders call themselves – must also be mediated by the fact that my observations are based largely upon living and working in the Waikato district, a conservative, agricultural region. I have lived in Hamilton, New Zealand for four years. But although New Zealand has only 3.67 million people, there is a very rich tapestry of cultures found in its many beautiful islands. I will make my brief observations about nonverbal behaviour based on my experience in the broad spheres of public and private life.

Public Differences

Queuing Kiwis require large spaces between themselves, especially in queues. I have stood in line outside of bank teller machines, for example, and a Kiwi might keep two or three metres distance from each other when using a teller machine. Kiwis keep a very large distance between themselves and others in almost every queue I have been in (with the exception of sport ticket queues, concert queues or giveaways). And they require a much larger area of personal space than people in the Midwest.

Boarding an Elevator Kiwis will dart on to an elevator before people have disembarked. Rather than waiting momentarily for people to disembark an elevator, Kiwis will rush on board especially if there is the slightest hesitation by an elevator passenger. It took me a while to not interpret this behaviour as rudeness; it is impatience. The same sort of behaviour can be seen while driving; the slightest hesitation and a Kiwi driver will pull out right in front of you!

Detecting an Accent Kiwis are very curious about a person's accent. They will interrupt your private conversation with another to ask 'Where does that accent come from?' It is as though they collect accents. Kiwis are very travelled and have loads of travel experience. It is that experience that generates their curiosity. It seems as though every shop you go into, a Kiwi will ask about your accent.

Group Nonverbal Behaviour Kiwis do everything in groups. It is very much a group-oriented culture. I have had other expatriates tell me that they feel it is amazing that anyone ever meets new people in this culture because of the rigidity of some group boundaries. There is a lot of friendly, touching behaviour in groups. Also there is a great deal of same dressing and same hair-styles as a price of group membership. This includes tattoos (very prominent throughout segments of the community), shaved heads, dread-locks, body piercing (nose, lips, etc.) and the Levi rock-band tee-shirt uniform.

Private Differences

Telling a Joke Kiwis keep a very straight face when telling a joke. They have inherited a rich sense of irony from their British forebears. Thus when telling a joke it is almost impossible to determine from their facial or vocal expressions whether or not they are serious or pulling your leg.

Volume of Voice Kiwis speak in very low tones compared to speakers in the States. I have been in meetings where expatriate group members have become quite upset about the low volume of Kiwi speakers. In one meeting I attended, an expatriate, after having asked a Kiwi group member to speak up, left the meeting. Kiwis are very soft spoken when compared especially to Americans who are loud, frequently obnoxious, and don't mind who hears what they say. I have been asked on numerous occasions to hold my voice down a little. And over the years I have been in New Zealand I have become considerably more soft spoken myself.

Physical Touching Kiwis touch each other a lot when playing sports. That is very similar to my experience in the States. One would think that Kiwis would be distant in their personal touching; cold and removed like the British. But they are not. I have found Kiwis to be very forward in their personal touching. My *marae*[9] experiences have been very pleasant with everyone kissing and hugging, and it all being a very natural and relaxed expression of belonging and familiarity. *Pakeha* culture too is very

---

[9] A *marae* is a Māori tribal meeting place, usually with spacious fields and several buildings.

touching, though not publicly. So that if you are having dinner at some-one's house they might play footsy with you under the table, which shocked me the first few times it happened. Public display of affection though, is not much in evidence in New Zealand. New Zealand is very much a touching culture, but in *Pakeha* experience it is much more private than in the States.

Make-up Kiwi women wear very little make-up. They seem to wear it only on special occasions or on nights out. American women will wear make-up anywhere and everywhere. Compared with American women, Kiwis are very conservative in the amount and the context of their wearing make-up.

Personal Dress One thing that struck my family when we first arrived in New Zealand is that it seemed as though Kiwis were all dressed as though they were on a camping trip. In other words, Kiwis dress very, very informally in almost all situations. Where I am from, a gentleman would never consider going to church on Sunday without a proper suit and tie. But in New Zealand, Kiwis come to church barefoot, in tank-tops (singlets) and shorts! Oh my! Kiwi men wear shorts year round. And they wear open toed shoes to work with socks. They also walk around barefoot at work; a practice which took some getting used to. Feet are best covered where I am from. Even my most eccentric relations never dress as informally as Kiwis do. Kiwis also have a hat for every occasion. They have gardening hats, running hats, drinking hats, camping hats, tramping hats, cricket hats, and beach hats. The list is endless. They must have closets full of hats!

Conclusion

These observations are very brief and anecdotal. They are based on my personal experience and reflect very much my personal cultural biases and sensitivities. But New Zealand, I feel, has a unique culture that has been born out of a pioneering independence and interdependence. It is a group-oriented culture whereas the culture in the States is, largely, individual-istic. There is something very informal and relaxed about New Zealand culture that is refreshing and very inviting. The mild weather, Polynesian location, and unique history have developed a nonverbal style that is quiet, relaxed, and easy going. This makes New Zealand a very pleasant place to live and to work.

Questions for Consideration

(1) Dyer says New Zealand is a group-oriented culture. Compare this view with that implied in Hofstede's table on page 68. In what ways do you think Dyer's observations support or belie his assessment that New Zealand has a collectivist culture.

(2) Draw a word picture of the nonverbal behaviour in your own culture, using Dyer's headings of public and private behaviour.

(3) Compare the observations in your word picture with observations of the nonverbal behaviour in any other culture you know.

(4) Consider your own nonverbal behaviour in any teaching or learning situation you are familiar with and jot down eight characteristics another person might notice. Which of them were you unconscious of until you deliberately thought about it?

(5) Give an example of some nonverbal behaviour you recall, which at the time caused embarrassment because of the cultural differences between the people present. Was the embarrassment resolved? If not, could it have been? How?

8 KNOWING AND LEARNING

'Mind differs from mind almost as much as body from body.'

Quintilian

Learning style is the way in which human beings concentrate on, absorb, process and retain new and difficult information (Dunn and Dunn, 1993). Understanding and appreciation of the different styles of learning are essential to the effective intercultural educator. As Hofstede (1991) pointed out, 'One of the reasons why so many solutions do not work or cannot be implemented is that differences in thinking among the partners have been ignored.'

The differences in culture, values, religion and verbal and nonverbal language are all important in intercultural communication at every level of education. The way people organise their thinking is reflected in the way they code and decode messages. How, then, are staff and students used to thinking in one way to communicate with those used to thinking in different ways? Hofstede (1986) alerts us to the problem:

> Teacher and student are an archetypal role pair in virtually any society. When teacher and student come from different cultures, as in the context of economic development programmes, many perplexities can arise.

Thought Patterns

Scholars like Ong and Kaplan have wrestled with the different ways of thinking which underpin different modes of knowing and learning. Ong (1982), in his work on orality,[1] linked linear thought with writing and holistic thought with speaking and used these links to explain the difference between oral and written cultures. Kaplan (1990), in his discussion on linear and

---

[1] By 'orality' Ong means the ability to communicate by speaking.

gyrating thought patterns, showed how unreasonable it is to penalise with low grades students who have been trained to base their thinking on images, abstractions and linkages rather than on step-by-step analytic Aristotelian logic. He suggested that speakers of other languages are just as logical as speakers of English but may be logical in a different way. Further, 'their logical orientation may make them appear illogical to readers anticipating a certain culturally-constrained demonstration of logic.'

One of the troubles is that language, especially written language, depends on a whole series of conventions which native speakers are sensitive to because they have been exposed to them all their lives, but which other speakers, however proficient, may never have come across. The order of a sentence, for instance, can affect the emphasis in a way a speaker of another language may not realise. The subtle difference between 'Because I think languages are so important, I am learning Russian' and 'I am learning Russian because I think languages are so important' is unlikely to be explained in any text book, but will almost certainly be grasped by a native speaker because of the English habit of stressing opening clauses.

Ong and Kaplan are concerned with differences in the language itself, with words linking with other words, phrases with other phrases, sentences with other sentences and combinations of all these. But differences exist also in structure. Samovar and Porter (1995) point out that the organisational pattern of many western documents and speeches with an introduction, body, and conclusion is by no means universal. In Middle East cultures, in both academic and business documents, diffuse language patterns, with liberal use of devices like alliteration, repetition and metaphor that westerners might think of as suitable only for poetry, are much admired.

In contrast, in the west the direct method is almost sacrosanct, at least in English business communication. It began with William Deming's now out-dated *Management by Objectives* philosophy which underlies the western determination to try to communicate as directly as possible, stating the purpose at the start of speech, report or letter and then fulfilling that purpose without any diversions. But Edward Hall (1976) reminds us, if reminding is necessary, 'Linearity can get in the way of mutual understanding and divert people unnecessarily along irrelevant tangents.'

Hall also points out that the western assumption that logic is synonymous with truth denies that part of the human mind that integrates unexpected material. The assumption is an academic one, seen in many western academic papers which start with theory and previous literature and then move to statement of a proposition, examination of that proposition and a final decision on its truth.

But truth itself is infinitely elusive. Karl Popper (1963) demonstrates that the notion that truth is manifest, a notion beginning with Plato and expanded by Bacon and Descartes, is in itself false. 'The world as we know it is our interpretation of observable facts in the light of theories which we ourselves invent.'

The 'logical' pattern westerners have inherited is not required in Asian academic papers and does not carry over into all types of western writing. For example, John Livingston Lowes (1951) in *The Road to Xanadu* traced the sources of Samuel Taylor Coleridge's poem, 'In Xanadu did Kubla Khan …'. Lowes found threads of information in a myriad of books Coleridge had read and in experiences he had had, and showed how Coleridge wove them together in a way that had a little to do with chronology but nothing at all to do with western logic. Lowes was saying that the mystical fusion of un-related facts and ideas has a magic all its own, a statement that most poetry lovers, western just as much as eastern, would accept.

Currently there is a great deal of debate regarding the nature of scholarly writing, a debate which is not confined to logical structure. Even in the same culture, university teachers do not always agree about what is acceptable academic work. The New Zealand poet and critic James K. Baxter, then a middle-aged man, failed a second year paper in English literary criticism at Victoria University of Wellington the same year as the same class used his critical work, *The Fire and the Anvil,* as a set text!

Most of the time, though, in the west, for every effect there must be a cause. Evidence needs to be processed, not to find relationships but to find causes. The typical western approach to an issue, in education as in business, is to cast it as a problem, tease out the steps in that problem and then sort out a solution. Westerners talk of isolating problems, of 'ironing out the bugs'. Conflict is seen as part of life. Even the law in western countries is worked out on the assumption that there is a right and a wrong to each set of circum-stances, though many people acknowledge that law and justice are not necessarily the same.

But many issues do not lend themselves to clear definition, let alone clear solution. In a society which stresses harmony and holistic thought, debate and confrontation are relatively unknown. As we saw in Chapter 6, in this kind of society, people asked a yes/no question to which they do not know the answer, may reply 'Yes' simply meaning they understand the question. Asked more complex questions, such as directions for getting to some place, they may promptly give any directions rather than have the questioner lose face and lose face themselves by admitting they do not know.

Maslow (1956) wrote of the two sets of forces each one of us is subject to: one towards safety and the other towards growth. The force towards safety has been called by later theorists convergent thinking, that towards growth divergent thinking. Sikkema and Niyekawa (1987) expand:

> Convergent thinking refers essentially to logical thinking, with a number of facts leading to one conclusion. In contrast divergent thinking, using a fact as a starting point, can go in different directions. There is no one correct answer in divergent thinking; a number of alternatives are available.

Okabe (1983) called western cause-to-effect thinking 'chain-like' and east relational thinking 'dotted' or 'point-like'. However we label them, both methods of thinking will exist in all cultures, but one or other will predominate.

Certainly those assessing academic writing and formal in-class presentations will expect students to conform as far as possible to the conventions of the institution and the language. To expect those used to different expectations to do so without help is not reasonable.

Ways of Knowing

Is knowing 'received' or probed for? In western cultures the view is that knowing is the result of searching and working. Teachers reward those who ask questions. The view is that knowledge, a product of thought, is an understanding of cause and effect, the result of thought which is linear, logical and analytic. Both induction, the scientific way of working from observed phenomena to a general principle, and deduction, the method often used in business by which a general principle is used to draw a conclusion useful in a specific situation, come from the teachings of the ancient Athenian philosophers. Thought is seen as an active process involving time and personal effort.

Similarly westerners tend to see the world in terms of opposites, of good versus bad, hot versus cold, and so on. Western law, in which people are found guilty or not guilty, works through opposites, the parties confronting each other. Debating is a western analytic intellectual exercise in which both sides present arguments, and one or other side wins.

As has been seen, people in low context cultures like detailed and exact written contracts. In contrast, Chinese and Japanese like the gist of the contract to be a tight base from which other matters can develop. Specific information is unnecessary. As Hellweg, Samovar and Skow (1991) put it:

'The Japanese view a contract as the beginning of an adaptive process rather than as the end of one.' Similarly in other high-context cultures – Chinese, Middle Eastern, Mexican and Polynesian – negotiators see trust and common sense as more important than a detailed written agreement.

The culture we belong to as individuals will affect not only the way we think, but also our attitude to information, and our access to that information. In a western culture we expect libraries and information systems to be central repositories of whatever up-to-date factual material we need, but in many cultures information is not so tidily available. The western fondness for classification and for systems for understanding that classification is not universal.

At the time this book is being written, statistics and public information can be hard to track down in China. In some substantial libraries, including some university libraries, there is very little up-to-date information, even on China itself. Different ministries have different statistics and reveal them – or do not reveal them – in different ways. One government body will have responsibility for some information and yet another for other related information, not necessarily with mutual access. Students being taught by a foreigner and asked to report on some current issue may be completely unused to seeking out information they have not been given. Considerable expansion of library and computer resources and substantial training in their use may well be necessary.

It will be intriguing to see if and how the Internet changes this situation. Change may be slow. First, for computers to make a marked difference, they would need to become as common as they are in the western world. Second, access to the World Wide Web would need to be freely available. However, even with the availability of, and access to, advanced computer technology, the holistic way of viewing knowledge is likely to persist, and has much to teach those not accustomed to it.

For example, a prominent Chinese scientist used the disease AIDS to show the difference between western and Chinese ways of knowing. Western scientists were busy trying to isolate the virus that caused the disease. But in China they were trying to find ways to strengthen the body's immune system (Varner and Beamer, 1995). The links which make a whole from the sum of the parts are what matter.

Categorisation and Integration

Chapter 5 showed that in some cultures separation between material and spiritual life was inconceivable. In such cultures, aggregation of everything, measurable and not, rather than categorisation, is the way people know and learn.

In a western society, we categorise and particularise. Gudykunst and Kim (1992a: 24) go so far as to say, 'Much of the work on social cognition is based on the assumption that categorization is the fundamental process of thought.' Both processes – placing stimuli in a general category and differentiating stimuli from one another – are likely to occur less often in a culture favouring holistic thought.

Western cognitive (as distinct from behavioural) psychologists focus much of their work on categorisation, using words like 'the individual' and the 'perceiver'. The categorisation process enables people to 'structure and give coherence to [their] general knowledge about people and the social world' (Cantor *et al.,* 1982).

Without categorising it would be impossible either to generalise or stereotype. But Billig (1987) points out that we need not only to be able to put particulars into categories, but also to be able to select and distinguish particulars. 'The paradox is that these two processes [categorising and particularising] seem to pull in opposite cognitive directions: the one pulls towards the aggregation of things and the other towards the uniqueness of things.' That does not mean we should stop categorising. We have to categorise but also to particularise to make sense of the world. Particularising on its own can be shallow and almost useless.

The complement to categorising and particularising is integrating and exploring. Speculation, inventiveness, innovation itself, develop out of the will to go beyond the bounds of logic. In collective cultures people are more inclined to see an issue intuitively and holistically. Gudykunst and Kim (1992a: 149) suggest:

> What seems to be of central importance in Asian thinking is a certain repose of the personality in which it feels it is grasping the inner significance ... The intuitive style of thinking provides a powerful cognitive mechanism for developing a harmonious rapport with the other person and the environment.

Ornstein (1976) called convergent thinking described earlier in this chapter and overlapping with linear, logical thinking, left brain; he called divergent thinking, 'intuition involving simultaneous perception of the whole', right brain. All people use both the left and the right brain, but in education in individualist cultures attention tends to be paid to the former, whereas in collectivist cultures emphasis is on the latter.

Ideally both the inferential and the intuitive ways of thinking are available to be used separately or together. The key thing is to be able to remain what Langer (1989) calls 'mindful', so that the mind is no longer 'trapped by stereotypes'. I once spent some time trying to help a student from the Cook Islands prepare for an examination on the early nineteenth century English romantic poets, and showed him how to comment on rhythm and imagery and the sense of the distant and so on. He looked at me in astonishment and simply said, 'Yes, but you lose all the poetry if you do that.' I had no answer.

Yet in retrospect it is clear that knowing how poetry works can enrich the enjoyment a reader can get from poetry. In many situations both students and teachers can benefit from learning about and adapting to meet the others' expectations.

Cultural Dimensions

The various cultural dimensions described in Chapter 2 and Chapter 4 all significantly affect the knowing and learning process.

High and Low Context

In low context cultures everything is worked out in detail. Disagreement and questioning are welcomed in a classroom. The students compete with one another; teachers may arbitrate as they decide on winning and losing points.

In high context cultures open conflict is almost always destructive. Confucian, Taoist and Buddhist philosophy all oppose debate and confrontation. Any interaction resulting in discord means one or all lose 'face'. There is a clear and acceptable distinction between what the Japanese call *hon'ne* (the true voice) and *tatenae* (the facade), depending on the level of acquaintance. Conflict must be suppressed, not talked out. Student questions and teacher disapproval alike will be indirect, accommodating, worded to ensure no face is lost. Repercussions of this in the classroom will be discussed more fully in the section on power distance.

Sometimes the terms 'field-dependent' and 'field-independent' are used with a meaning very similar to those of high context and low context. Those from field-dependent cultures see the big picture, the whole before the parts; those from field-independent cultures see discrete items, the parts before the whole. Is teaching and learning a holistic process or is it a series of separate identified parts? At Foshan University, as in universities throughout much of Asia, there seemed to be no set curriculum. This has implications for teaching and learning.

Polychronic and Monochronic Time

The western linear, sequential way of thinking and planning with timetables and set dates for each item can be compared in education with the synchronic approach, where several different activities are rhythmically undertaken together. Those used to one approach can be uncomfortable with the other.

In a polychronic culture, several tasks can be done at the same time. Even if tasks are organised and carefully put in order of priority, the arranged order can be altered at any time. Goals are long-term.

In monochronic cultures, appointments are made and full attention is expected to be paid to the arranged matter at the appointed time. Westerners are used to keeping a daily diary and allowing it to order their days. Attendance at classes and due dates for assignments become a routine to be followed almost automatically. In contrast a Pacific Island student told me he had never kept a diary and no one he knew at home had one. Missing a class or a deadline could easily occur for such a student unless practical help in time management is given, whether by administration in training sessions and regular checking, by teacher in extra time and explanations or – perhaps best of all – by fellow students urging and reminding their friend from another culture that not conforming to the imposed timetable can interfere with the likelihood of success.

Fons Trompenaars (1993) tells of an interesting attempt by Shell International Petroleum Company, which works in both monochronic and polychronic cultures, to fuse the two approaches in planning long-term developments. Analysts were asked to write scenarios for three alternative futures, as if they were contemporary commentators. In other words they had to synchronise the past, the present and the future and use the combination to project the work they would be involved in eventually. That combination of sequential and synchronic planning produced certain forecasts. For instance, for the year 2003 Shell foresaw the launching of the electric car in California.

Power Distance

The *Analects* of Confucius give as the first two approved attitudes for students submission to authority – parents, elders and superiors – and submission to the mores of society.

The basic rule is: 'Honour the hierarchy first, your vision of truth second'. The superior must always be accorded face, so one first agrees with what he or (occasionally) she has said. Only then is difference voiced, if possible through a third party, *and* in private. (Bond, 1991: 83)

In high power distance cultures, students expect to be told what to do and do not question a superior's instructions. Ideas are taken at face value. This has implications for study in a culture where students are expected to generate their own ideas. Even when original work is not being demanded, a person who moves from a culture with high power distance to one with low power distance, or the other way round, may be extremely uncomfortable in the classroom.

In cultures in which the focus is on development of relationships in any situation rather than on solving a problem, institutions seeking scholarships and financial aid may deliberately adopt a dependent pose as though to acknowledge power distance. Universities from Bangladesh applying to organisations like the World Bank for funding for particular projects may couch their requests in what, for a westerner, seems sycophantic language. To those not used to such a style, these applications read like pleas from the poor begging their due from the rich rather than analytic, reasoned requests.

Collectivism and Individualism

A significant difference exists in educational situations in individualist and collectivist cultures. In individualist cultures, from birth onwards, children are encouraged to have wants and views of their own and to express them. If they disagree with parents or teachers they say so and from the disagreement a solution is reached. In Hofstede's (1991) words, 'Confrontation can be salutary; a clash of opinions is believed to lead to a higher truth.' The attention that accompanies disagreement with teacher or classmate, like that which comes when a person is singled out for praise, is seen as desirable. In contrast, in a collectivist culture, students would be uncomfortable with either kind of attention.

Even Milton Rokeach (1979), who aims throughout *Understanding Human Values* at avoiding making value judgments himself, suggests that the ultimate educational values are individual growth and self-actualisation which would hardly seem the ultimate aim for many people from a collectivist culture.

In collectivist homes and schools the children are expected to take their opinions from others, and to go along with what is best for the group. Reward for excellence goes to the group and responsibility for performance is owed to the group. Even the choice of study and occupation is a group decision rather than a personal one. Interdependence is always important and go-betweens are relied upon. The relationship matters more than success. In Varner and Beamer's (1995) words: 'If success eluded you this time, you can always try again if the relationship is intact.'

In collectivist cultures, decisions are often based on means, not ends. Decisions about careers and tertiary study fields are made by family, not individuals. Students may have their fees and living expenses paid by their extended families. The assumption is that they will always return to their homes and when they do all the family will share in the greater income the graduate can then earn. Little wonder that such students abroad are distressed when they fail, when they take longer than they planned to complete a thesis or degree, or even when their marks are lower than they expected.

Studies such as that by David McClelland (Bond, 1991: 17) have shown achievement motivation is above the world average for the Chinese. But the achievement goals are seen as being collective (for the state or the family) rather than for the individual. In China doing well academically has long been the *only* means of moving into a different station in life. Now that private ownership of wealth is accepted, this may no longer be true. The peasant whose rice fields and small farm happen to be in a desirable area can suddenly become very wealthy. Possessions and travel, at least within China, can unexpectedly become available.

Most people, though, do not own land or housing or transport. For them and perhaps more importantly for their children, academic excellence remains the way for the group to advance. In Foshan University in 1996 parents would avoid social functions in the evening altogether or go to them only briefly if attendance might mean their four or five-year-old children could not do their regular several hours of homework a night. The homework was not the play-work a western child might have a little of, but arduous and repetitive copying of Chinese characters or memorising information.

Uncertainty Avoidance

In cultures where tolerance of uncertainty is high, format and rules become very important. In the teaching and learning process, this leads to certain preferences. Hofstede (1991: 119) describes what he observed when teaching in an international teachers' programme in 1980:

> Most Germans, for example, favor structured learning situations with precise objectives, detailed assignments, and strict timetables. They like situations in which there is one correct answer which they can find. They expect to be rewarded for accuracy. Their preferences are typical for strong avoidance countries. Most British participants, on the other hand, despise too much structure. They like open-ended situations with vague objectives, broad assignments and no timetables at all. The suggestion that there could be only one correct answer is taboo with them. They expect to be rewarded for originality. Their reactions are typical for countries with weak uncertainty avoidance.[2]

As was noted before, China was not included in Hofstede's research. However, Hong Kong and Singapore which both have a strong Chinese heritage, were included in the updated survey, and came even lower in the uncertainty avoidance scale than Great Britain. This suggests that Chinese people may have extremely low uncertainty avoidance. Perhaps that accounts, at least partly, for the astonishment I met from my classes in Foshan University in south China when I distributed a course outline on the first day of class. To do so had taken great effort, since I had trouble finding what was needed and what they had already done. The effort was appreciated but my students, even in the graduating class, told me they had never seen a course outline before. Chinese friends from universities in other parts of the country told me that they too had rarely had their course of study planned ahead by the lecturer as far as they knew. Nor did they feel it necessary. The students simply accepted each day as it came.

To try to ensure that no mistakes will be made, students from high avoidance cultures where access to authority is always mediated will use people they have met to introduce them and speak for them. Even so, international students will always face uncertainty, which will add to their other difficulties. When individuals from one culture are forced to adopt a very different cultural pattern, they are likely to 'experience high levels of stress, a reduction in positive outcomes, lower self esteem, anomie and general demoralization' (Albert and Triandis, 1985). Our self-esteem depends on those close to us who support us in culturally patterned ways. In a foreign culture a student will probably be without his or her support system.

---

[2]   The programme Hofstede was writing about was sponsored by the Institute for Research on Intercultural Co-operation, Arnhem, The Netherlands. It was a summer refresher course for teachers in management subjects.

Anxiety is a normal response to this loss.

There are two special dangers: one is that anxiety produces avoidance, so that anxious students miss classes. The other is that negative stereotypes held by the teacher can bias assessment. That which is unfamiliar may be seen as less acceptable than that which is familiar.

If either a student or a lecturer is inclined to make hostile attributions, any attempt, however earnest, to improve teaching or learning may be affected. A student who says little in a tutorial even when the teacher knows he or she is particularly well informed on the topic under discussion may be considered lazy, arrogant or both by a teacher who does not appreciate the student's need to ensure the teacher does not lose face. A student who always asks questions after class may similarly be seen as demanding when in reality the student cannot bear the thought of publicly drawing attention to him or herself. And a lecturer who keeps asking questions of an international student in an attempt to encourage him or her to participate comfortably may appear to the student to be racially prejudiced.

Masculinity and Femininity

Even the masculinity-femininity dimension can have its repercussions in a learning situation. In a culture where independence is valued, the international student who is for ever asking for guidance, even in personal matters, can seem demanding. When that student is being supervised for a thesis the requests for help may seem disproportionate.

Students from cultures where gender is a significant factor in the hierarchy may be disturbed when they find themselves in situations in which gender is irrelevant. Tae Woo Kim (1997: 157) describes how the help a young female tutor was giving new settlers to enrol in English as a Second Language classes was unappreciated by one middle-aged male student who demanded 'to see the director, to see a man'.

To start with, in his culture a fifty-year-old man would not be a student in a classroom. The very concept of a mature student is unfamiliar in Korea. His annoyance was compounded by the feeling that he was being treated as a second-class person when he found a young woman representing the institution in its dealings with him. 'Status of their counterpart is regarded as very important for Koreans in interactive communication.' The issues of age, gender and status were interacting.

Doing, Being and Becoming Cultures

Clifford Clarke, foreign student adviser at Yale, first observed the correlation between *doing* cultures where activity is valued – almost for its own sake at times – with *being* cultures where silence is valued. Members of *doing* cultures view silence as a waste, when 'Nothing is happening'. On the other hand, members of *being* cultures often value silence. They wait patiently, confident that if truth is to be known it will show itself. This quiet acceptance of what is, of the *status quo,* means that aggressive behaviour is rare in *being* cultures like Japan. Bond (1991: 14) analyses the situation:

> Firstly wilful actions by an individual put family or group cohesion at risk and hence are avoided. Secondly, there are many clear indicators of status, such as age, sex and title. The prerogatives of each party in the hierarchy are widely acknowledged. Any challenge to this established order by a junior will be regarded as 'revolutionary' and is thus promptly suppressed. Thirdly, aggression will backfire, bringing harm to its instigators. The demands for filial piety require the child not to take this risk by instigating attacks on others.

The western way of creating new categories can be 'mindful' to quote Langer or sensitive to the complexities of a particular situation, but even mindful thought is still very different from meditation in eastern cultures in which the mind becomes quieter and active thought is discouraged. The goal is to rise above the mind so that thought simply does not exist.

Physical Setting

Three environmental matters can cause special difficulty for international staff and students: geography, buildings and population density.

Early theorists pointed out that agricultural societies encouraged co-operation and emphasised obedience whereas hunting societies encouraged independence and initiative. It is improbable that these tendencies persist now. However, a culture which encourages *interdependence* will foster group interpersonal skills and teachers will set group work; one which encourages *independence* will also encourage individual work.

Whether individual or group, study can be hard in a climate which is hotter or colder or wetter or drier than the familiar climate. As a result, absenteeism can be a major problem. In Hamilton in New Zealand the winter temperature rarely drops below 12 degrees Celsius, yet one Melanesian student told a classmate:

> The cold has a physiological effect on us. We don't like taking papers scheduled before 11 am. The cold is so depressing and the sun has no warmth in it. I would say that failing to cope with the cold has cost me time, grades and money. (Cameron, 1993)

Another, a Tongan student, admitted to me:

> I found the cold so troubling that I could not get out of bed in the morning. I was not keeping up with my work. My grades went down and I did not mention this problem to my friends or my parents because I felt so ashamed. I realised I should have asked for an extension. But how do I explain that the cold weather is keeping me away from lectures?

How might students from such climates manage if they went to study in Alberta or Staffordshire?

Similarly, as was seen in Chapter 2, hot and humid climates are conducive to an after-lunch siesta. Even when they are in a very different climate, foreign students from countries like China who have been used to sleeping after lunch all their lives, may find it extremely difficult to study in the early afternoon when classes, tests and even examinations may be scheduled.

Western teachers and students in less affluent cultures will encounter aspects of the 'built environment' which will have a direct effect on the teaching and learning process. Classrooms with rows of fixed seating make flexible group work difficult if not impossible. Libraries and computer laboratories will not only be different in what they provide, but also in their hours of opening. And expectations of housing will differ markedly. Western students might have their study habits disrupted by having to share bedrooms with several other students and by the common practice in many Asian campus hostels of switching off the electricity at, say, 11 pm.

Population density will also affect the comfort of the international staff member or student. A person from Canada, Australia or New Zealand may cower for some time before daring to cross the street in a crowded Asian city. And a person from a densely populated place may be appalled at the lack of public transport and evening entertainment in a more sparsely populated place.

Even the size of a student in an unfamiliar culture may become an issue. For instance, lanky Australians may be uncomfortable in the fixed narrow desks used in the classrooms in some Chinese and Japanese universities. And two aspirin, the normal adult dose in the west, may be far too much for a tiny Vietnamese girl (Victor, 1992: 47).

Perception

In Chapter 3 perception was defined as 'the internal process by which we select, evaluate, and organize stimuli from the external environment' (Hall, 1976). It includes what we see and what we fail to see.

Appearances may be deceptive. Students from abroad who wear western dress and speak fluent English will still have very different cultural backgrounds from those raised in the host country. Even students raised in a particular place and on the surface very like other locals may come from homes in which a different language is spoken and in which cultural expectations may be very different. For instance, Punjabi girls who have lived all their lives in a western culture may have been brought up to expect an arranged marriage.

Even assumptions about intelligence are culturally biased. Intelligence tests in the west, notoriously biased towards middle class children, measure verbal and mathematical skills. However, Andersen and Powell (1991) tell us that in Iran a child who has memorised the *Qur'an* and mastered the Arabic language is thought to be of high intelligence.

Teaching and Learning Styles

Gross (1991), in discussing individual differences rather than cultural differences, plainly states: 'No particular learning style is in itself superior to another.'

Learning can occur in several ways: through inspiration, religious vision or meditation; through explicit teaching or written instruction; through personal reading or observing; through watching television or through pooling information and experience. Most people learn in a variety of ways. The ways that are most often common for any individual will depend on the culture.

Hofstede (1986) has drawn attention to the fundamental problems that arise in cross-cultural learning situations. He traces them to four types of difference:

(1) Differences in the social positions of teachers and students in different societies.

(2) Differences in the relevance of the curriculum in different societies. This can occur in countries like the United States where Indian MBA students may be taught mathematical modelling of United States stock.

(3) Differences in profiles of cognitive abilities between the populations from which teacher and student are drawn. Hofstede is referring, in particular, to the memory of Chinese children who, because of the nature of Chinese script, develop great ability in pattern recognition.

(4) Differences in expected patterns of teacher/student and student/ teacher interaction.

Hofstede considers it is preferable to teach the teacher how to teach rather than to teach the learner how to learn, though he points out that if there is one foreign student in a class of thirty the second strategy, teaching the learner how to learn, is required.

International students and teachers and local students and teachers need to recognise that in some countries teaching is heavily structured and in others the students are encouraged and expected to take much of the initiative themselves. Changing from one process to the other may be slow and difficult.

Similarly in some countries technological aids will be readily available and students will be able to use them easily. In others they will be practically unknown, their availability will be restricted, or their use will be forbidden. Myanmar (Burma), for example, has outlawed the unauthorised possession of networking computers on pain of fifteen years' imprisonment (*The Economist*, 19 October 1996: 15). International students from such places, when they go to study in the west, especially if they fear to lose face over their inexperience with tools like word-processors and the information sources like the Internet, will be reluctant to acknowledge their unfamiliarity. After all, technical expertise is not seen to be as important in ascriptive cultures as it is in the achievement-oriented cultures of the west.

Bond (1991: 24) cites the Japanese philosopher, Hajime Nakamura, as saying of the Chinese: 'For the purposes of instruction, they resort to images that have the appeal of direct perception.' Bond goes on to say that comparative research has shown that the Chinese are more concrete and practical than Americans and therefore less creative. He gives no evidence for either assertion.

The Role of the Teacher

In cultures where attribution matters more than achievement, students have enormous respect for their teachers, greatly desire their approval, and rarely challenge their opinions. The teacher knows, and will help the student know. In Asia, for example, teachers are considered wise, authority figures whose word has great weight. Students bow to them in the street.

Confucius himself is often referred to as the great teacher. In Islamic cultures, too, teachers have a key role. In Gudykunst and Kim (1992b: 418) Rahman (1966) writes that 'the role of the *ulama,* a central core of scholars, is as significant as that of the ruling *caliph.'*

The Egyptian proverb: 'Whoever teaches me a letter, I should become a slave to him for ever' has its equivalent in various other cultures. Mei Young Noh, a Korean student, said she was brought up to believe: 'I dare not walk even on the shadow of the teacher.'[3]

This standing brings with it reciprocal obligations. The teacher is expected to give full support to the student. I once had a heartrending letter from a failing Chinese student addressed to 'My Margaret' and clearly intended to persuade me to pass him on the grounds of his need to pass.

This feeling of dependence does not disappear when a student moves to a culture where it is unrecognised. Pitt and MacPherson (1974: 103) comment:

> Samoan students may feel rebuffed and discouraged by what they interpret as coolness in a teacher's manner when this is simply a normal European cultural trait; and European teachers may be unable to understand their students' consequent lack of interest.

This sense of relationships in education continues throughout life. The Chinese saying, 'If you have been my teacher for one day I will treat you as my father for ever' is not taken lightly. When I was in China a friend, a full professor in engineering at Foshan University, took me some hundreds of miles to visit the professor who had supervised his degree work. Since the Foshan professor did not own a car – indeed I knew no professors who did – the trip took considerable organising. However, maintaining the relationship and justifying his former supervisor's confidence in him were clearly an important part of the young professor's obligation to his teacher. Another

---

[3]   Noh, Mei Young (1996: 3) student paper.

Chinese saying, quaint in translation, 'Green comes from blue but better than blue', picks up the student's sense of debt to the teacher and determination to repay the debt to the community by developing what was learnt still further.

The general manager of a Korean forestry corporation provided another example:

> An interesting relationship I always encountered in business is [that between] the senior, junior [staff] ... They had a little booklet: all the graduates from Seoul National Forestry Academy over the last thirty years. Everyone's there, you can see who's my senior, who's my junior. And you can ring up a 'junior' in another company. There is some sort of debt owed ... The first thing that they tell me is: 'He is my high school senior' or 'He is my university junior.' They want me to understand that sort of power relationship that they have. (Kim, Tae Woo, 1997: 67)

These relationships produce loyalty and service from the juniors, and responsibility and support from the seniors.

Hofstede (1986) contrasts this kind of Confucian view of teaching as an almost revered profession with the attitude of the British aristocrat who is supposed to have said about his son's private tutor, 'I cannot understand why Mr Jones cannot get along with Charlie – all the other servants can.'

It is, of course, easy to oversimplify. Attitudes change not only with place but also with time. Oliver Goldsmith's description of the English village schoolmaster in the poem *The Deserted Village* could hardly be more reverential:

> And still they gazed, and still the wonder grew
> That one small head could carry all he knew.

Teachers who belong in a culture where teachers are members of a community no more or less respected than other people will rarely be prepared to take on the new role. If they have international students, however, they will need to understand the background that produces the veneration. Conversely, older people in China have told me that 'Teachers' Day' was introduced in China because it was felt that the young were not respecting their teachers appropriately.

Behaviour in the Classroom

The way a classroom is set up to some extent controls teaching and learning. A classroom in which the teacher has a long podium and a formal chair, both on a raised platform in front of rows of desks, invites lecture-style teaching, whereas a circle in which all students can see one another, or a fluid arrangement of movable chairs so groups can work together for some of the time and then join as a single unit, invites student-centred shared learning. Students and teachers used to one arrangement may find another arrangement uncomfortable.

Miscommunication can occur even when international staff and students adjust to the physical setting. The universal tendency to stereotype and to see others from an ethnocentric viewpoint can cause problems.

Albert and Triandis (1985) recommend attribution training, 'a technique designed to teach persons from one culture to interpret events as persons from another culture do'. The teacher can learn to try to cure, say, absenteeism or lateness. The student can learn to accept adverse criticism as a contribution to his or her development.

Students and teachers used to high power distance will expect more direction, closer supervision and less participation in both planning and delivering the course content. When teachers ask students for their opinion and Asian students say nothing, it is not rudeness. Students will speak only when the teacher invites them to do so. When they do speak it will be in the tradition of decision making by consensus which Indonesians call *musyawarah mufakat*. Self-deprecating rituals, the Japanese *enryo*, are used to maintain group harmony. Debate and confrontation between teachers and students are most unusual. To quote Tao Te Ching: 'A good man does not argue; he who argues is not a good man' (Bond, 1991: 55). In the unlikely event that there is conflict between teacher and student, parents are expected to side with the teacher.

Although students from high power distance cultures are reluctant to disagree with their teachers, sometimes in a group they can be what one lecturer in a western institution called 'tough':

> There was a lot of difficulty for the teachers. Korean students basically refused, a number of students, to do what they were asked and it was very difficult to persuade them round to another way of thinking. They were very set on their idea and the importance of their idea ... If they see the advantage in compromising or bending, then they will do so. But I don't

think that they are going to be persuaded by other people, unless they themselves think that is the way to go. (Kim, Tae Woo, 1997: 66-7)

Those used to small power distance will expect to be involved in deciding what will be done in class and will demonstrate independence, questioning and spontaneous challenge of both teacher and other students. 'What if' questions are asked. Planning usually involves subdividing points and issues. Clear details are laid out so that the whole can be seen. Both teachers and learners argue from cause to effect and back.

Administrators measure needs and employ staff for specific reasons. Even small children work out how to allocate their time and spend their pocket money. In a school, if conflict arises between teacher and student, parents will be expected to side with the student. In a university, every student matters and has a right to individual advice.

Contrast this with a situation which occurred when a visiting 'foreign expert' – to use the common if over-flattering Chinese term – asked if classes could be made smaller than sixty so that the students could receive some individual attention. The departmental head reacted with shock and horror: 'Students here do *not* want individual attention nor do we want them to have it. It would be most undesirable.'[4] Albert and Triandis (1985: 415) cite this example from their own research:

> A Hispanic child who did not speak much English was given a workbook and told by the teacher to work on her English lessons for a while, while the rest of the class worked in groups on a different task. In this particular case, the teacher probably intended to help her learn English in the most effective way, but due to a greater need for personal attention and the more communal nature of her culture, the child experienced the situation in a very negative way.

In a western classroom stimulation is expected. Open-ended questions, repeating, paraphrases, are all seen as useful ways to check comprehension with difficult material. The teacher will try to motivate students with praise, a strategy that will not work well with those who are reluctant to be singled out for attention in the classroom.

For written work in business communication the direct style with plain

---

[4]   Briefing meeting between four new 'foreign experts' and the senior academics of the School of International Business at Foshan University, 25 August 1996.

English and active voice is preferred. Tentative hedging words such as 'possibly', 'quite', 'somewhat', 'fairly' are disapproved of. Instead, the term 'you-attitude' is common in North American textbooks (for example, Locker, 1995; Lesiker, Pettit and Flatley, 1996). The implication is that a communicator has always to point out how the recipient will gain.

But for effective business communication in Japan, Hirokawa and Miyakawa (1986) show that managers appeal to duty ('It is your duty as a responsible employee to start work on time') or altruism ('For the sake of the company, please share your ideas with us'). When questions are asked, it is usually to verify information more than to understand something. Asking questions is also a way to get to know your student or your teacher.

In Israel the teachers use *dugri* or 'straight talk'; Arab teachers, on the other hand, use elaborate language, flowery and exaggerated. In the classroom in China two-thirds of the time are spent on Chinese and mathematics. There are frequent breaks during the day for fitness drill and eye exercises.[5]

Naoki Kameda (1996: 26) compares the way of teaching language control in Japan with that common in the west, suggesting the different approach is partly responsible for the less exact style common in much Japanese business writing and speaking. He shows that in Japan emphasis is on the whole, and that incidental errors may be totally overlooked:

> If statements full of artistic effect are written [in Japan], for instance, in correct chronological order, such a composition is considered good. In the western world, however, compositions … are returned with the teacher's comments pointing out grammatical mistakes, mistaken expressions or lack of consistent logic.

This shift in emphasis does not mean that Japanese students do not work hard. They do. A New Zealand high school student on an exchange scholarship in Japan said she was shocked at first when she saw Japanese students sleeping in class, but she began to sympathise with them when she found that students regularly studied until two in the morning (Asia 2000, 1996).

In the Thai culture, students are accustomed to listening to the lecturer and accepting what he or she says, so that it is difficult for them to start asking questions in class. For one thing, they are afraid of losing face. For another, they are afraid of causing the lecturer to lose face, as though

---

[5]   Personal communication from Zhang, Yu Rou, 24 February 1997.

disagreeing with what he or she says is adverse criticism, implying that the lecture is less than perfect. Private questions afterwards are entirely acceptable. Thai students in a western institution can be misunderstood when they are thought to be agreeing with teachers but are only refraining from disagreeing. Thai etiquette requires that no one openly disagrees with a superior.

For students from some collectivist cultures both class attendance and private study may suffer when friends call or relations come to visit. Even though the students know they need to attend class or laboratories or study in other ways, obligations to kin and friends are a cultural priority over scheduling. In one New Zealand university, in a university hostel, a Tongan student, worried about a test the next day and simply unable to tell his friends who arrived for a party to go away, went to the local cemetery to sleep in a vault all night. Most Tongan students in that position would have joined the party.

For other students religion may affect class attendance. Muslim students are serious about their prayer times and will either miss class or take turns in attending so that there is always some one there to take notes. At the University of Waikato in New Zealand, the Muslim students run a roster among themselves so that the same person does not repeatedly miss class. Tests and examinations are scheduled in such a way that clashes do not occur. All teaching institutions need to consider whether an official policy on such timetabling issues is practicable for them.

Face-Saving

Both inside and outside the classroom, face-saving is an important aspect of intercultural communication in the knowing and learning process. In the past so many scholars (Argyle, 1969; Samovar and Porter, 1991; Gudykunst and Kim, 1992) have pointed out the importance of face in Asian cultures that it is easy to assume that in class a wish not to appear foolish is a characteristic of Asians alone. However the wish to retain a sense of personal dignity and pleasant interpersonal relations is universal.

Colleen Mills' 1996 research, comparing perceptions of New Zealand and Malaysian students, bears this out. She found that more New Zealand than Malaysian students wished to remain anonymous in class. Malaysian students were slightly more scared to participate in case other students might laugh at them but few students in either group were prepared to disagree with a lecturer in class. The Malaysian students, however, wanted to make sure their lecturers knew them so they were aware of their needs and concerned about their welfare.

O'Sullivan (1994) explains that though 'face' and politeness are important in cultures, the way to be polite will differ markedly according to the culture. For educators, as for anyone else, four approaches are possible.

(1)   We can avoid communicating altogether. We then avoid the risk of losing face, but we achieve nothing.

(2)   We can communicate indirectly, hinting rather than saying anything outright. A teacher might say that a previous student had been very helpful in the classroom. This can seem a tactful way of asking for help. It might, though, seem a comment in its own right with no relevance to what a present student should do. Or it might seem a devious and even insulting way of asking for help, as though the student should have realised help would be appreciated.

(3)   We can ask directly. For example, 'Give me a hand with these dishes we've just used.' This method is sure to be understood but gives the listener no way out. A visitor wanting to catch the last bus home might feel bound to help and so incur a huge taxi bill or make it necessary for the host to drive him or her home.

(4)   We can ask directly but with some softening words. We might ask, 'Have you time to clean the blackboard?' This method is likely to be understood and unlikely to give offence.

Both circumstances and the tone of voice with which the statement is made will make a difference to a wise speaker's choice.

In high context cultures, other people matter above all else. In China, for example, *mianzi* ('face') and *ren qing* ('human feelings') are of crucial importance. People in high context cultures feel shame; those in low context cultures are more likely to feel guilt.

Conventions are important in high context cultures. Meetings will often be very formally conducted. Each group will describe themselves – who they are and what they do – with many statistics. In some cultures, such as the New Zealand Mäori, speakers begin by acknowledging their debt to their ancestors, a practice which can take a long time.

Student Concerns

Research on Thai postgraduate students in Australia revealed that they suffer from linguistic and cultural problems. Isolation and loneliness were seen as critical issues. Problems included accommodation, finance, health, religion, recreation and political matters. The trouble was that when students were worried or upset, they tended to use face-saving strategies like profuse apologies, ignoring the situation or 'pretending that nothing had happened' (Nuangwong and Simkin, 1996). They felt insulted when help was offered and tended to insist that their ability to solve a problem was much greater than it actually was. Similar worries could be expressed by international students anywhere.

The main worries of international students seem to be these:

(1)   Language: speaking and listening

Many international students and some international staff members say how worried they are about their oral command of the target language, both for speaking and for understanding what is said. Having locals as friends, having access to specialised language help, and being encouraged to use tape recorders so that they can go over lectures and instructions afterwards to check and fill in notes are among the possible strategies that can be helpful.

(2)   Thesis writing

Another problem is that in their own country they may never have had to write anything of any length or complexity. When they did write they were probably describing events rather than tussling with ideas. They may have relied totally on the authority of written texts and revered authorities. Writing a thesis proposal, let alone a thesis itself, becomes a daunting task to a student with limited experience of this kind.

For example, six Chinese students who had studied at Staffordshire University reported afterwards that their greatest worry was writing. They had never had to write more than 300 words before and even that was following precise directions. Suddenly they had to plan essays, reports, projects and a dissertation 5,000 to 20,000 words long. The sustained library research and the writing and editing combined into a prolonged nightmare.

Systematic workshops in sustained writing and research skills may well be needed for any students who are unfamiliar with the academic demands of their host institution.

(3)   Nonverbal messages

Unfamiliar teacher-student relationships and teaching styles can be a constant problem. Some students tend to avoid looking speakers in the eye because that signifies to them both defiance and confrontation. The lecturers assume they are uninterested in the work.

(4)   Different academic and cultural traditions

Students may be used to rote learning, with great respect for received opinions and may be totally unused to challenging or being challenged. The scholarships they hold may not have been awarded for 'academic' reasons and the field of study they are in may have been decided on by others.

(5)   Culture shock

Homesickness and loneliness may be severe. Having been members of close-knit groups they are suddenly away from all they are used to relying on. Two international students who came to New Zealand were delivered to their apartment late on a Sunday morning and left there. It was assumed they would find somewhere to eat on or off campus. They waited, expecting someone to call as they would have done at home, not leaving their rooms, till next morning when a person from the university's international students' office did come.

(6)   Personal confidence

Sometimes a graduate student will have spent years as a teacher and will be worried about reverting to the role of student.

(7)   Family and government expectations

Often students are under enormous pressure not to fail. They are also very worried that failure would reflect badly on their families.

(8)   Money

Worry may be about sheer survival, about the difficulties of actually getting promised money, and about the financial situation of the family left behind. Some take on jobs to earn a little extra while away, and worry about the time this work takes. They may also find themselves in debt after spending money on toll calls home or heating, items they had not planned for but find indispensable.

(9)   Uncertainties at home

They may be separated from spouses and small children or elderly parents. The family left behind once provided the support and peace of mind they now desperately miss.

(10) Prejudices – perceived and actual

Some behaviour common in the host culture may be distressing to international students not accustomed to it. Singling out individuals publicly to answer questions or to give praise or blame, for example, may be interpreted in a way never intended.

9 CONCLUSIONS

'There are many roads to truth and no culture has a corner in the path or is better equipped than others to search for it.'

Edward Hall

No culture can impose its values on another. Robert M. March (1996: 89) warned: 'Cross-cultural communication is a minefield of problems in business or private life, the seriousness of which should never be underrated.'

For people of different cultures to work together, all have to have respect for value systems other than their own. Chan Heng Yee, head of Singapore's Institute of South-East Asian Studies, on a visit to the New Zealand Asia 2000 Foundation of New Zealand, compared the Asian sense of community with the western admiration of individualism, the Asian respect for authority and hierarchy with the western clamour for independence and change, the Asian tendency towards a centralised bureaucracy, a strong state and stress on moral values with the hedonism and glamour of Hollywood. Anglo-Saxon liberal democracy, she believes, is not admired or wanted in Asia, though western style economic development is (Asia 2000, 1996).

Selective learning has gone on for centuries. Consider the English language. The western calendar has week days named after Norse gods, months after Roman emperors and legendary figures, years (inaccurately) from the birth of Christ and digits themselves from India through Arabic (Dasenbrock, 1991). But such learning is only a small part of intercultural communication.

To become 'intercultural' we need to work at the three competencies labelled by Gudykunst and Kim as cognitive, affective and behavioural and discussed throughout this book. Let us call them, more simply, knowledge, feeling and skills. These three are interdependent. Without understanding and appreciation of differences, which depend on knowledge, we cannot fully feel for others and respect other ways of acting. Without empathy and insight into our own behaviour, we cannot unjudgementally accept sets of values held by others which are different from our own. And without skills we cannot act in a way that is quietly acceptable to others. We can work successfully to reduce our own and others' uncertainty and anxiety only if we understand the differences that exist, care about them, and work at our own skills for ensuring that they do not prevent effective communication. For teaching and learning, for conducting business, and for developing satisfying intercultural relationships, a fusion of all three competencies is important. This book has been an attempt to stretch all three competencies. The emphasis, as is inevitable with a text, has been on knowledge, not as more important than, but rather as a bridge to, empathy and skills.

Two incidents, both minor though the second could have had widespread repercussions, will illustrate the overlapping nature of these three competencies. In the first one a Japanese man was ending a visit as leader of a group of secondary students who had come to a western country for some weeks for total language immersion. The organiser of the visit and her husband were standing with the crowd, waiting for the buses to leave. As the Japanese man approached the organiser she walked towards him, hand outstretched. He *almost* walked straight past, but suddenly realised, turned round and shook hands first with her and then with her husband. Though nothing was said, both realised what had happened. The Japanese man had been conditioned to put men and older people first, especially those of high status. However, he knew from his study and experience that in western cultures the custom is to shake hands with the woman first, whatever her status, especially if she is standing closer. Because he was sensitive to the feelings of others, he instantly reacted to her recognition that she was being bypassed. Because he had travelled extensively, he had the skill to recover the situation quickly.

In a much more important incident the prime minister of a western country was officially opening a new school building. A small Tongan girl had been delegated to give flowers to his wife. As soon as she had done so he patted her on the head in an avuncular way. The crowd seethed. He smiled benignly and proceeded to speak on the significance of the occasion.

The prime minister was totally unaware that in many cultures, including the Tongan culture, the head is regarded as sacred, the seat of the soul, and should never be touched. He did not have the skill to behave appropriately in a formal situation. Nor did he sense the reaction of those watching, especially the Pacific Islanders, of whom there were many in the crowd. For many reasons, one of which may have been his lack of intercultural competence, his time in office was short.

Such incidents may cause temporary bad feeling but they are not as serious as the long-term tensions which may develop if intercultural knowledge, awareness and skills are lacking. The three cannot be separated because each is so dependent on the others, but if one is more important than the others that one is surely skills, or the way we behave towards others. The unskilled may not even begin to communicate.

To increase our knowledge and so be able to hone our skills, we need to learn all we can about cultures outside our own. The extent we do this will depend on our particular situations. Knowledge of a specific culture, for example, will be of great importance to a person intending to live and work in another culture, or a person closely involved with an individual from another culture, for instance supervising a doctoral thesis. More general knowledge of many cultures and the underlying differences among those cultures will matter to the person whose work involves contact with people from a wide range of cultures.

The most important knowledge for intercultural competence, knowledge of the language, is also the most difficult to acquire, especially when the language is not cognate and in addition has a different script. Certain matters which are an integral part of communication, like humour, are extremely dependent on language. However, acquiring fluency in a language in adult-hood might be too much to expect. Lack of a language by one party need not impede intercultural communication unduly, so long as the monolingual person is not harsh about the other's attempts to use the shared language, but willingly gives constant, patient help.

To communicate well with international staff and students we also need to know something of their home culture, history, geography, political system and outstanding leaders. We need to know and appreciate the particular contributions their culture has made to the world. And we need to be able to generalise about their values and social systems, and at the same time observe individual differences in the people we meet.

Technology has changed the access to knowledge and has broken the barriers of time and space for those who have access to it. An e-mail message takes four seconds to reach its destination on the other side of the world. Internet gives almost instant access to information that once would have taken years to track down.

The problem is that we can never know enough. We learn, for instance, from the literature and from some Chinese friends that four is an unlucky and eight a lucky number in Mandarin and so in China. However in populous Hunan province the reverse is true: four is a lucky number because there are four seasons and each can bring good fortune; eight is an unlucky number because eight people carry a coffin.

Also, cultures change all the time. In China where authority once rested unchallenged with the elders, young people are now given special responsibilities and parents often ask their children for advice. In Korea, at least in the business world, the vertical hierarchical nature of society, with guaranteed long-term employment, is giving way to an individualist, achievement-oriented society, where able, highly-educated people vie for top posts and less able and less educated people lose them. And in many cultures with high power distance, women, whose place used to be in the home, now work in organisations and sometimes reach senior positions.

Since no one can know in advance how to deal with every intercultural pressure point, we must be ready to use our intuition, or affective response, to sense the reaction of those from other cultures to any specific situation. Affective and behavioural skills are of critical importance. They are hard to separate. They involve language, appreciation of art and music, dance, food. Understanding feelings leads to acceptable behaviour, especially for those who have had time immersed in a culture. For instance, those who realise that in a particular culture respect of status and age are imperative and is shown by bowing will find themselves bowing automatically in appropriate situations. Others may be totally insensitive. In Hofstede's (1991: 230) words :'Without awareness, one may travel around the world feeling superior and remaining deaf and blind to all clues about the relativity of one's own mental programming.'

A three-step approach may work well in a situation which calls for effective intercultural communication. First, describe to yourself what is happening. Second, interpret what you believe that means. Only then decide on a course of action in the particular circumstances. Recognise always that your own bias is likely to have affected that evaluation. Let us take a real situation:

> Two young men, recently arrived from China, are talking with a senior woman who is the faculty's Director of Graduate Studies. One of them asks her how old she is.

If we describe the behaviour objectively, we can then consider several possible interpretations:

- They are rude.
- They want to find out all they can about her.
- Since factual, personal questions are considered natural and commonplace in China, they are using a normal question in order to be able to treat her with due respect.

The first and second interpretations can be rejected, since the students are both courteous and serious. The last one leads to useful understanding. The students have not yet had a chance to learn about usual western patterns of speech at initial meetings between staff and students. They are therefore using questions which are acceptable at home when attempting to socialise.

Gudykunst and Kim (1992a: 240) draw attention to the need to attend to our own behaviour and to the process of communication rather than the outcome. They list attributes associated with intercultural adaptation: tolerance for ambiguity and risk-taking, gregariousness, willingness to take responsibility, cognitive complexity and flexibility, a hardy or resilient personality and readiness for change. If we go about communicating in a consciously sensitive manner, the outcome can take care of itself.

Developing the necessary sensitivity is a difficult process. Hanvey (1979) suggests it has four stages:

(1)   The stage of stereotypes, of awareness of superficial or very visible cultural traits. This limited awareness usually comes from brief travel and from reading popular magazines. The differences noticed seem exotic and bizarre.

(2)   The stage when a person notices unfamiliar significant and subtle cultural traits. This often comes from cultural conflict situations and seems frustrating and irrational.

(3)   The stage when a person notices unfamiliar significant and subtle cultural traits but analyses them intellectually, accepting them and trying to understand them.

(4)   Finally the stage where the person is aware what it is like to belong in another culture. This comes from cultural immersion, from living the culture. The person not only understands, as at stage 3, but personally empathises with the culture.

Social Skills

Accepting different sets of values in a positive way makes heavy demands on both teacher and student. In comparison, working on our overt behaviour may seem to have more practical and immediate results. Those involved do not change themselves but pick up a set of skills to apply in interactions with those from a culture different from their own.

For intercultural competence, the host educators need understanding of other cultures, respect for them and appreciation of differences. There are many ways of increasing cultural competence: language learning, cultural learning, role playing, interaction with people from other cultures, and a combination of all four.

For their part, international staff and students will need information about the host country, cultural awareness including knowledge of such issues as high and low context expectations, and attribution training to help them understand host behaviour and personal interaction with hosts. For example, to avoid the embarrassment of asking personal questions which may seem too blunt, students would probably be grateful for a session on customary patterns of speech in early meetings.

Reading and training can help with the first three. But, fortunately, life is not so simple that books can teach everything. Each of us and each of those we meet is both a member of a culture and an individual. To be truly intercultural both hosts and international staff and students need to get to know people from other cultures well.

Scholars like Gudykunst, Wiseman and Hammer recommend that good communicators should not rely on either their own way of seeing things, or on that of the other person. Rather they should develop a third perspective combining their own cultural perspective with that of the other.

Those who share this new perspective are likely to be open-minded toward new ideas and experiences, empathetic toward people from other cultures, and able to perceive accurately similarities and differences between people from the host culture and their own. They are inclined to describe behaviour they do not understand rather than evaluating unfamiliar behaviour as bad, nonsensical, or meaningless; they are relatively astute noncritical observers of their own behaviour and that of others, and they are better able to establish meaningful relationships with people from the host culture. In short they are less ethnocentric than they would have been if seeing other cultures entirely from their own perspective.[1]

Suggestions for Teachers, Administrators and Students

The following list summarises the discussion in all preceding chapters of this book. It is part of the beginning of an exploration into those differences between people which make the study of intercultural communication such an exciting challenge.

(1)   Realise that cultural differences exist and matter. The assumption

---

[1]   Adapted from Gudykunst, Wiseman and Hammer (1977: 424).

that underneath we are all the same can lead to all sorts of trouble. Misunderstandings occur not because communicators have different cultural orientations, but because they assume they share the same orientations and so misinterpret messages from each other.

(2) Read about, observe, and interact with people of other cultures so that you can recognise cultural differences and their meanings. Even in the very first meeting these may be crucial. Expect first meetings to be formal, often through an intermediary, and primarily intended to establish trust.

(3) Learn to recognise different ways of handling space and time. This does not mean that we need to accept other cultures' ways of handling space and time but that we need to sort out a system that is mutually acceptable to those we work with. And we need to remember that our own assumptions may penalise some students. For instance, as Andersen and Powell (1991: 211) point out, tests which are graded on the number of questions a student can answer in a given, limited amount of time disadvantage those who have not been brought up to use every moment in a productive, task-oriented way.

(4) Watch for unfamiliar and subtle signs for respect and formality which may be very different from those you are used to. Asking how old you are, for instance, may be a way of showing deference.

(5) Be alert to the differences in nonverbal meanings between people of different cultures. Shrugging the shoulders, for example, may be a courteous way of admitting lack of foresight, but may seem insolent to those not used to that meaning. Be particularly careful with eye contact and touching in cultures different from your own.

(6) Learn to question your own stereotypes and to remember that, even if as stereotypes they are reasonable, they may be inaccurate for particular people in particular circumstances.

(7) If you have to criticise, do so sensitively. Remember that in a high-context culture, to condemn a deed is to condemn the doer, not just the deed. Further, the shame is felt not only by the person criticised but by the whole group, so anything adverse should be said gently and privately to minimise the discomfort. And in a low-context culture people have feelings which can interfere with learning if not respected.

(8) Be wary of lists of 'dos and don'ts'. Laray M. Barna (1991: 348) points out that the same action can have different meanings in different situations, so any list of simple instructions about what to

do can be fraught with danger. Instead concentrate on recognising your own assumptions and values, and considering how these may be interfering with your intercultural communication.

(9) Pay special attention to questions and answers involving 'Yes' and 'No'. Remember that in some cultures it may be impolite to say 'No' so a student may agree to have work done by a particular date, knowing very well it will not be done. A student who says 'No thank you' to an offer of a second helping of a meal may be waiting hopefully to be asked again, since in his or her culture immediate acceptance would imply that insufficient was given the first time.

(10) Avoid negative questions in English altogether. Imagine a student has not been put in a tutorial yet. If you ask, 'Were you not put in a tutorial?' some would reply 'Yes', meaning, 'Yes, your pre-supposition is right. I have not been put in a tutorial.' Others would answer 'No,' meaning 'No, I was not put in a tutorial.' If the question had been 'Were you put in a tutorial', there would be no ambiguity about the answer.

(11) When you are perplexed about the way someone from another culture has reacted to a situation, consider the matter not from the view point of the individual concerned, but from that of the group to which he or she belongs. And remember that groups are flexible in an individualist culture but relatively fixed in a collective culture. It is, therefore, unwise to attempt to help international students from collectivist cultures by sharing them out among the groups of western students instead of allowing them to form their own groups. Although well-intended, such a procedure may be counter-productive, and will depend on the particular situation. The most successful international students are those who have links and friendships with two groups of fellow students: their own cultural peer group and the local peer group.

(12) Finally, remember that in any communication between native and non-native speakers of a language, the native speaker is in a position of advantage which should not be exploited. Habermas (1990) repeatedly pointed out that an ideal communicative situation requires equality of participants, which is rare in an educational institution anyway, if only because usually the teacher is also the evaluator of the student. Be grateful for the level of your language that a non-native speaker has, and try to learn at least something of his or her language. Even one word of greeting in another language is better than none. A serious attempt to improve in another

language helps the learner appreciate the efforts constantly being made by speakers of other languages. Alternatively, or as well, a teacher may find some guide such as Swan and Smith's *Learner English* a help to anticipating difficulties speakers of other languages may have with English.

Long as the road may seem, the journey towards intercultural awareness, knowledge and skill is itself a pleasant one. For educators, intercultural competence may give insights into difficulties they and others have, understanding of students from other cultures, and many wonderful friendships.

BIBLIOGRAPHY

Given names or initials have been used, depending on each author's choice as seen on the title page.

Achebe, Chinya (1958) *Things Fall Apart.* London: Heinemann.

Achebe, Chinua (1975) "The African writer and the English language" in his own collection of essays *Morning Yet On Creation Day.* London: Heinemann.

Albert, R.D. and Triandis, H.C. (1985) "Intercultural education for multicultural societies", *International Journal of Intercultural Relations*, 9: 391-7. Reprinted in Samovar and Porter (1991) *Intercultural Communication: a Reader.* (6th edn) Belmont CA: Wadsworth.

Adler, P.S. (1975) "The transition experience: an alternative view of culture shock", *Journal of Humanistic Psychology*, 15: 13-23.

Adler, P.S. (1987) "Culture shock and the cross-cultural learning experience" in L.F. Luce and E.C. Smith (eds.) *Towards Internationalism.* Cambridge, MA: Newbury.

Al-Hajj, A. (1994) "Overseas Students" in David Black *A Guide for Research Supervisors.* Dereham: Peter Francis Publishers.

Allport, G.W. (1954) *In The Nature of Prejudice.* Garden City: Anchor Books.

Almaney, A. and Alwan, A. (1982) *Communicating with the Arabs.* Prospect Heights, IL: Waveland Press.

Amit-Talai, Vered and Knowles, Caroline (1996) *Resituating Identities*: *The Policies of Race, Ethnicity and Culture.* Toronto: Broadside Press.

Andersen, Janis F. and Powell, Robert (1991) "Intercultural communication and the classroom" in Samovar and Porter *Intercultural Communication: a Reader* (6th edn). Belmont CA: Wadsworth.

Argyle, Michael (1969) "Intercultural communication" in S. Bochner (ed.) (1982) *Cultures in Contact: Studies in Cross-Cultural Communication.* Oxford: Pergamon Press.

Argyle, M. and Cook, M. (1976) *Gaze and Mutual Gaze.* Cambridge: Cambridge University Press.

Asante, Molefi and Gudykunst, William B. (1991) (eds.) *Handbook of International and Intercultural Communication.* Newbury Park, CA: Sage.

Asia 2000 Foundation of New Zealand (March-April 1966) "Asia is our future", *Newsletter*, 7.

Barna, M. LaRay (1991) "Stumbling blocks in intercultural communication" in Samovar and Porter (1991) *Intercultural Communication : a Reader*: (6th edn) Belmont CA: Wadsworth.

Baring, Evelyn (1908) *Modern Egypt.* New York: Macmillan.

Barnlund, Dean (1975) "Communication in a Global Village" in Samovar and Porter (1991) *Intercultural Communication: a Reader.* (6th edn) Belmont CA: Wadsworth.

Basso, K.H. (1970) *Portraits of "The Whiteman".* Cambridge: Cambridge University Press.

Bates, Daniel G. and Plog, Fred (1990) *Cultural Anthropology.* (3rd edn) New York: McGraw-Hill.

Beaver, R. Pierce (ed.) (1982) *Eerdman' s "Handbook of the World's Religions".* Grand Rapids MI: Eerdman.

Becker, Carl B. (1988) "Reasons for the lack of argumentation and debate in the Far East" in Samovar and Porter (1991) *Intercultural Communication: a Reader.* (6th edn) Belmont CA: Wadsworth.

Beeby, C.E. (1992) *The Biography of an Idea: Beeby on Education.* Wellington, NZ: New Zealand Council of Educational Research.

Berger, Charles R. (1992) "Communicating under uncertainty" in W.B. Gudykunst and Y.Y. Kim (eds.) *Readings on Communicating with Strangers.* New York: McGraw-Hill.

Berger, Charles R. and Calabrese, R.J. (1975) "Some explorations in initial interaction and beyond", *Human Communication Research*, 1: 99-112.

Berlin, B. and Kay, P. (1969) *Basic Color Terms.* Berkeley: University of California Press.

Bernstein, Basil (1964) "Elaborated and restricted codes: their social origins and some consequences" in John J. Gumperz and Dell Hymes (eds.) "The ethnography of communication", *American Anthropologist*, 66 (6), Part II: 55-69.

Berris, Jan Carol (1991) "The art of interpreting" in Samovar and Porter *Intercultural Communication: a Reader.* (6th edn) Belmont CA: Wadsworth.

Billig, Michael (1987) "Categorization and particularization" in W.B. Gudykunst and Y.Y. Kim (eds.) (1992) *Readings on Communicating with Strangers.* New York: McGraw Hill.

Birdwhistell, R.L. (1970) *Kinesics and Context: Essays on Body Motion Communication.* Philadelphia: University of Pennsylvania Press.

Bisong, Joseph O. (1992) "The native speaker's burden", *ELT Journal*, 46 (1): 12-18.

Bisong, Joseph O. (1995) "Language choice and cultural imperialism", *ELT Journal*, 49 (2): 122-32.

Bock, Philip (ed.) (1970) *Culture Shock: a Reader in Modern Cultural Anthropology*. New York: Alfred A. Knopf.

Bochner, Stephen (1979) "Cultural diversity; implications for modernization and international education" in K. Kumar (ed.) (1979) *Bonds without Bondage*. Honolulu: University of Hawaii Press.

Bochner Stephen (ed.) (1982) *Cultures in Contact: Studies in Cross-Cultural Communication*. Oxford: Pergamon Press.

Bond, Michael Harris (1991) *Beyond the Chinese Face*. Hong Kong: Oxford University Press.

Borden G.A. (1991) *Cultural Orientation*. Englewood Cliffs, N J: Prentice Hall.

Bowe, Heather and a'Beckett, Margaret (1994) "Convergence and divergence: language universals and intellectual communication". Paper presented at the International Communication Conference. Sydney, July 11-15.

Brick, Jean (1991) *China: A Handbook in Intercultural Communication*. Sydney: NCELTR.

Brislin, Richard (1993) *Understanding Culture's Influence on Behavior*. Fort Worth, TX: Harcourt Brace Jovanovitch College Publishers.

Butterfield, Fox (1982) *China: Alive in the Bitter Sea*. New York: Hodder and Stoughton.

Cameron, William (1993) "Differing time concepts". Unpublished master's thesis, University of Waikato, New Zealand.

Cantor, N., Mischel, W. and Schwartz, J. (1982) "Social knowledge: structure, content, use and abuse" in A.H. Hastorf and A.M. Isen (eds.) *Cognitive Social Psychology*. New York: Elsevier.

Carson, Rachel (1987) *Silent Spring*. London: Hamish Hamilton.

Chaney, Lillian H. and Martin, Jeanette S. (1995) *Intercultural Business Communication*. Englewood Cliffs, NJ: Prentice Hall.

Chang, Jung (1993) *Wild Swans: Three Daughters of China*. London: Flamingo.

Cohen, Raymond (1991) *Negotiating across Cultures*. Washington DC: United States Institute of Peace.

Collett, P. (1971) "On training Englishmen in the nonverbal behaviour of Arabs: an experiment in intercultural communication", *International Journal of Psychology*, 6, 209-15.

Collins, Beth, Tesdell, Les S. and Wei, Yong-Kang (1996) "Redefining reader responsibility: a cross-cultural study". Paper presented at Chicago: ABC International Convention.

Collins, Ian (1996) "Putting relationships on the ice", *Education Review*, 10 July: 11.

Condon, John (1991) ' " ... so near the United States": notes on communication between Mexicans and North Americans' in L.A. Samovar and R.E. Porter (1991) *Intercultural Communication: a Reader*. (6th edn) Belmont CA: Wadsworth.

Condon John C. and Yousef, Fathi S. (1975) *An Introduction to Intercultural Communication.* New York: Bobbs-Merrill.

Conrad, Joseph (1928) *A Personal Record*. London: Nelson & Sons.

Crapanzano, Vincent (1988) "Growing up white in South Africa" in C.J.Verburg *Cross Cultural Readings for Writers*. New York: St Martins Press.

Dasenbrock, Reed Way (1991) "The multicultural West" in Irene L. Clark *Writing about Diversity*. Fort Worth: Harcourt Brace.

De Keijzer, Arne J. (1992) *China: Business Strategies for the Nineties.* Berkeley, CA: Pacific View Press.

De Mente, Boye Lafayette (1994) *Chinese Etiquette & Ethics in Business.* Lincolnwood, IL: NTC Business Books.

Deener, R. Elvina and Adelman, Mara B. (1982) *Beyond Language.* Engelwood Cliffs, NJ: Prentice-Hall.

Di Stephano, J.J. (1979) "Case methods in international management training" in M.K. Asante, E. Newmark and C.A. Blake (eds.) *Handbook of Intercultural Communication*. Beverley Hills, CA: Sage.

Dickens, Charles (1837; reprinted 1986 ed. James Kinsley) *The Pickwick Papers*. Oxford: The Clarendon Press.

Dodd, Carley H. (1991) *Dynamics of Intercultural Communication*. (3rd edn) Dubuque, IA: Wm C. Brown.

Draine, Cathie and Hall, Barbara (1986) *Culture Shock: Indonesia.* Singapore: Times Books International.

Dunn, Rita and Dunn, Kenneth (1993) *Teaching Secondary Students through Their Individual Learning Styles.* Boston: Allyn and Bacon.

Durrani, Tehmina (1994) *My Feudal Lord*. London: Bantam.

Eco, Umberto (1979) *The Role of the Reader*. Bloomington: Indiana University Press.

Edwards, John (1994) *Multilingualism.* London: Routledge.

Eibl-Eibesfeldt, I. (1975) *Ethology: the Biology of Behavior.* New York: Holt, Rinehart and Winston.

Ekman, P. and Friesen, W.V. (1969) "The repertoire of nonverbal behavior: categories, origins, usage and coding", *Semiotica*, 1: 49-98.

Elgin, Duane (1981) *Voluntary Simplicity.* New York: William Morrow.

Evans, Richard (1993) *Deng Xiaoping and the Making of Modern China.* New York: Viking.

Farb, Peter (1974) *Word Play.* New York: Knopf.

Fielding, Henry (1749; reprinted 1974) *The History of Tom Jones.* Oxford: The Clarendon Press.

Finegan, Edward (1994) *Language: Its Structure and Use.* Fort Worth: Harcourt Brace.

Freilich, Morris (1970) *Marginal Natives: Anthropologists at Work.* New York: Harper and Row.

Furnham, Adrian (1988) "The adjustment of sojourners" in Y.Y. Kim and W.B. Gudykunst (eds.) *Cross-Cultural Adaptation.* Newbury Park, CA: Sage.

Graham, J.A. and Argyle, M. (1975) "A cross-cultural study of the communication of extra-verbal meaning by gestures", *International Journal of Psychology*, 10: 57-67.

Greenbaum, Sidney (1988) *Good English and the Grammarian.* London: Longman.

Gross, Ronald (1991) *Peak Learning: A Master Course in Learning How to Learn.* Los Angeles: Tarcher.

Gudykunst, W., Wiseman, R. and Hammer, M. (1977) "Determinants of a sojourner's attitudinal satisfaction" in B. Rubin (ed.) *Communication Yearbook 1.* New Brunswick, NJ: Transaction Books.

Gudykunst, W.B. (1983) "Uncertainty reduction and predictability of behavior in low and high context cultures: an exploratory study", *Communication Quarterly*, Winter 31, (1): 49-65.

Gudykunst, W.B., Chua, E. and Gray, A. (1987) "Cultural dissimilarities and uncertainty reduction processes" in M. McLaughlin (ed.) *Communication Yearbook 10.* Beverly Hills, CA: Sage.

Gudykunst, W. and Hammer, M. (1987) "Strangers and hosts: an uncertainty reduction based theory of intercultural adaptation" in Y.Y. Kim (ed.) *Cross-Cultural Adaptation.* Newbury Park, CA: Sage.

Gudykunst, William B. and Ting-Toomey, Stella (1988) "Verbal Communication Styles" in L.A. Samovar, and R.E. Porter (eds.) (1991) *Intercultural communication: A Reader.* (6th edn) Belmont CA: Wadsworth.

Gudykunst, William B. and Kim, Young Yun (1992a) *Communicating with Strangers.* New York: McGraw-Hill.

Gudykunst, William B. and Kim, Young Yun (1992b) *Readings on Communicating with Strangers.* New York: McGraw-Hill.

Gudykunst, William B. and Ting-Toomey, Stella (1992) "Nonverbal dimensions and context regulation" in Gudykunst and Kim (1992b) *Readings on Communicating with Strangers.* New York: McGraw-Hill.

Habermas, Jürgen (1990) *Moral Consciousness and Communicative Action.* Translated by Christian Lenhardt and Shierry Weber Nicholsen. Cambridge: Polity Press.

Hall, Edward (1959) *The Silent Language.* New York: Doubleday.

Hall, Edward (1966) *The Hidden Dimension.* New York: Doubleday.

Hall, Edward (1972) "Context and Meaning" in Gudykunst and Kim, (1992b) *Readings on Communicating with Strangers.* New York: McGraw-Hill.

Hall, Edward (1976) *Beyond Culture.* New York: Doubleday.

Hall, Edward (1983) *The Dance of Life.* New York: Doubleday. Reprinted in Samovar and Porter (1991) *Intercultural Communication: a Reader.* Belmont CA: Wadsworth.

Hall, Edward T. and Reed, Mildred (1987) *Doing Business with the Japanese.* New York: Anchor Press and Doubleday.

Hall, Edward T. and Reed, Mildred (1990) *Understanding Cultural Differences: Germans, French and Americans.* Yarmouth, ME: Intercultural Press.

Hall, Stuart (1992) "The question of cultural identity" in S. Hall, D. Held and T. McGrew (eds.) *Modernity and its Futures.* Cambridge: Polity Press.

Halliday, M.A.K. (1978) *Language as Social Semiotics.* London: Edward Arnold.

Hamilton, David L., Sherman, Steven J. and Ruvolo, Catherine M. (1992) "Stereotype-based expectancies" in W.B. Gudykunst and Y.Y. Kim (eds.) (1992b) *Readings on Communicating with Strangers.* New York: McGraw-Hill.

Haneda, Saburo and Shima, Hirosuke (1982) "Japanese communication behavior as reflected in letter writing", *The Journal of Business Communication,* 19 (1): 19-32.

Hanvey, Robert G. (1979) "Cross-cultural Awareness" in Elise C. Smith and Louise Fiber Luce (eds.) *Toward Internationalism.* Rowley. MA: Newbury House.

Harris, Marvin (1979) *Cultural Materialism: the Struggle for a Science of Culture.* New York: Random House.

Harris, Phillip R. and Moran, Robert T. (1991) *Managing Cultural Differences.* Houston, TX: Gulf Publishing.

Hecht, M., Ribeau, S. and Sedana, M. (1990) "A Mexican-American perspective on interethnic communication", *Communication Monographs,* 56: 385-410

Heider, F. (1958) *The Psychology of Interpersonal Relations.* New York: John Wiley and Sons.

Hellweg, Susan A., Samovar, Larry A. and Skow, Lisa (1991) "Cultural variations in negotiation styles" in Samovar and Porter *Intercultural Communication; a Reader.* (6th edn) Belmont CA: Wadsworth.

Hirokawa, R. and Miyakawa, A. (1986) "A comparison of influence strategies utilised by managers in American and Japanese organisations", *Communication Quarterly,* 34: 250-65.

Hoebel, E. Adamson and Frost, Everett L. (1976) *Cultural and Social Anthropology.* New York: McGraw-Hill.

Hofstede, Geert (1980) *Culture's Consequences: International Differences in Work-Related Values.* Beverly Hills, CA: Sage.

Hofstede, Geert (1984) "Cultural dimensions in planning and management", abridged version published in W.B. Gudykunst and Y.Y. Kim (eds.) (1992b) *Readings on Communicating with Strangers.* New York: McGraw-Hill.

Hofstede, Geert (1986) "Cultural differences in teaching and learning", *International Journal of Intercultural Relations,* 10: 301-20.

Hofstede, Geert (1991) *Culture and Organizations: Software of the Mind.* London and New York: McGraw-Hill. Paperback (1994) London: Harper Collins.

Hoijer, Harry (1954) "The Sapir-Whorf hypothesis" in Samovar and Porter (1991) *Intercultural Communication: a Reader.* Belmont CA: Wadsworth.

Hsu, F.L.K. (1971) "Psychological homeostasis and jen: conceptual tools for advancing psychological anthropology", *American Anthropologist,* 73: 23-44.

Hughes, Robert (1994) *The Culture of Complaint.* London: OUP and Harvill Publishers.

Humboldt, Wilhelm von (1799) *Uber die Verschiedheit des Menschlischen Sprachbaues.* Translated by Peter Heath (1988) *On Language: The Diversity of Human Language.* Cambridge: Cambridge University Press.

Hutton, W. (1995) *The State We're In.* London: Jonathan Cape.

Hymes, Dell (ed.) (1964) *Language in Culture and Society.* New York: Harper and Row.

Kameda, Naoki (1993) "Business English a an international trade language" *Doshisha Business Review* 45 (2 & 3).

Kameda, Naoki (1996) *Business Communication towards Transnationalism.* Tokyo: Kindaibungeisha.

Kaplan, Robert B. (1966) "Cultural thought patterns in intercultural education", *Language Learning*, 16 (1-2): 3-15.

Kaplan, Robert B. (1990) "Writing in a multilingual/multicultural context", *The Writing Instructor*, Fall: 7-17.

Kelley, H.H. (1972) "Attribution theory in social psychology" in *Nebraska Symposium on Motivation* 15: 192-238. Lincoln: University of Nebraska Press.

Kim, Jin K. (1980) "Explaining acculturation in a communication framework: an empirical test", *Communication Monographs*, 47: 155-79.

Kim, Tae Woo (1997) "Communicating with Koreans". Unpublished master's thesis, University of Waikato, New Zealand.

Kim, Young Y. (1991) "Intercultural personhood: an integration of Eastern and Western perspectives" in Samovar and Porter *Intercultural Communication: a Reader*. (6th edn) Belmont CA: Wadsworth.

Kim, Young Yun and Gudykunst, William B. (eds.) (1988) *Theories in Intercultural Communication.* Newbury Park, CA: Sage.

Kim, Young Y. (1988) *Communication and Cross-Cultural Adaptation.* Newbury Park, CA: Sage.

Kluckhohn, Florence and Strodtbeck, Frederick (1961) *Variations in Value Orientations.* New York: Row & Peterson.

Knapp, Mark L. and Hall, Judith A. (1992) *Nonverbal Communication in Human Interaction.* Fort Worth: Holt, Rinehart and Winston.

Kogawa, Joy (1981) *Obasan.* Markham, Ontario: Penguin.

Konishi, A., Kondo, T. and Ogata, S. (1990) "Behind the screen: three prominent Japanese candidly discuss the future of their country and its changing relations with the United States", *The World and I*, 5 (11): 44-51.

Korzenny, Felipe (1991) "Relevance and application of intercultural communication theory and research" in Samovar and Porter *Intercultural Communication: a Reader*. (6th edn) Belmont CA: Wadsworth.

Kroeber, Alfred and Kluckhohn, Clyde (1954) *Culture: A Critical Review of Concepts and Definitions.* New York: Random House.

Kreuger, J. And Rothbart, M. (1998) "Use of categorical and individuating information in making inferences about personality", *Journal of Personality and Social Psychology*, 55 (2): 187-95.

Lago, Colin (1996) *Race, Culture and Ethnicity.* Milton Keynes, UK: Open University Press.

Langer, E.J. (1989) *Mindfulness.* Reading, MA: Addison-Wesley.

Langer, E.J. (1992) "The nature of mindfulness" in Gudykunst and Kim (eds.) *Readings on Communicating with Strangers.* New York: McGraw-Hill.

Lederer W.J. and Burdeck, Eugene (1958) *The Ugly American.* New York: Norton.

Letts, Malcolm (translator) (1957) *Hans Staden: the True History of His Captivity.* London: Routledge and Kegan Paul.

Leung, K. and Iwawaki, S. (1988) "Cultural collectivism and distributive behavior", *Journal of Cross-Cultural Psychology*, 19: 35-49.

Levine, Deena R. and Adelman, Mara B. (1982) *Beyond Language.* Engelwood Cliffs, NJ: Prentice-Hall.

Lewin, Kurt (1951) *Field Theory in Social Science.* New York: Harper & Row.

Lin, Zhi (1994) "When Westerners Meet Chinese". Unpublished master's thesis, University of Waikato, New Zealand.

Lindholm, Cherry and Lindholm, Charles (1988) "Life behind the veil" in C.J. Verburg, (ed.) *Cross Cultural Readings for Writers.* New York: St Martin's Press.

Lustig, Myron W. and Koester, Jolen (1996) *Intercultural Competence.* (2nd edn) New York: Harper Collins.

Lynch, James (1983) "Multicultural education: the context and the case" in *Multicultural Curriculum.* London: B.T. Batsford.

Ma, Zhenling (1992) *Aspects of Chinese Culture.* Tianjin: Nankai University Press.

Mahmoody, Betty (1987) *Not Without My Daughter.* New York: St Martin's Press.

Malmberg, R. (1992) "Culture and communication: a video training programme", *Language Training*, 12: 3.

Mandelbaum, David, G. (ed.) (1960) *Selected Writings of Edward Sapir.* Berkeley and Los Angeles: University of California Press.

Maquet, Jacques (1970) "An African world view" in Philip Bock (ed.) *Culture Shock : a Reader in Modern Cultural Anthropology.* New York: Alfred A. Knopf.

March, Robert M. (1996) *Working for a Japanese Company: Insights into the Multicultural Workplace.* Tokyo: Kodansha International.

Marcus, Stacey and Slansky, Nuala (1994) "Teaching the unwritten rules of time and space", *ELT Journal*, 48 (4): 306-14.

Maslow, Abraham (1954) *Motivation and Personality.* New York: Harper & Row.

Maslow, Abraham (1956) "Defense and growth", *Merrill-Palmer Quarterly*, 3 (1): 503-7.

Mbiti, J.S. (1970) *African Religions and Philosophy.* New York: Anchor Books.

McCallen, Brian (1989) "A world commodity". *The Economist Intelligence Unit*, special report 1166: 1.

McLuhan, Marshall (1989) *The Global Village: Transformation in World Life and Media in the 21st Century.* Oxford: Oxford University Press.

Mead, Richard (1990) *Cross-cultural Management Communication.* Wiley, Chichester.

Mehrabian, Albert and Wiener, Morton (1967) "Decoding in inconsistent messages", *Journal of Personality and Social Psychology*, 6: 109-14.

Metge, Joan and Kinloch, Patricia (1978) *Talking Past Each Other: Problems in Cross-Cultural Communication.* Wellington, NZ: Victoria University of Wellington Press.

Mills, Colleen (1996) "Three perspectives on experiences in multicultural classrooms." Paper presented at the Higher Education Research and Development Society of Australia Conference, University of Western Australia, Perth. June 1996.

Minae Naila (1988) "Women in early Islam" in C.J. Verburg (ed.) *Cross Cultural Readings for Writers.* New York: St Martin's Press.

Montiero, Kenneth P. (1995) *Ethnicity Psychology.* Dubuque: Kendall Hunt.

Moore, Alexander (1978) *Cultural Anthropology.* New York: Harper & Row.

Morris, D., Collett, P., Marsh P. and O'Shaughnessy, M. (1979) *Gestures: Their Origins and Distribution.* London: Cape.

Murphy, Herta A. and Hildebrandt, Herbert W. (1991) *Effective Business Communications.* New York: McGraw-Hill.

Nelson, Frances (1995) *Journal*: 60.

Nida, Eugene (1991) *Language, Culture and Translating.* Shanghai: Shanghai Foreign Language Press.

Niehaus, Carl (1993) *Fighting for Hope.* Capetown: Human and Rousseau.

Nuangwong, B. and Simkin, K. (1996) "Adapting Australian universities to international students; a case study of Thais". Paper presented at the 9th World Congress of Comparative Education Societies, Sydney, July.

Oberg, K. (1960) "Culture shock and the problem of adjustment to new cultural environments", *Practical Anthropology*, 7: 177-82.

Oddou, Gary and Mendenhall, Mark (1992) "Person perception in cross-cultural settings" in Gudykunst and Kim (1992b) *Readings on Communicating with Strangers.* New York: McGraw-Hill.

Okabe, R. (1983) "Cultural assumptions of East and West: Japan and the United States" in W.B. Gudykunst (ed.) *Intercultural Communication Theory: Current Perspectives.* Beverly Hills, CA: Sage Publications.

Ong, Walter (1980) "Literacy and orality in our times", *Journal of Communication*, 30: 197-204.

Ong, Walter (1982) *Literacy and Orality.* London: Methuen.

Ornstein, Robert (1976) *The Nature of Human Consciousness.* New York: Viking Press.

Ornstein, Robert (1976) *The Nature of Human Consciousness.* New York: Viking Press.

Osmond, Warren (1996) "International students in our construction of racism on campuses. *Campus Review*, 9: 17-23, July.

O'Sullivan, Kerry (1994) *Understanding Ways.* Sydney: Hale and Iremonger.

Park, M.S. and Kim, M.S. (1992) "Communication practices in Korea", *Communication Quarterly*, 40: 4.

Pease, Allan (1987) *Body Language: how to read others' thoughts by their language.* Avalon Beach, N.S.W.: Camel Press.

Pedersen, A. and Pedersen, P. (1989) "The cultural grid: a framework for multi-cultural counselling", *International Journal for the Advancement of Counselling*, 12 (4): 299-307.

Pedersen, Paul (1988) *A Handbook for Developing Multicultural Awareness..* Virginia: American Association for Counselling and Development.

Pedersen, Paul (1990) "The culture-bound counselor as an unintentional racist", working paper. University of Syracuse.

Phillipson, Robert (1992) *Linguistic Imperialism.* Oxford: OUP.

Pitt, David and Macpherson, Cluny (1974) *Emerging Pluralism.* Auckland: Longman Paul.

Popper, Karl (1963) *The Spell of Plato.* London: Routledge and Kegan.

Popper, Karl (1968) *Conjectures and Refutations: The Growth of Scientific Knowledge.* (3rd edn) London: Routledge and Kegan Paul.

Prashnig, Barbara (1996) *Diversity is our Strength: the Learning Revolution in Action.* Auckland, NZ: Profile Books.

Pratt, Douglas (1993) *Religion: A First Encounter.* Auckland, NZ: Longman Paul.

Pye, Lucien (1982) *Chinese Commercial Negotiating Style.* Cambridge, MA: Oelgeschlager, Gunn and Hain.

Quinlin, Joseph P. (1989) *Vietnam: Business Opportunities and Risks.* Berkeley: Pacific View Press.

Quirk, Randoph (1962) *The Use of English.* London: Longmans Green.

Ricks, David (1983) *Big Business Blunders: Mistakes in Multinational Marketing.* Homewood, IL: Dow Jones-Irwin.

Rokeach, Milton (1968) *Beliefs, Values and Attitudes.* San Francisco: Jossey-Bass.

Rokeach, Milton (1973) *Human Values.* New York: Free Press.

Rokeach, Milton (1979) *Understanding Human Values: Individual and Societal.* New York: Macmillan.

Ross, L.D. (1977) "The intuitive psychologist and his shortcomings: distortions in the attribution process" in L. Berkowitz (ed.) *Advances in Experimental Psychology*, 10: 173-220. New York: Academic Press.

Ruesch, Jurgen and Kees, Weldon (1956) *Nonverbal Communication: Notes on the Visual Perception of Human Relations*. Berkeley: University of California Press.

Said, Edward (1979) *Orientalism*. New York: Random House.

Said, Edward (1993) *Culture and Imperialism*. New York: Knopf.

Samovar, Larry A. and Porter, Richard E. (1991) *Intercultural Communication: a Reader*. (6th edn) Belmont CA: Wadsworth.

Samovar, Larry A. and Porter, Richard E. (1995) *Communication between Cultures*. (2nd edn) Belmont CA: Wadsworth.

Sanjaya, Santosa (1996) "Bahasa Indonesia as the language of unity in diversity". Unpublished master's thesis, University of Waikato, New Zealand.

Schaefer, Francis (1968) *The God Who Is There*. Downers Grove, IL: Inter-Varsity.

Scharfstein, B.A. (1974) *The Mind of China*. New York: Delta.

Schnapper, Melvin (1979) "The Volunteer" in Elise C. Smith and Louise Fiber Luce, *Toward Internationalism*. Rowley. MA: Newbury House.

Seelye, H. Ned and Seelye-James, Alan (1995) *Culture Clash*. Lincolnwood, IL: NTC Publishing.

Seligman, S.D. (1990) *Dealing with the Chinese: a Practical Guide to Business Etiquette in the People's Republic Today*. New York: Warner Books.

Setiadi, B.N. (1984) "Schooling, age and culture as moderators of role perceptions". Unpublished doctoral dissertation, University of Illinois, Urbana.

Sikkema, Mildred and Niyekawa, Agnes (1987) *Design for Cross-Cultural Learning*. Yarmouth, Maine: The Intercultural Press.

Simmel, Georg (1906) *Der Fremde* in K. Woolf (ed. and trans.) (1950) *The Sociology of Georg Simmel*. New York: Free Press.

Smith, Adam (1776. Reprinted 1970) *Wealth of Nations*. London: Penguin.

Smith, Elise C. and Luce, Louise Fiber (1979) *Toward Internationalism*. Rowley, MA: Newbury House.

Sperber, James P. and Wilson, Deirdre (1986) *Relevance: Communication and Transition*. Oxford: Blackwell.

Spitzberg, Brian and Cupach, William (1984) *Interpersonal Communication Competence*. Beverly Hills, CA: Sage.

Spradley, James P. and McCurdy, David W. (1990) *Conformity and Conflict: Readings in Cultural Anthropology*. (7th edn) Glenview, IL: Scott, Foresman/Little Brown.

Sumner, William Graham (1906) *Folkways*. Boston: Ginn.

Swan, Michael and Smith, Bernard (1987) *Learner English: a teacher's guide to interference and other problems*. Cambridge: Cambridge University Press.

Taft, R. (1977) "Coping with unfamiliar cultures" in N. Warren (ed.) *Studies in Cross-cultural Psychology*, 1: 121-53. London: Academic Press.

Taylor, Robert B. (1980) *Cultural Ways*. (3rd edn) Boston, MA: Allyn and Bacon.

Thomas, Yoke Leng Natrah (1996) "Whose rules rule: an investigation of intercultural communication between New Zealand People and Asian People". Unpublished master's thesis, University of Waikato, New Zealand.

Ting-Toomey, Stella (1988) "A face negotiation theory" in Y.Y. Kim and W. B. Gudykunst (eds.) *Theories in Intercultural Communication*. Newbury Park, CA: Sage.

Triandis, Harry (1972) "Collectivism v. Individualism" in W.B. Gudykunst and Y.Y. Kim (eds.) (1992b) *Readings on Communicating with Strangers*. McGraw-Hill, New York.

Triandis, Harry C., Brislin, Richard and Hui, C. Harry (1991) "Cross-cultural training across the individualism-collectivism divide" in Samovar and Porter *Intercultural Communication: a Reader*. (6th edn) Belmont CA: Wadsworth.

Trompenaars, Fons (1993) *Riding the Waves of Culture*. London: The Economist Books.

Valdes, Joyce Merrill (1986) *Culture Bound: Bridging the Cultural Gap in Language*. Cambridge: Cambridge University Press.

Varner, Iris and Beamer, Linda (1995) *Intercultural Communication in the Global Workplace*. Chicago: Irwin.

Verburg, Carol J. (ed.) (1988) *Cross Cultural Readings for Writers*. New York: St Martin's Press.

Vernon, Philip E. (1982) *The Abilities and Achievements of Orientals in North America*. New York: Academic Press.

Victor, David A. (1992) *International Business Communication*. New York: Harper Collins Publishers.

Wanguri, Delores McGee (1996) "Diversity, equity and communicative openness", *The Journal of Business Communication*, 33 (4): 443-57.

Ward, L. (1967) "Some observations of the underlying dynamics of conflict in foreign students", *Journal of the American College Health Association*, 10: 430-40.

Waugh, Evelyn (1958) *The Loved One*. London: Chapman and Hall.

Whorf, Benjamin L. (1962) *Language, Thought and Reality*. New York: Massachusetts Institute of Technology and John Wiley.

Williams, Frederick, Whitehead, Jack L. and Miller, Leslie M. (1971) "Ethnic stereotyping and judgments of children's speech", *Speech Monographs*, 38: 166-70.

Williams, Raymond (1958) *Culture and Society, 1780-1950*. London: Chatto and Windus.

Wittgenstein, Ludwig (1958. Reprinted 1963) *Tractatus, Logico-Philosophicus*. D.F. Pears and B.F. McGuinness (trans.) London: Routledge and Kegan Paul.

Yoshikawa, M. (1988) "Cross-cultural adaptation and perceptual development" in Y.Y. Kim and W. Gudykunst (eds.) *Cross-cultural Adaptation*. Newbury Park, CA: Sage.

Yum, J. (1987) "The practice of *uye-ri* in interpersonal relationships in Korea" in D.L. Kincaid (ed.) *Communication Theory from Eastern and Western Perspectives*. New York: Academic Press.

Zak, Michele (1996) "Deep structure of the field", *The Journal of Business Communication*, 33 (4): 503-11.

Zhang, You Ru (1997) "Chinese culture and its implications for international business". Unpublished master's thesis, University of Waikato, New Zealand.

Zigler E. and Child I.L. (1969) "Socialization" in G. Lindzey, and E. Aronson *The Handbook of Social Psychology*, 3: 450-589. Reading, Mass: Addison-Wesley.

AUTHORS

This list includes student papers not given in the bibliography.

INDEX